THE CUSTODIAN OF TRUST

ADVANCE PRAISE FOR THE BOOK

'Rajnish Kumar has had a stellar career as India's banker, which is why his autobiography makes for both insightful and exciting reading. Through his work one gets a ringside glimpse of the challenges that the Indian banking system constantly faces and how it rises to surmount them.

As Chairman, State Bank of India, he was responsible for some of the most critical financial developments that contributed extensively towards making India what it is today.

This is a book that is not just about the banking system of our country, but a chronicle of contemporary economic history.'

—**Ratan N. Tata**, Chairman, Tata Trusts;
Chairman Emeritus, Tata Sons

'I congratulate Shri Rajnish Kumar for penning an illuminating and engrossing memoir of his long and illustrious career at the State Bank of India, an institution where he started as a probationary officer and rose to become the chairman.

The book gives a rare insight into the inner workings of the oldest and most prestigious bank in our country, and what it takes to preserve and uphold the one thing that matters the most in the business of banking: Trust.

His roadmap—based on some tumultuous episodes in the interaction between the corporate and banking sectors in India—for restoring the confidence of bankers, both public and private, could serve as a blueprint for charting India's rapid growth and also for facilitating the full blossoming of our entrepreneurial class.'

—**Mukesh D. Ambani,** Chairman and Managing Director,
Reliance Industries Ltd

'As India works its way towards finding its rightful place as one of the largest economies in the world, we are also witnessing wide-scale changes and transformation in the country's financial sector: the failing corporates and the faltering banks, structural reforms by the government, opening up new growth possibilities; and finally, the pandemic, posing immense challenges and yet opening up new opportunities. Rajnish Kumar, who chaired the nation's largest bank, the State Bank of India, in this book titled *The Custodian of Trust*, gives us a ring-side view of this rather turbulent phase. Rajnish blends his inimitable simplicity with his deep understanding and knowledge of the financial sector to pen a gripping account of his travails at SBI, and how the Bank is navigating challenges to play an important role in India's growth story. This book captures Rajnish Kumar's inspirational journey from a small town in India to the Chairmanship of a venerable financial institution. I am sure each one of us, be it a student, an entrepreneur or a business leader, can learn from the experiences shared by one of the doyens of the financial sector in this book.'

—**Sanjiv Mehta**, Chairman and Managing Director, Hindustan Unilever Limited; President, Unilever South Asia

'Rajnish Kumar ran India's largest bank at one of the most turbulent times in the Indian financial sector. His book reflects his personality. Down-to-earth, sleeves-rolled-up, real-world banker at the scene of action when a lot happened.

He was open to out of the box thinking and execution. The book captures his candour. I read with interest his chapter on 'Trouble in the Corridors of Money' and can relate to the many challenges we in the financial sector faced. He has captured the SBI's transition to new-age digital banking with YONO. Rajnish's book is a refreshing narration of stories from our sector, many of which have the potential to be a Bollywood blockbuster.'

—**Uday Kotak**, CEO, Kotak Mahindra Bank

'The SBI enjoys the trust of all Indians as India's leading bank with a history of over 200 years. As the Chairman of SBI during a particularly critical period in India's economic and political history, Rajnish Kumar provided the leadership to face many a crisis with great distinction. His memoir make for a fascinating reading and gives an insider's view of many momentous events. A must read for all.'

—**T.V. Mohandas Pai**, Chairman, Aarin Capital Partners

'Rajnish Kumar led the banking behemoth SBI through its more difficult period with a quiet fortitude and unmatched personal confidence. This book gives a fascinating glimpse into the building blocks that went into the making of the man from his humble beginnings in Meerut to a seasoned banker who took the bank to new heights and laid a firm foundation for its continued sustenance. A must-read for anyone who wants to understand how the Indian financial system works.'

—**Harsh Goenka**, Chairman, RPG Enterprises

'Rajnish Kumar is a no-frill banker. He calls a spade a spade and believes execution is as important as vision for running a bank. This book, from cover to cover, bears testimony to his philosophy as a finance professional. Whether the success of the YES Bank rescue act, led by the State Bank of

India, or the failure of the banking system in reviving Jet Airways promptly, Kumar has written the behind-the-scenes stories dispassionately. He is a good raconteur. The book also offers insights into what it takes to be a leader to run India's biggest and one among the world's 50 largest banks by assets, representing little less than one-fourth of the nation's GDP.'

—Tamal Bandyopadhyay,
bestselling author and award-winning columnist

THE CUSTODIAN OF TRUST

A BANKER'S MEMOIR

RAJNISH KUMAR

PENGUIN
VIKING
An imprint of Penguin Random House

VIKING

USA | Canada | UK | Ireland | Australia
New Zealand | India | South Africa | China

Viking is part of the Penguin Random House group of companies
whose addresses can be found at global.penguinrandomhouse.com

Published by Penguin Random House India Pvt. Ltd
4th Floor, Capital Tower 1, MG Road,
Gurugram 122 002, Haryana, India

First published in Viking by Penguin Random House India 2021

The author is committed to using the royalty from this book for charitable purposes.

10 9 8 7 6 5 4 3 2 1

The views and opinions expressed in this book are the author's own and the facts are as reported by him which have been verified to the extent possible, and the publishers are not in any way liable for the same.

ISBN 9780670095773

Typeset in Adobe Caslon Pro by Manipal Technologies Limited, Manipal
Printed at Replika Press Pvt. Ltd, India

www.penguin.co.in

In loving memory of Aakanksha Agarwal (1985–2005)

Contents

Part Three: My Journey with SBI

Abbreviations

AA	:	Appellate Authority
AEL	:	Aurora Enterprises Limited
ALCO	:	Asset Liability Committee
APIs	:	Account Information and Payment Initiation (portals)
APL	:	Adani Power Limited
APTEL	:	Appellate Tribunal for Electricity
ARCs	:	Asset Reconstruction Companies
ATIs	:	Administrative Training Institutes
ATMs	:	Automated Teller Machines
AUM	:	Assets under Management
BARC	:	Bhabha Atomic Research Centre
BFSI	:	Banking, Financial Services, and Insurance (sector)
BG	:	Bank Guarantee
BHEL	:	Bharat Heavy Electricals Limited
BOT	:	Build–Operate–Transfer
CA	:	Chartered Accountant
CAG	:	Corporate Accounts Group
CAGR	:	Compound Annual Growth Rate

CAIIB	:	Certified Associate of the Indian Institute of Bankers
CBS	:	Core Banking System
CCG	:	Commercial Clients Group
CCO	:	Chief Credit Officer
CDMs	:	Cash Deposit Machines
CDS	:	Career Development System
CENMAC	:	Central Management Committee
CERC	:	Central Electricity Regulatory Commission
CFOs	:	Chief Financial Officers
CGM	:	Chief General Manager
CGPL	:	Coastal Gujarat Power Limited
CIDCO	:	City and Industrial Development Corporation
CIR	:	Corporate Insolvency Resolution
CIRP	:	Corporate Insolvency Resolution Procedure
CITU	:	Centre for Indian Trade Union
CLG	:	Credit Light Group
CoC	:	Committee of Creditors
CRD	:	Credit Review Department
CrPC	:	Criminal Procedure Code
CRPSs	:	Cumulative Redeemable Preference Shares
CRR	:	Cash Reserve Ratio
CSAs	:	Coal Supply Agreements
CXOs	:	Chief Experience Officers
DFI	:	Development Finance Institution
DFS	:	Department of Financial Services
DHBVN	:	Dakshin Haryana Bijli Vitran Nigam
DHFL	:	Dewan Housing Finance Limited
DPC	:	Dabhol Power Company
DSIBs	:	Domestic SIBs
EASE	:	Enhanced Access Service Excellence (award)
EPCs	:	Engineering, Procurement and Construction (companies)
EPGL	:	Essar Power Gujarat Limited
ESAHL	:	Essar Steel Asia Holdings Limited

ESIL	:	Essar Steel (India) Limited
FCA	:	Financial Conduct Authority
FCs	:	Financial Creditors
FDI	:	Foreign Direct Investment
FI	:	Financial Institution
FIMM	:	Financial Inclusion and Micro market
Fintech	:	Financial Technological Company
FOB	:	Free on Board
FSA	:	Financial Services Authority
FSA	:	Fuel Supply Agreement
FTDPM	:	Fast Track Disciplinary Proceedings Management
GAIL	:	Gas Authority of India
GCF	:	Gross Capital Formation
GCV	:	Gross Calorific Value
GDP	:	Gross Domestic Product
GERC	:	Gujarat Electricity Regulatory Commission
GHG	:	Greenhouse Gas
GMDC	:	Gujarat Mineral Development Corporation
GRM	:	Group Relationship Manager
GST	:	Goods and Services Tax
GUVNL	:	Gujarat Urja Vikas Nigam Limited
HPC	:	High Power Committee
HPGCL	:	Haryana Power Generation Corporation Limited
HRMS	:	Human Resources Management System
HUL	:	Hindustan Unilever Limited
IACs	:	Internal Advisory Committees
IAS	:	Indian Administrative Service
IBA	:	Indian Banks' Association
IBBI	:	Insolvency and Bankruptcy Board of India
IBC	:	Insolvency and Bankruptcy Code
IDC	:	Interest During Construction
IDPs	:	Individual Development Plans
IEX	:	Indian Energy Exchange

IFCI	:	Industrial Finance Corporation of India
IFFCO	:	Indian Farmers' Fertiliser Cooperative Limited
IIFCL	:	India Infrastructure Finance Corporation Limited
ILFS	:	Infrastructure Leasing & Financial Services
KLPL	:	Konkan LNG Private Limited
KRAs	:	Key Result Areas
KRIBHCO	:	Krishak Bharati Cooperative Limited
KYC	:	Know Your Customer
LC	:	Letters of Credit
LNG	:	Liquefied Natural Gas
MCG	:	Mid-Corporate Group
MCL	:	Mahanadi Coalfields Limited
MIAL	:	Mumbai International Airport Limited
MLA	:	Member of the Legislative Assembly
MoCA	:	Ministry of Civil Aviation
MOD	:	Merit Order Dispatch
MoPNG	:	Ministry of Petroleum and Natural Gas
MoU	:	Memorandum of Understanding
MSEB	:	Maharashtra State Electricity Board
MSEDCL	:	Maharashtra State Electricity Distribution Company Limited
NBFCs	:	Non-Banking Financial Companies
NBG	:	National Banking Group
NBI	:	National Banking Institute
NCLAT	:	National Company Law Appellate Tribunal
NCLT	:	National Company Law Tribunal
NHAI	:	National Highways Authority of India
NIIF	:	National Investment and Infrastructure Fund
NPAs	:	Non-Performing Assets
NPL	:	Non-Performing Loans
NTPC	:	National Thermal Power Corporation
OCs	:	Operational Creditors

OMDA	:	Operation Management and Development Agreement
ONGC	:	Oil and Natural Gas Corporation Limited
OSD	:	Officer on Special Duty
PAPL	:	Pre-Approved Personal Loan
PCA	:	Prompt Corrective Action (framework)
PE	:	Private Equity
PIL	:	Public Interest Litigation
PLF	:	Plant Load Factor
PMC	:	Punjab & Maharashtra Cooperative Bank
PMLA	:	Prevention of Money Laundering Act
PMO	:	Prime Minister's Office
POS	:	Point of Sale
POs	:	Probationary Officers
PPA	:	Power Purchase Agreement
PPP	:	Public–Private Partnership (model)
PRA	:	Prudential Regulation Authority
PSB	:	Public Sector Bank
PSU	:	Public Sector Unit
RA	:	Reviewing Authority
RBI	:	Reserve Bank of India
RfP	:	Request for Proposal
RGPL	:	Reliance Gas Pipelines Limited
RGPPL	:	Ratnagiri Gas and Power Private Limited
RIL	:	Reliance Industries Limited
RM	:	Regional Manager
ROE	:	Return on Equity
RP	:	Resolution Professional
SBA	:	State Bank Academy
SBFI	:	State Bank Foundation Institute
SBI CAPS	:	SBI Capital Markets
SBI	:	State Bank of India
SBICB	:	State Bank Institute of Consumer Banking
SBICRM	:	State Bank Institute of Credit and Risk Management

SBIHRD	:	State Bank Institute of Human Resource Development
SBIICM	:	State Bank Institute of Information and Communication Management
SBIIT	:	State Bank Institute of Innovation and Technology
SBIL	:	State Bank Institute of Leadership
SBIM	:	State Bank Institute of Management
SBIRB	:	State Bank Institute of Rural Banking
SBIRD	:	State Bank Institute of Rural Development
SBNs	:	Specified Bank Notes
SBSC	:	State Bank Staff College
SBT	:	State Bank of Travancore
SCOD	:	Scheduled Commercial Operation Date
SEBI	:	Securities and Exchange Board of India
SIBs	:	Systemically Important Banks
SIDBI	:	Small Industries Development Bank of India Ltd
SLR	:	Statutory Liquidity Ratio
SOPs	:	Standard Operating Procedures
SPPA	:	Supplemental PPA (Power Purchase Agreement)
SPVs	:	Special Purpose Vehicles
SSB	:	Services Selection Board
STU	:	Strategic Training Unit
TOs	:	Trainee Officers
TRA	:	Trust and Retention Account
UHBVN	:	Uttar Haryana Bijli Vitran Nigam
UIDAI	:	Unique Identification Authority of India
UMPP	:	Ultra Mega Power Project
UP	:	Uttar Pradesh
VMVSs	:	Vision, Mission, and Value Statements
YONO	:	You Only Need One

Preface

On 6 October 2020, I completed my three-year term as the Chairman of the State Bank of India (SBI), the largest bank in the country and amongst the top 50 banks in the world. Prior to me, 24 chairpersons had had the honour of leading the bank in this executive position. The SBI carries a legacy of more than 210 years behind it, and occupies a special place in the socio-economic history of India. The bank was created in its current form under an Act of the Parliament on 1 July 1955.

That the SBI is a unique institution in the world is largely due to the fact that it is the only bank across nations that funds the largest corporates and infrastructure projects while at the same time offering inclusive banking to meet the needs of the most underprivileged citizens of the country. The fact that it is a listed entity on stock exchanges with a majority of its stake being owned by the Government entails its own challenges of governance and the mandate to fulfil the high expectations of all its stakeholders. Thus, there is never a dull moment in the life of the SBI Chairman even in normal times.

My tenure as Chairman was even more momentous as the period during which I shouldered this responsibility cannot be termed as 'normal' under any circumstances. The Indian banking industry was going through one of its most tumultuous phases. The problem of non-performing loans (NPLs) had severely impacted the balance sheet and profitability of banks, especially those in the public sector. The failure of a few prominent non-banking financial companies (NBFCs) and the near-collapse of the fourth largest private sector bank in the country, YES Bank, posed a serious threat to the private sector banking system of the country. Further, the rise of Financial Technological Companies (Fintechs) was changing the fiscal landscape by creating competition for conventional banks.

The other unprecedented events that occurred just before and during my stint as the SBI Chairman, which had a lasting impact on the nation's economy, included demonetization, introduction of the Insolvency and Bankruptcy Code (IBC) and the Goods and Services Tax (GST), and the rise of e-commerce companies, all of which fostered a paradigm shift in the operating environment for banks. All these developments have inspired me to write this book to share my experiences at SBI with readers and invite them to join my eventful journey aboard this huge ship.

The book is divided into three sections. Part I provides details about the YES Bank fiasco and the rescue of the bank, the behind-the-scenes tale of Jet Airways, assessment of NPLs from a banker's perspective, and the case of Essar Steel, a trailblazer in terms of the resolution of stressed assets under the newly introduced IBC.

Part II details the SBI's handling of the challenges of demonetization and of the merger of six banks with it, cleaning up of the bank's balance sheet, the advent of a significant technological advancement through the introduction of its YONO App, and most importantly, harnessing of the latent talent in the bank that has enabled it to sail through rough waters.

In Part III, I have offered glimpses of my personal life, including my struggles before and after joining SBI, how I survived a serious childhood illness, completion of my education in trying financial circumstances, the many hits and misses in my career, and above all, a monumental personal tragedy that took a heavy emotional toll on me and my near and dear ones. It was in the midst of all these conundrums that I got the opportunity to lead one of the most coveted institutions in the country, an outcome I would never have expected when I humbly began my career in the narrow streets of the small town of Meerut in Uttar Pradesh.

To end it all, the final year of my assignment as the top functionary of the SBI was marked by the advent of the biggest ever health and economic crisis faced by the world, the COVID-19 pandemic. It also had a devastating impact on the bank with many staff members succumbing to the disease. Keeping the bank's operations up and running, and witnessing the unfettered compassion and empathy in these circumstances have been the lasting testimony to the unimpeachable character and strong willpower of the staff at the State Bank of India to perform their duty in the most adverse circumstances. The book is a tribute to this spirit.

Rajnish Kumar
21 July 2021

PART ONE

The Crisis

Was It a Lehman Brothers Moment for India?

Dedicated to Late Shri Arun Jaitley,
erstwhile Finance Minister,
who guided me in many crucial decisions.

1

Trouble in the Corridors of Money

In September 2018, the financial markets in India got a shock when the financial arm of Infrastructure Leasing & Financial Services Ltd (ILFS) defaulted on its payment of Rs 1,000 crore loan to Small Industries Development Bank of India Ltd (SIDBI). The ILFS group was engaged in financing and development of infrastructure projects. The parent company and its financial services subsidiary enjoyed the highest credit rating of AAA, indicating the lowest probability of default. In January 2019, the Cobrapost website, known for journalistic sting operations, alleged that Dewan Housing Finance Limited (DHFL), a company engaged primarily in housing finance, had siphoned off Rs 31,000 crore. In 2008, DHFL also enjoyed the highest credit rating of AAA. Though the owners of DHFL, the Wadhawans, vehemently denied any wrongdoing, its lending practices and the books came under question and in November 2019, DHFL was eventually put under administration by the Reserve Bank of India (RBI). In September 2019, the RBI placed the Punjab & Maharashtra Cooperative Bank (PMC) under moratorium and put it under administration. It was not the first cooperative bank to face action by the RBI. It was, however, one of the largest cooperative banks having operations in more than one state and had a balance sheet size of Rs 13,000 crore, which made it larger than many small finance banks. There were many banks, both in the private and public sectors, which were facing trouble and put under Prompt Corrective Action (PCA) framework, a policy tool used by the RBI to deal with the banks in trouble. The most problematic of all was YES Bank, the fourth largest private sector bank owned by Rana Kapoor and family. The bank was put under a moratorium in March 2020. The discussion was rife in financial circles as to whether India was facing its Lehman Brothers moment.

Lehman Brothers was the fourth largest investment bank in the United States and had US$639 billion in assets. The failure of Lehman Brothers in 2008 caused a global financial crisis. To put things in perspective, the balance sheet of the largest bank in the country, State Bank of India (SBI), is smaller than that of Lehman Brothers. The fear was not unfounded because the impact of the debt crisis started impacting the mutual fund industry and six debt schemes of Franklin Templeton Mutual Fund had to be recently wound up, causing immense loss to its investors. The mutual fund industry had invested heavily in long-term debt instruments and the commercial papers, a short-term money market instrument issued by the non-banking financial companies (NBFCs). Any default was sure to have a spiralling effect. These were really unnerving times not only for financial market players and regulators but most importantly, for investors in mutual funds and depositors of YES Bank. The credibility of the entire banking and financial system was at stake, with huge implications for the economy of the country and its standing in the global markets. A crisis is a terrible thing to waste, they say—the economic crisis faced by India in 1991, when the country had to mortgage its gold, and the securities and stock market scam of 1992 led to an overhaul of the system and many path-breaking reforms of the economy and the financial markets were carried out, which changed the face of the country and its financial system. The timely interventions by the government and the RBI, through provision of liquidity support, helped the country escape its Lehman Brothers moment. However, long-term reform measures are still needed to fix the system. Although a few measures have already been initiated, only time will tell if these are enough.

The Saga of YES Bank

The successful rescue of YES Bank in a short period of time is a unique example of perfectly coordinated action by the government, the RBI, and Public–Private partnerships. Of all the names, I have picked YES Bank to write about because of this uniqueness.

The saga of YES Bank started unfolding in June 2018 for me, when I received a request for an appointment from GVK Reddy of the GVK Group, a company in the construction business. My brief for the meeting with Reddy was to discuss the financing of the Navi Mumbai International Airport. GVK Group had built international airports at Mumbai and Bengaluru under the Public–Private Partnership model (PPP) and now had been awarded the contract to build another International Airport at Navi Mumbai. Although the SBI had re-financed Mumbai International Airport Limited (MIAL) a few years ago, it was not otherwise involved in financing any other project for the GVK Group. However, that was no reflection on the credibility or stature of the Group that had created world-class international airports at Bengaluru and Mumbai, especially the latter, which is undoubtedly one of the finest airports in the world. The infrastructure at airports in other countries may be better than at the Mumbai airport but the unique artworks at *Amchi Mumbai* never fail to fuel a deep sense of pride in Indian traditions and culture among travellers like me. I was actually looking forward to the meeting, mainly because of the deep impact created by MIAL in India's infrastructural space.

It was fascinating to learn from Reddy how he had entered the infrastructure business exactly after his return from the USA, and how the GVK Group had subsequently become one of the leading infrastructure companies in India, at par with other large south-based infrastructure companies like the Grandhi Mallikarjuna Rao (GMR) Group, Iragavarapu Venkata Reddy Construction Limited (IVRCL), Lagadapati Amarappa Naidu and Company (LANCO), and Ramky Infras. In addition, many other smaller companies have mushroomed in the South, especially in Hyderabad, arousing my curiosity about the business environment in southern India that nurtures their growth and what distinguishes them from their counterparts in the North. While each of these companies deserves admiration for creating a unique niche for itself, I later learnt from one of the promoters that political patronage had also played a critical role in their success.

The Mumbai airport is also a reminder of the rapid economic progress made by India over the last 25 years, especially when compared to the pathetic conditions witnessed at the Delhi and Mumbai airports in the mid-1990s with stinking carpets and toilets. The modernization of many of the airports in the country has been carried out successfully under Public Private Partnership (PPP) between the Airports Authority of India and a private developer. The PPP model has been relatively successful because of the capability to generate higher revenue by levying higher user fee and development of real estate around the airport.

YES Bank, the Lender of Last Resort

During discussions with the GVK Group, it became clear that the proposed project of the new international airport in Mumbai would be a highly complex one. Construction of the airport entailed flattening of an entire hill and re-routing of a rivulet that flowed right through the land designated for the project. It also necessitated a huge amount of earth work. Of course, the future of the project was never in any doubt as Mumbai badly needed a second airport. The existing airport was running to its maximum capacity and flying in and out of Mumbai had become a nightmare for passengers. The departure and landing of most flights were inevitably delayed and it was very rare for any flight to take off or land on time at Mumbai. Since the existing airport was surrounded by slums, there was no scope for its expansion. Both the Ministry of Civil Aviation (MoCA) and City and Industrial Development Corporation (CIDCO), the local authority, which was responsible for the development of New Mumbai, were keen for work on the project to commence at the earliest.

The mandate for appraisal and arranging of financial closure for the project was accepted by SBI without much persuasion. The project finance team started working earnestly on the project. The MoCA, CIDCO, and the Maharashtra Government were keen to ensure an early financial closure, and 'in principle' approval had already been given by SBI. However, there was a lot of apprehension and unease within SBI on one issue, that of defaults on loans by group companies in the power and road sectors, as a result of which the bank had been insisting that the promoters should settle the default payments of the group companies. In the midst of this, suddenly one day, I learnt that YES Bank had sanctioned the entire loan amount enabling achievement of the financial closure. Simultaneously, reports were doing the round that YES Bank had charged a very hefty fee for the transaction. These developments took the entire team at SBI by surprise. Reddy called to explain the urgency for achieving the financial closure and the difficulty the Group was facing in complying with the terms stipulated by SBI. Deciding to end the matter then and there, I wished him good luck and did not discuss the issue again with him. The lending model of YES Bank was apparently to be a lender of the last resort for borrowers who were under stress or were unable to raise borrowings from other banks, and to charge a high fee for this service. These dealings were shrouded in a degree of ambiguity, and only ongoing investigations by the Enforcement Directorate would reveal whether a part of the fee was being diverted to group companies owned by the family members of the management of the bank. However, one thing that my team found in most of the cases was that the promoter of YES Bank, Rana Kapoor, had secured the loans well.

Behind the Scenes

The former MD and CEO of YES Bank, Ravneet Gill, had alleged that the private lender had, as on 31 March 2018, released a credit watch list naming several large corporate borrowers, including Reliance ADAG Group, Essel Group, Cox & Kings, Dewan Housing Finance, and several others. What is less clear is why the RBI took its own time in deciding on the re-appointment of Rana Kapoor as MD of YES Bank, since his term was ending in August 2018. However, regardless of the reason, once the decision on the appointment was delayed, the RBI was probably left with no choice but to offer a three-month extension up to January 2019 to Rana Kapoor.

There was an avid interest in financial circles about the prospective successor to Rana Kapoor. One of the prominent industrialists, who was always equipped with all the information about developments in the corridors of power, mentioned Ravneet Gill's name as a likely successor to Rana Kapoor and possibly also a shadow MD with Rana Kapoor still in control of the bank as a back seat driver. I paid little heed to this rumour. I was also sceptical of the idea that Ravneet would leave his cushy job at Deutsche Bank and agree to take responsibility of running a troubled bank. Moreover, my impression about Ravneet was that he was a perfect gentleman, an all-weather friend, and belonging to a respectable category of bankers armed with foreign degrees and strong communication skills. He also ostensibly represented the culture of foreign banks and their paradigm of cutting one's losses and moving on in case of an adverse event. It thus came as a total surprise to me when Ravneet accepted the offer.

Since YES Bank had exposure on Jet Airways, I had the opportunity of interacting with Ravneet on a couple of occasions. He and his team had agreed to support the resolution plan on many issues but failed to secure approval from their board. I understood his position because most of the banks were extremely reluctant to support a resolution plan for Jet Airways. For me too, this was one of the most challenging cases with even the SBI board being uncomfortable in backing me on this issue, not because I did not enjoy their support or goodwill but because they felt that it posed a huge risk to the reputation of the bank. Consequently, they did not want to be party to such a decision without receiving an explicit letter of support from the Department of Financial Services (DFS) or the MoCA. I had not faced such a difficult situation throughout my two-year long tenure at the helm of affairs at SBI, but I viewed it as a major learning experience that came in handy in resolving the YES Bank crisis.

The Quest for Partners to Save YES Bank

Soon, the grapevine was rife with rumours that Ravneet and the board of YES Bank were not on the same page, and the news spread rapidly in financial circles, which were also aghast at the manner in which the capital raising issue was handled by YES Bank. It was clear that senior staff at YES Bank were totally unaware of both the RBI as well as Securities and Exchange Board of India (SEBI) regulations. Analysts had already started predicting an unsavoury end for the bank. Inevitably, the one question that always emerged at every meeting of analysts and during discussions of quarterly earnings was whether SBI would have to jump in to save YES Bank. This question was also regularly asked by TV anchors and in the columns of almost every financial daily across the country.

What the analysts and media failed to realize was that SBI was a Government-owned entity and also a listed one, and that YES Bank too was a listed entity. Hence, any word about the matter from me would have huge ramifications for the stock prices of both banks, and under the circumstances, no chairman of any bank could offer an unequivocal statement on the issue. Secretly, I also started harbouring the fear that eventually the analysts and newspaper columnists would be proved right, for if not SBI, who else could become a saviour for YES Bank? On a lighter side, Uday Kotak, the owner of the Kotak Mahindra Bank, and I would keep pulling each other's leg. He would say, 'YES Bank is yours', and I would respond that private sector banks should be saved only by their counterparts in the private sector, and since his bank had deep pockets, it was best suited to act as a Good Samaritan in this case. Providentially, our discussions held in jest, proved to be prophetic, and eventually both of us had to step in together to save YES Bank. Initially, I believed that after having achieved the mergers of six banks, SBI would be spared the task of saving yet another bank. The last bailout by SBI had been that of Kashi Nath Seth Bank, a family owned bank, operating in a few districts of Uttar Pradesh (UP). The takeover of the bank was a complete disaster at the local levels, and had severely impacted the performance of the bank in many districts of Uttar Pradesh. But 2020 was not the same as 1990. Neither SBI nor Kashi Nath Seth Bank was a listed entity and SBI was not competing with new-generation private sector banks then.

SBI Emerges as Saviour of YES Bank

Stephen A. Schwarzman, MD of Blackstone Group and the author of one of the bestselling books *What It Takes: Lessons in the Pursuit of Excellence*, was on a visit to India in the first week of March 2020. On the evening of 5 March 2020, Mukesh Ambani had organized an event at his residence, Antilia, in honour of Stephen and for the release of his book in India. The who's who from the financial industry of India were present at the event. While the event was going on, the news broke about the moratorium on

YES Bank by the RBI. I also got a call from the RBI that Prashant Kumar, Deputy Managing Director and Chief Financial Officer at SBI, was being appointed as the administrator and needed to report at YES Bank next morning at 8 a.m. I asked Prashant to submit his resignation. The entire process of his resignation and its acceptance was completed within the next two hours. He came with his resignation letter to the Altamount Road, where Antilia is located, and I accepted his resignation, sitting in his car.

Earlier, during the day, I had made a courtesy call on Schwarzman and briefly the situation of YES Bank was discussed. It was an exploratory meeting to discuss whether Blackstone could be a potential investor with SBI in the lead. My first parallel action was to send a message to my team at SBI to reach out to Amit Dixit, who was heading Indian Operations of Blackstone as well as other private equity (PE) investors. On the same night (5 March) itself, I saw a missed call from Sonjoy Chatterjee, the head of Goldman Sachs in India. Sonjoy was a good friend and among the very few with whom I enjoyed socializing.

I called back Sonjoy early in the morning on 6 March. He wanted to discuss the YES Bank situation with me, as Goldman Sachs was interested in investing in it and he was one of the first potential investors. My next meeting was with Amit Dixit and Deepak Parekh, involving one of the most serious discussions I would have in my capacity as head of SBI. I found that Amit Dixit was quite knowledgeable and had done his homework. Amit felt that the action of placing YES Bank under moratorium had complicated the things. Nevertheless, Blackstone was willing to participate in the deal and consider taking up a share of up to 20 per cent. HDFC, on the other hand, was willing to invest around Rs 1,000 crore, and between the two of them, Amit wanted two board seats. All these demands were, of course, subject to the deal being in accordance with the RBI criteria and willingness to allow an investment of beyond 5 per cent. The estimate by Blackstone for the losses incurred by YES Bank was around Rs 45,000 crore.

A consensus was already emerging around this figure amongst investors based on the information gathered from various sources. It would require a write-down of the entire equity and AT-1 bonds besides the loan loss provisions already held. Further, there was the issue of liability on account of income tax, for which exemption was a must and would be a pre-condition for investment.

The potential names for the board members as well as the names of the MD and CEO were also discussed in the meeting. Amit Dixit expressed some reservation about whether Prashant could handle a bank of the size of YES Bank. I had to tell him politely but firmly that at the current juncture, we needed a 'nuts and bolts' person who had dirtied his hands at the ground level, and could ensure culmination of the deal. From all accounts, Prashant was the right choice with the capability of handling the situation and enjoyed the confidence of everyone concerned with the matter. He had earlier been instrumental in turning around the fortunes of the Kolkata circle of SBI, which had branches in West Bengal and Sikkim. There was a great deal of negative perception about the work culture in West Bengal, which was, in fact, almost considered to be incorrigible due to its many limitations as a business destination. However, the turnaround started under Prashant, and today West Bengal is consistently amongst the top-performing circles in the bank. SBI has divided the entire branch network into 17 circles, with each circle typically controlling 1,200 to 1,600 branches. The business handled by each circle of the bank is higher than the cumulative business of many mid-sized banks, and the experience of running a circle is considered as a pre-requisite for becoming a Managing Director or Chairman in the bank.

I was quite impressed with the depth of knowledge of the subject exhibited by Amit and my interaction with him provided crucial inputs for my subsequent discussions with the RBI. Amit was very clear about two issues, one, that the bank should be fully capitalized and the entire capital of a minimum of Rs 22,000 crore should be infused into it in one go; second, that the RBI should provide an unsecured committed loan of Rs 50,000 crore to YES Bank. Just to reiterate, the Government had put YES Bank under a moratorium till 3 April and capped deposit withdrawal at Rs 50,000 after severe deterioration of the bank's financial position. There was also a fear that there may be a run on the bank as soon as the moratorium was lifted.

The Nitty-Gritty of the Resurrection Plan

Simultaneously, I had been discussing the matter with several other potential investors like Brookfield, Carlyle, and KKR. One fund which showed remarkable speed and willingness to conclude the deal was Tilden Park. They had reportedly discussed the funding with their existing management and a strict timeline had reportedly been stipulated by the RBI to report visibility of funds. Tilden Park had actually transferred US$500 million. Rakesh Jhunjhunwala, Premji Invest, and D Mart had also shown willingness to chip in Rs 500 crore each. The efforts were proceeding in the right direction and I became very optimistic that the target of INR Rs 22,000 crore was achievable with SBI contributing around Rs 7,000 crore, for a stake of 30 per cent in YES Bank. The only problem in mobilizing foreign funds for the deal was the timeline as foreign investors had to go through their own processes involving approval from investment committees and legal approvals. Although everyone realized the need for maintaining a tight timeline, it was clear that funding the transaction before 13 March, as desired by the RBI, was virtually impossible.

The legal challenge posed by the AT-1 bond holders was also weighing on the minds of investors. Achieving a full write-off, as proposed in the draft scheme, was in the interest of the new investors. The AT-1 bond-holders had proposed to YES Bank for converting the entire amount of Rs 8,700 crore into a 20 per cent equity at a cost of Rs 51 per share. This implied that the cost of acquisition for new investors would go up by 20 per cent. While the new investors were not averse to the idea, it was proposed that the matter should be left to the administrator and that the RBI should take a call on it.

Both Amit Dixit and Deepak Parekh discussed the issue with Stephen Schwarzman, CEO of Blackstone Group, and conveyed the urgency of concluding the deal to him. I was told that the earliest date when the funding could happen was 19 March, and accordingly, I sent an update to the RBI officials handling the matter. On the evening of 8 March, which also happened to be the date for celebrating the festival of Holi, I met both the Deputy Governors at the RBI guest house, updating them on the discussions and the terms at which the potential investors were willing to invest in YES Bank. I also made it clear that there was no way for the funding to happen before 19 March and that I would prefer to mobilize as much equity as possible. However, the RBI was not willing to wait till the 19th, and were insisting that the funding must happen on or before 13 March. I also mentioned in the meeting that even domestic investors, particularly HDFC and Kotak, had developed cold feet and were not willing to put in any money unless all the other potential investors joined in the deal. There was also reluctance to obtain equity from other domestic investors lest it leads to criticism of selling the equity cheap and thereby allowing profiteering.

It was also clear that at this stage, the RBI was not concerned about the impact of these events on AT-1 bond markets and felt that YES Bank would eventually be on a strong footing legally by adjusting the AT-1 bonds. The RBI officials asked me why SBI did not proceed as planned earlier and acquire a stake of only 49 per cent by subscribing to 245 crore shares. I told them candidly that the moratorium had changed the entire scenario, resulting in a real risk of a run on YES Bank. Thus, SBI would not be able to manage alone, and it was important to ensure that a few more investors joined in the deal. Simultaneously, I was also not confident of the ability of YES Bank to raise the required capital in the second stage or even before the financial results at the end of the fiscal year were announced on 31 March 2020. I strongly felt that if an investor met the fit and proper criteria of the RBI and the rules pertaining to Know Your Customer (KYC) and anti-money laundering, at this stage, YES Bank should raise capital from any such investors. The lock-in requirement of three years would prevent any allegations about allowing profiteering from taking ground. It was, eventually, decided to carry forward the discussions next day though everyone was more or less in agreement that the process would be completed in two stages, with SBI and a few other banks contributing equity before 13 March in the first stage. It was also felt that the Deputy Governors concerned would perhaps need to discuss the matter with the Governor too.

The Perils of Networking

I reached out to Uday immediately after the critical meeting and discussed the situation with him in detail, as to why a few domestic banks needed to come forward and join hands with SBI. In view of the current situation, wherein many public sector banks (PSBs) were having shortage of capital for their own operations, and the rest were busy in mergers, there was no possibility of any other public sector bank being able to make any contribution. The mantle of bailing out YES Bank thus naturally fell on the private banks.

We discussed the volatile situation at length and the need for some of the private banks to step in to save YES Bank. The failure of YES Bank would definitely pose a significant threat to the franchise of private banks in the country, particularly the smaller banks. While banks like HDFC Bank, ICICI Bank, Axis Bank, and Kotak Mahindra Bank were better placed to face similar situations, other private banks would be hit hard. Meanwhile, many state governments had already issued direction for withdrawing money from private banks, compelling the RBI to step in for damage control by writing to all the state governments to assure them about the safety of funds parked in private sector banks.

Uday told me that he was going to meet Deepak Parekh to discuss the issue with him urgently, and would thereafter meet me the next day at around 10.30 a.m. In the interim period, Deepak Parekh and Uday had touched base with Sandeep Bakhshi and Amitabh Chaudhry, the CEOs of ICICI Bank and Axis Bank, who agreed, in principle, to contribute Rs 1,000 crore and Rs 600 crore respectively, which again was a very pragmatic view taken by both the gentlemen. There were a few expectations from the RBI, which we decided to convey to the RBI. The foremost was the grant of an unsecured credit line of Rs 50,000 crore to YES Bank from the RBI. Although the RBI was willing to extend liquidity support, it had expressed a preference to offer the support through SBI. Since I was not in a position to shoulder such a huge responsibility, I clearly conveyed to all concerned that the liquidity support for YES Bank had to come directly from the RBI with no obligations on SBI.

There would be no tax liability on account of preferential pricing, which was to be decided and certified as fair value by the RBI. We also wanted clarity on the AT-1 bonds in order to avoid litigation. However, the final decision was left to the administrator of YES Bank and the RBI. The security trustee of Axis Bank had submitted a consent of 75 per cent of AT-1 bond holders for converting the entire amount into equity with 20 shares for approximately 100 shares held. All of us were of the view that we should bring in as many investors as possible so that from day one after the moratorium, the bank would start with a sound capital base.

For my scheduled meeting with Deepak Parekh and Uday on the morning of 9 March, I was quite tense because I was not sure of the response of private sector banks. However, I breathed a sigh of relief when I came to know that apart from HDFC and Kotak Mahindra, two other major banks, viz. ICICI Bank and Axis Bank, had also been roped in to participate in the deal. These four banks were willing to collectively contribute Rs 3,100 crore rupees. All of us were also on the same page with regard to other issues such as tax exemption on the investment, unsecured line of credit by the RBI, accepting investment from other willing investors, and the need for clarity on the treatment of AT-1 bond holders. All the issues agitating the minds of the investing bankers were conveyed to RBI. Finally, the RBI advised that the share allotment and funding process had to be completed by 13 March. Since there were still strong reservations among some of the stakeholders about allowing other investors to buy shares, it was decided to take up the matter strongly with the Finance Ministry to offer income tax exemption and leave it to YES Bank to take a call on the treatment of AT-1 bonds as per the terms and conditions of such bonds, while the RBI had to finalize the scheme for reconstruction of YES Bank.

The issue around the existing equity holders was also deliberated at length. There was a proposed lock-in period of three years for 75 per cent of the shares bought for all investors other than SBI. The lock-in requirement for SBI would be a 26 per cent shareholding for a minimum of three years and a four-year window to bring in the shareholding below 30 per cent in compliance with the Banking Regulation Act. A question was raised that if there would also be a lock-in requirement for new investors and if the AT-1 bonds would also be written off, then how could the existing equity holders, who otherwise would be the first to bear the loss, be allowed to have no sacrifice. The best solution was to place similar restrictions on them as for the new investors. All of us were aware that such an arrangement would entail complications but there was no other option.

Anxious Moments for All . . .

All the potential foreign investors called off their due diligence except Tilden Park, who were very keen to invest at least US$500 million. The other investors, who were willing to invest, included Premji Invest, IIFL, and Damania. I also tested the waters with the Life Insurance Corporation of India (LIC). While Kumar, the Chairman of LIC, was also inclined to make an investment of up to Rs 250 crore, one limitation in this offer was that between SBI and LIC, we were not willing to go beyond a total investment of 49.9 per cent. Another difficulty was to achieve the transfer of funds on 14 March, which was a Saturday.

In view of all the above complications, it was finally decided to keep LIC out of the deal. In the meantime, Shyam Srinivasan of Federal Bank reached out to me and conveyed his willingness to take up with his Board for approval to invest about Rs 250 crore. V. Vaidyanathan of IDFC First Bank also chipped in as a surprise late entrant with a commitment of Rs 150 crore. Despite all these commitments, however, I was still falling short of the target of Rs 10,000 crore. In an effort to bridge the gap between the offers and the required investment, I called Ghosh of Bandhan Bank. He reluctantly agreed to put in another Rs 250 crore, which was a big relief. Uday asked me why I had decided to back out of the arrangement wherein SBI would first acquire a 49 per cent stake by investing Rs 2,450 crore. I reiterated that there was no backing out but after my discussions with all the investors, I came to the conclusion that it would be impossible to save YES Bank with so little capital and the end result would be disastrous for all concerned. I did not share with him my fear that such a misadventure would also bring the entire blame at the doors of SBI and it would be my head on the guillotine.

The proposed scheme was finally approved by the Government of India and notified on 13 March 2020. It was announced that the moratorium would be lifted from 18 March and the office of the administrator would be dissolved a week thereafter. Prashant Kumar was appointed as the MD and CEO of YES Bank and Sunil Mehta, former Non-Executive Chairman of Punjab National Bank, was designated as the Non-Executive Chairman of the newly constituted board of YES Bank. Two board seats were reserved for SBI as the largest shareholder and two others were reserved for the RBI nominees. The scheme was broadly in line with the requests made by the investing banks, with the only surprise being the absence of any mention of AT-1 bonds. The ostensible reason for this omission was that it was in the domain of YES Bank and the regulator.

The D-day, 14 March, was a hectic day for all the private banks and HDFC. I learnt that all the boards were going through a lot of anxiety. However, eventually, HDFC and all the banks were able to secure the approval of their boards and the share application money came into an escrow account with SBI. YES Bank proceeded with allotment of shares on the same day, and also announced its December quarter results late into the same night. When the books were cleaned and the losses booked, the fact that the real loss was less than the estimated figure came as a pleasant surprise to us. With all the pieces finally falling into place, this rapid restructuring of a commercial bank was achieved in perhaps the shortest possible time in the history of banking across the world. I had made an appearance on several news channels during the week, pointing out that after the deal was through, the YES Bank depositors would be able to withdraw their money very soon, and in fact, much before the timeline of 4 April mentioned in the draft restructuring scheme. There was all round disbelief at my declarations but eventually my statements and the timelines I had predicted were becoming a reality. Although the suspense was still not over, everyone was waiting with bated breath to watch what would actually happen on 18 March when the moratorium was to be finally lifted. It was a big relief for everyone that there was no panic amongst the retail investors. The bulk deposits by many state governments and corporates were withdrawn. The liquidity support of Rs 50,000 crore from the RBI prevented the collapse of YES Bank. The rest is history and need not be recounted here.

None of us were aware of the impending lockdown because of COVID-19 in the last week of March. With hindsight, I can say that the pressure from the RBI to implement the resolution plan by 14 March 2021 proved to be a providential escape for YES Bank and the depositors. A delay of 15 days would have led to disastrous consequences for both YES Bank and the banking system in the country. This time, it was a stitch just in time!

YES Bank could not have been saved without the resolute and astute leadership provided by the RBI Governor, Shaktikanta Das, and the two Deputy Governors, M.K. Jain and N.S. Vishwanathan. Another critical factor was the practical wisdom shown by Deepak Parekh and Uday Kotak, who correctly read the threat of a huge loss of liability franchise for private banks, if YES Bank was allowed to go under, and rallied their respective boards and the other private sector banks. The possibility of run on other private banks could not be ruled out, if YES Bank failed. The merger with SBI would have been a disaster for SBI, from integration perspective, in view of contrasting cultures. From balance sheet perspective, digesting YES Bank was not such a big problem for SBI.

One of the most important learnings from the entire crisis was that liquidity alone matters in the short term when dealing with a financial institution in crisis.

Uncomfortable Questions That Need Clairvoyant Answers

In hindsight, however, the YES Bank saga raises many questions. Could the RBI have acted faster? And if so, did the ostensible delay by the RBI have any long-term ramifications? These questions bear some thought and explanations here.

It was clear that YES Bank's plan to raise capital was not well thought out and the Board and management of the bank had not applied their minds sufficiently to prepare a proper revival plan. YES Bank had started losing deposits since around September and later was in breach of the requirements of Statutory Liquidity Ratio (SLR) and Cash Reserve Ratio (CRR). They were perhaps hoping against hope that YES Bank would be able to raise equity as per the SEBI regulations with regard to pricing and the take-over code. In this context, the action that the RBI took as late as March 2020 could probably have been taken as early as November 2019. But everyone is wiser in retrospect.

Licensing Policy for Banks

It would be an interesting exercise to assess the experiences of new-generation private sector banks in India, and to determine if any lessons have been learnt at all from the grim experiences of leading banks or if they have been conveniently forgotten. After the economic crisis of 1991, reforms were initiated in the country, with banking and financial sector reforms accounting for a major part of the agenda. As part of these reforms, five new banking licences were allotted in 1994. These included HDFC Bank promoted by HDFC, which had by then created a name for itself in housing finance; UTI Bank promoted by UTI; ICICI Bank promoted by the ICICI Group; IndusInd Bank promoted by the Hindujas; and Global Trust Bank, promoted by Ramesh Gelli and a few other professionals. Until then, the banking system had been dominated by public sector banks, with only a few smaller old-generation private sector banks to give them company. However, on receipt of licences, the new-generation private sector banks started making their presence felt rapidly. These banks had swanky branches, and were using the latest core banking platform, which radically opened up the consumer banking space. This development coincided with the growth of the neo-rich in India, who were clearly beneficiaries of the reform era.

The new-generation private sector banks functioned with much fewer constraints than their public sector counterparts as they had no legacy issues and enjoyed the flexibility to hire the best talent, to devise a suitable salary structure, and to fire non-performers. They also had the complete liberty to choose their business strategy with a focus on maximizing returns for shareholders. Public sector banks, on the other hand, had highly unionized staff with a very rigid human resources policy, which has not changed at all over the years except the fact that the role of unions has been sharply curtailed by the expansion of technology and the emergence of alternate channels. While government ownership has ensured continued faith of the customers in the banking system, as they feel safe in keeping their money in public sector banks irrespective of the performance of these banks, private sector banks have been able to wean away the creamy layer of profitable business from public sector banks. However, not all the five new banks that were allotted licences have had a free run. The Global Trust Bank incurred heavy losses in the stock market scam allegedly perpetrated by Ketan Parekh in the year 2001. This forced its main promoter, Ramesh Gelli, to resign; though he tried to make a comeback. The bank was eventually merged with the Oriental Bank of Commerce in 2004, the year YES Bank was born. It may be a coincidence but 16 years later, in the year 2020, history repeated itself with the near failure of YES Bank. In complete contrast, Kotak Mahindra Bank promoted by Uday Kotak has become one of the 10 most-valued companies in terms of market capitalization along with the HDFC twins and ICICI Bank and SBI.

In a surprise move, two more licences were given to private sector banks by the RBI after 10 years in 2014–15. While one of these was for Bandhan, a microfinance company with assets of Rs 5,000 crore, the second was an infrastructure finance company,

IDFC, which had been facing huge stress in its infrastructure financing portfolio.

It brings to question whether the RBI really had a rational policy for licensing. The policy for granting a licence may have had a rationale but it is perplexing to an outsider. The logic for granting licences to individuals immediately in the aftermath of the failure of Global Trust Bank defies logic. Uday still had a reputed partner like the Mahindras and was successfully running an NBFC. But, other than the requirement of a net worth of Rs 100 crore, what was the due diligence for three individuals who had come together to undertake as serious a task as floating a bank? They may have had the requisite professional experience for such a venture but the messy family dispute between Rana Kapoor and the family of late Ashok Kapur and the poor corporate governance at YES Bank put several question marks around the licensing process.

Does Ownership Matter?

The apparent answer to the above question is 'No'. Of the eight new-generation private sector banks, three, that is, HDFC, ICICI, and Axis, were originally promoted by institutions; three others, that is, Kotak, Bandhan, and IDFC First, have been driven by individuals, whereas one, IndusInd, has been promoted by a group, the Hindujas.

At the one end of the spectrum is HDFC Bank, one of the top performers, led for more than 26 years by Aditya Puri, the longest serving bank chief who created huge wealth for the bank's shareholders, before he stepped down in October 2020. His iron grip on the functioning of the bank, booming voice, and typical Punjabi accent have become part of folklore. The success of Kotak Mahindra Bank can largely be attributed to its owner Uday Kotak. ICICI Bank too benefited tremendously from the leadership of K.V. Kamath, who was at its helm for a sustained period, though ICICI Bank failed to command the same respect as that earned by HDFC Bank. During the Global Financial Crisis of 2008, there was a panic amongst the depositors of the bank and only the timely intervention of the RBI, coupled with help from SBI and other public sector banks, saved the day for it.

The performance of Axis Bank and IndusInd Bank is average when compared to the other three large peers. Bandhan and IDFC First Bank are too new and their performance needs to be watched. YES Bank was a failure and only time will tell how it performs in its new avatar.

One learning that clearly emerges from these developments is that the system should always be wary of high-profile CEOs flaunting flashy lifestyles, irrespective of ownership of the company. They can dazzle and bring success in the short term but in the long term, many such enterprises have ceased to exist.

India has a dream of becoming a 5 trillion dollar economy in the next five years. A sound banking and financial system is a sine qua non for achieving this dream. The proposed privatization of a few public sector banks is a significant step in this direction. A transparent licensing and ownership policy for the banks is required to support these efforts.

Capability of the RBI to Supervise a Large and Complex System

One also needs to ask if the RBI really has the necessary infrastructure to effectively supervise the banking system in the country. The banking and commercial spaces are chock-a-block with a multitude of various financial intermediaries, scheduled commercial banks, NBFCs, housing finance companies, deposit taking and non-deposit taking organizations, and cooperative banks, among other such institutions. The failures of ILFS, Dewan Housing and PMC Bank, and the near-failure of YES Bank have exposed chinks in the armour of the RBI. To their credit, the crisis has led to a real overhaul of the system and several steps have been taken around strengthening the corporate governance in the banks, auditing, process for licensing, tough regulatory stance and no-nonsense approach with regard to recognition of non-performing loans and provisions, which hopefully will lead to a healthier banking system in the country.

Role of Deposit Insurance Corporation

Yet another question that remains pertains to the purpose of deposit insurance. Deposit-taking institutions pay a huge fee to the Deposit Insurance Corporation. However, apart from a few cooperative banks, none of the commercial banks have been allowed to be liquidated, and remedies have instead been sought in amalgamation with another bank. Deposit insurance does not even have the capability of meeting the obligations to depositors of a small-sized commercial bank, not to speak of mid-sized commercial banks. Public sector banks have an implied sovereign guarantee by virtue of their ownership but because of the contagion effect, even a private sector bank works under the implicit comfort, if not guarantee, that it would not be allowed to fail. What then is the relevance of the Deposit Insurance Corporation? There is an immediate need to put in place a proper resolution framework for financial entities. In the absence of the same, each case has been dealt with differently. In the case of ILFS, the Central Government exercised powers under Section 241 (2) of the Companies Act 2013 to supersede the Board of the company and put a new board in place under the chairmanship of Uday Kotak. In case of Dewan Housing, the RBI initiated a Corporate Insolvency Resolution process under Section 227 of the Insolvency and Bankruptcy Code (IBC) framework. For PMC Bank, the search for a suitable new promoter has ended only recently. The cases of many other stressed NBFCs are still in limbo. The depositors of Laxmi Vilas Bank were lucky that a foreign bank, DBS of Singapore took it over. The lenders to

ILFS and its group companies as well as Dewan Housing are still waiting for recovery of their money.

How Small Is Too Small to Be Allowed to Fail?

The last but not the least question that one needs to ponder over is: How big is too big to fail or how small is too small to be allowed to fail? The Basel framework provides for additional capital buffers for Systemically Important Banks (SIBs). The RBI has identified three Domestic SIBs (DSIBs), viz., SBI, HDFC Bank and ICICI Bank, for providing an additional capital of 0.625 per cent to DSIBs as compared to other banks. These three banks have been chosen to play this role as they are considered to be too big to fail. Time and again, it has been proved that the failure or near-failure of even a small bank has disastrous consequences for the banking system and the economy because of the interconnectedness among all banks and financial institutions. The provision of an additional capital buffer offers little comfort as a coping mechanism in case of such a failure. There is, thus, a need to rethink about safety protocols in the banking system, and buffers of pooled risk capital and liquidity need to be built up that can be used to save a bank in distress.

2

The Jet Airways Conundrum

The Rise and Fall of a Trailblazer in the Airlines Sector

A rewarding facet of my tenure at SBI was that my learning was not just limited to the banking space but also offered me a window into the functioning of many key players in other leading sectors of the economy. Here, I recount the tale of one such player in the airlines sector, viz., Jet Airways, which had earned renown as one of the best airlines providing premium service and excellent connectivity to many international destinations. In contrast, the state carrier in the sector, Air India, was perceived to be on the decline despite sincere efforts at the higher levels of governance to improve its customer service and performance. However, the problems at Air India had become so deep-rooted and widespread that flyers had en masse started shifting their loyalties to private airlines like Jet Airways. Among other carriers, Vistara was the new kid on the block and was slowly acquiring new customers by flaunting its brand new aircraft and polite and courteous crew. Its only constraint was its limited connectivity as compared to Jet Airways and Air India. As for the rest of the airlines, they were much lower in the hierarchy of operators because they were budget airlines offering a much scaled down flying experience to customers, who were now spoilt for choice due to the expanding reach of the private sector airlines.

The rise of Jet Airways symbolized a remarkable achievement for its promoter, Naresh Goyal, an erstwhile travel agent with a an affable personality, who had made it big in the airline business through the sheer dint of his enterprise and hard work. Way back in 2010 or 2011, when I was heading the UK Operations of SBI, I had come across both Vijay Mallya and Naresh Goyal at a social event in London. The two were contrasting personalities—one was rich, flamboyant, and ostentatious while the other was a low-profile businessman, perhaps not highly educated but a very amicable person. In fact, looking at him, one could hardly believe that he was the man instrumental in creating such a successful airline in terms of both adroit branding and high-quality service. I have flown almost all major airlines across the globe, and found Jet to be a perfect match for many of the best international airlines like Emirates, Korean Air of South Korea, Lufthansa, and Singapore Airlines. For Indians, Jet offered another unique selling proposition—a familiar and comfortable environment stemming from its typical 'Indian-ness'. However, I soon learnt that trouble was brewing in this apparent paradise.

The Beginning of the End for Jet Airways

In the middle of 2019, Naresh Goyal and one of the topmost investment bankers hired by Jet Airways reached out to SBI for sanction of additional loans. The loans were to be secured by the pledge of shares of JP Miles, a frequent flyer programme being offered by the airline but which was managed by a separate company that Jet jointly owned with Etihad Airways. The valuation being talked about for this financial deal was in excess of US$1 billion.

While Jet was holding shares worth 49.9 per cent, the remaining 51.1 per cent were held by Etihad. It was obvious that Jet was facing shortage of working capital funds. My first intuitive reaction was that SBI should stay away from Jet's woes rather than enter into its messy financial waters. My perception seemed justified as subsequently many issues unfolded with regard to the valuation of Jet Privilege Private Limited pertaining to JP Miles, being closely held as also because its valuation would be inextricably linked with the performance of Jet Airways

Another proposal suggested for resolving the issue was that of financing against six Boeing 777, three Boeing 737 and three Airbus planes owned by Jet. Since SBI had no experience of financing aircraft, this proposal too could not be carried further and the company was advised to explore funding from other banks that had some understanding of financing aircraft. Meanwhile, the financial problems being faced by the company became more and more evident. The investment bankers concerned had probably underestimated the common sense and intelligence of officials at public sector banks, who were assumed to provide assistance without giving much thought to the issue.

Word of trouble at Jet Airways soon spread in the public domain. Jet's problems had started with the acquisition of Sahara Airlines, as a result of which it ended up managing two brands for many years, one of which was a premium full-service carrier while the other was a budget airline that had somehow diluted the original Jet brand. The company was thus falling apart because of its inability to compete with budget airlines, and Indigo had rapidly started capturing the market share. There was huge pressure on the revenue per seat kilometre for Jet whereas its cost per seat kilometre was substantially higher that of other budget airlines. Governance at Jet was reportedly poor amid allegations that the CEO and the management were not being given due authority to run the airline professionally.

Mistrust between Partners

Later on, I realized that the bigger problem, which had beset the company, was a complete lack of trust between the two partners, Jet and Etihad. In 2013, Jet had brought in Etihad as a joint venture partner with a 24 per cent stake. Further, it sold a 50.1 per cent stake in Jet Privilege to Etihad, and went on to sell its three slots at Heathrow Airport in London, with the right to buy them back after three years for US$70 million. Etihad had arranged funding from one of the bankers of Etihad, which was to be reportedly secured by pledging shares held by Jet Airways. In hindsight, it appeared, at least to me, that Naresh Goyal had got a raw deal and had effectively mortgaged the interest of Jet Airways, considering that the agreement between Etihad and Jet Airways had opened up a huge and attractive market of Indian flyers for global players like Etihad by an increase in its revenue. As the obvious mistrust between the two partners became public knowledge, it started becoming evident that one of the major irritants was the non-perfection of security on the shares of Jet Airways. Etihad had guaranteed its repayment. Under the rules, foreigners are not allowed to hold more than a 49 per cent share in an airline, and it was not clear if this rule applied to the Jet Privilege wherein Etihad had a 50.1 per cent stake. Since no clarification on the issue came from the MoCA, Etihad started believing that Naresh Goyal was using his influence with MoCA to prevent it from issuing the clarification.

Tony Douglas, the CEO of Etihad, flew down to Mumbai in October 2018, after Naresh Goyal had met me. The visit by Douglas underscored the seriousness of the situation. Jet was fast running out of cash and hurtling towards an imminent shutdown unless a major infusion of cash happened. Tony wanted SBI to invest in Jet Privilege, against security of Jet's shareholding in Jet Privilege, following which Etihad was willing to take over the operations without any financial commitment in case of an emergency.

Hunting for Solutions

The next six months at SBI were characterized by hectic activity centred around finding a solution for the Jet Airways predicament. The bank proactively started the formal resolution process on 1 November 2018 under the resolution framework of the RBI. The requirement for the equity to be infused into the company was assessed at Rs 3,000 to 4,000 crore, as lenders had realized that increasing the debt further was not an option, even in short term. Efforts by the bank to find an acceptable resolution plan in such a situation entailed coordination among several players, including the promoters and joint venture partners in the business, lessors, vendors, financial creditors led by the banks, operational creditors, representatives of the government, and regulators. Bringing everyone on the same page was tried in right earnest by the lenders but it was turning out to be an uphill task.

Innumerable meetings were held to discuss the matter, both jointly and with all the stakeholders, as per the banking protocol and practices. At one end of the spectrum were Naresh Goyal and his son, who were in denial of the emergency-like situation, refusing to believe that Jet was actually sinking and thus could not command a valuation of US$2 billion as per their expectations. At the other end, were potential investors, whose participation Naresh Goyal desperately wanted at these valuations but without giving up control of the airlines. Naresh once confided to me that Tatas were also seriously pondering about getting involved and were undertaking due diligence through a team positioned in London. However, this deal too did not make any progress like many others as none of the potential investors was willing to put in money in the sinking Jet ship unless Naresh gave up complete control. But for Naresh, Jet Airways was his baby that he had reared since birth, and for him giving up a company which he had built from scratch was unthinkable.

This problem of inexorable control by promoters has plagued many failing businesses though there have been exceptions like that of Manoj Gaur of the JP Group, who willingly sold one business after another to curtail his debts. Naresh was meanwhile insisting on keeping permanent chairmanship for himself and Board seats for both his son as well as his nominee. This was not acceptable either to Etihad or to any other potential investor. Qatar Airways was the only possible investor that was willing to retain him as a partner. However, in view of the geopolitical situation prevalent in the Gulf at the time, wherein UAE and Qatar were sworn enemies, it would have been impossible for the Government of India to approve of the entry of Qatar Airways in the deal.

The Battle for Control over the Airline

Muddled thought process and inability to read the writing on the wall made Naresh Goyal a huge stumbling block in the resolution of Jet's financial crisis. The smartest move on his part would have been to make an honourable exit in July 2017 itself but sadly his emotional attachment to his company proved to be too strong for him to take a rational decision. Two of his trusted advisers and ex-bureaucrats, Ashok Chawla and Nasim Zaidi, who were on the Board of Jet Airways, were present in a couple of meetings, but even they failed to convince their mentor to give up his control over the company.

Another complication was that it was not merely Naresh Goyal who failed to read the writing on the wall. The Etihad team, led by its CEO Tony Douglas, was equally indecisive and vacillating about handing over control. Tony had first met me in October 2018. The situation at the airlines had already become quite precarious by then and it was becoming difficult to keep the operations up and running. Sustaining the airlines' operations was perhaps even more important for Etihad than for Naresh as nearly half of the passenger load of Etihad on highly lucrative international routes was coming from the Indian market. Tony was looking for financial support from banks against a pledge of shares of Jet Privilege valued at about US$800 million. However, financing against shares that were closely held, with no secondary market for trading was not SBI's cup of tea. The company was, therefore, advised to work out a resolution plan that would be acceptable to all the lenders and creditors.

Jet Airways, meanwhile, was fast running out of cash. The lenders, who had financed receivables, had started squeezing its working capital and were refusing to release cash from escrow accounts. Several rounds of discussion were held at the State Bank Bhawan, which had become the hub of activity for the resolution of the problem of the stressed assets but all solutions were running into insurmountable roadblocks. Despite all efforts, Etihad and Jet could not agree on either the composition of the Board or control of the company. Etihad wanted more say and control, which Naresh Goyal was not willing to give up.

The most difficult issue defying resolution was that of the SEBI rules under which the price at which preferential allotment could happen was Rs 270 per share as against Rs 140, which Etihad was willing to invest. It was a good price for a distressed airline. An investment beyond 25 per cent by Etihad or any other investor requires an open offer to the existing shareholders. This is an onerous condition for any potential investor to acquire a stressed company. Several representations to SEBI to grant an exemption went unheeded. These very rules had also brought YES Bank to a situation of near collapse. Such exemptions were earlier available under the Debt Restructuring Scheme of the RBI as well as in respect of companies going through the IBC process but not for the February 2018 scheme aimed at resolution of the RBI's stressed assets. Fortunately, the rules have since been amended, now exempting applicability of both the above SEBI rules in respect of the resolution of stressed companies outside the IBC framework. Better late than never!

Naresh Goyal always had the apprehension that the real interest of Etihad was limited to acquiring full control of Jet Privilege Private Limited so that they could open up the privilege programme to other airlines as well and make up for the loss incurred on their investment in Jet Airways. The team at SBI had also started veering around to the same view, and in one of the meetings over the issue, when out of sheer frustration, Arijit Basu, then MD of SBI, mentioned this to Tony, he became aggressive and started moving towards Arijit menacingly. It was only my strong intervention that stopped Tony in his tracks. Things were indeed beginning to get ugly, and we were running out of time for resolving the Jet Airways quandary!

The Inevitable Collapse

The company failed to submit the resolution plan within the given timelines. In the meantime, the lenders were also actively engaged with prospective potential investors like TPG Wholesale Private Limited but no agreement could be worked out. From December 2018 onwards, the lessors of aircraft started losing patience and grounding notices had begun to be served. Salaries of the pilots and other staff were not paid, and the pilots were threatening to go on strike. Fortunately, better sense prevailed among them as a strike by the pilots would have led to a complete shut-down and nullified all efforts to keep the airline afloat. Things were, however, slowly coming to a head as on many occasions the company did not have funds to pay for the fuel and the passengers often got stranded. Only an emergency infusion of some funds collectively by Naresh Goyal, Etihad, and banks kept the airline flying till as long as possible, which was crucial for keeping the investors' interest alive. It is virtually impossible to revive a grounded airline, which is what prevented lenders from initiating the IBC process until they were left with no other alternative.

In contrast to the volatility exhibited by the promoters of the company, the lessors and operational creditors were more practical in their approach and were more interested in an early resolution. In fact, much to their credit, they even held back from invoking their rights till quite late in the resolution process. The operational creditors had also realized that if the airlines failed, which it ultimately did, they would lose much more than if the issue were resolved urgently. The lessors, also, for some time avoided immediate grounding of the aircraft to keep the airline up and running. In a subsequent large meeting of operational creditors and lessors organized by SBI in January 2019, Naresh came across as a stubborn leader who was losing his clout and control but who still wanted to dictate terms rather than seek the cooperation of those who were trying to resurrect his company. The meeting soon disintegrated into a melee of frayed tempers, which could be brought under control only by the intervention of Arijit Basu.

Since the company failed to submit an acceptable resolution plan, the lenders prepared a provisional resolution plan. Meanwhile, the cost of reviving the company was going up day by day. The requirement of infusion of equity, which was initially assessed at Rs 3,000 to 3,500 crore in November 2018, had gone up to more than Rs 5,000 crore. The total funding requirement worked out by SBI Capital Markets and McKinsey & Co, which were appointed by Jet Airways, exceeded Rs 10,000 crore. The lenders, proactively, prepared a provisional resolution plan. After several rounds of discussions and fine-tuning of the plan, the meeting of joint lenders was held at Hotel Trident on 27 February 2019 to discuss the interim resolution plan. Different lenders had different security structures but to their credit, all the lenders, in a spirit of mutual understanding and the larger interest of the aviation industry, managed to broadly agree with the plan. None of the lenders was willing to take additional exposure but all of them were willing to convert debt into equity at Re 1, with a controlling stake. The shareholders had given their approval for this plan during their Annual General Meeting. Naresh Goyal also agreed to bring down the equity below 25 per cent and to cap it at 22 per cent, and infuse fresh equity. Further, he agreed to continue to be the promoter of the company in compliance with the relevant laws requiring an Indian to be the promoter of an airline operating in the country. Finally, he also seemed to be coming around over the issue of total control as he expressed his willingness to relinquish the chairmanship of the board and become Chairman Emeritus. Etihad also reiterated their commitment to revive Jet Airways. However, while Naresh Goyal was agreeable to pledge his shareholding in Jet Airways in favour of the lenders, Tony Douglas refused to pledge his shareholding either in Jet Airways or in Jet Privilege.

The implementation of the proposed plan was subject to approval by the boards of both Jet Airways and Etihad as well as the acquisition of an RP 4 rating from two credit rating agencies. An interim funding of Rs 750 crore was also agreed upon subject to the perfection of security and infusion of their share of funds by Naresh Goyal and Etihad. The meeting at which the contentious issues started seemingly moving towards a resolution ended at around 11.30 p.m., offering a ray of hope about an end to the conflict. Seeking approval from MoCA for pledging of the shares of Jet Airways in Jet Privilege, which had been a sore point between the two partners, was also ironed out and the lenders were able to secure approval for the pledge of shares in favour of the domestic lenders, including the nominated Indian branch of lenders to Etihad. The lenders initiated the process of obtaining the sanction of their respective Boards, including interim funding and the appointment of A.K. Purwar, ex-Chairman of SBI, and Kapil Kaul, an aviation sector expert, as the nominees of lenders on the Board of Jet Airways. Expression of interest was also invited from the investors.

The optimism generated by these developments proved to be short-lived. Jet's Board approved the Bank Led Provisional Resolution Plan conforming to framework for resolution of stressed assets by the RBI. The shareholders of Jet Airways also gave their approval for operating components of the Plan during their Extraordinary General Meeting held on 21 February 2019. However, for some inexplicable reasons, the Board of Etihad rejected the resolution plan. With mounting losses, a large number of planes started being grounded and the airline was left with only half its fleet, leading to large-scale cancellation of flights and stranded passengers. The airline's pilots too had issued a notice for a strike. It was evident that the airlines had entered a downward spiral and was about to be grounded. The daily collection from the flights was barely enough to pay for the fuel or parking charges. Taking note of the grim state of affairs, then the Finance Minister convened a review meeting to assess the situation in the third week of March 2019. The paramount question was whether to invoke IBC and appoint an administrator but it was a Hobson's choice. Invoking IBC would have led to immediate grounding of the airline and putting off all the potential investors like TPG, Etihad, National Investment and Infrastructure Fund (NIIF), Tatas, and a few others who had shown preliminary interest in acquiring the company or bailing it out. There was an outside chance of potential investors stepping in if the airline was not grounded. The fear was not unfounded as revealed by subsequent events. All the potential investors wanted Naresh Goyal to give up control, but by the time he decided to step down and some of the security conditions were about to be fulfilled, the number of Jet planes flying had fallen below the requisite level of 20, which was one of the conditions to be complied with by any airline flying its aircraft on international routes. However, to keep the concern alive and protect enterprise value, lenders sought a special dispensation from MoCA to keep the airline's licence valid and to protect slots for its planes at the airports. Eventually, the company stopped operations on 17 April

2019, a sad day in the history of civil aviation in India, when one of the best airlines in the country had to be grounded. As expected, the bidders' interest started waning and at the end, only Etihad gave a conditional offer which was impossible for the lenders to accept.

An Uncertain Future

Revival of a grounded airline has virtually no precedence.

Most airlines hardly own any assets and planes are mostly taken on lease. The slots given to them for their aircraft at most of the airports are not their property. Thus, in case of any financial crunch, their liabilities start mounting rapidly. Credit card receivables are also of little value if the flights get cancelled. The money needs to be refunded to passengers who have booked the tickets. Operating profits are also hard to come by. Most of the profits are, in fact, earned through financial engineering of the sale and lease back of aircraft. Unlike the RBI, which has wide-ranging powers for rescuing a financial entity, the aviation sector has no such authority. The financing of airlines remains a high-risk business for banks, as has been repeatedly proven by the losses incurred by banks in high-profile cases like the failures of Kingfisher Airlines and Jet Airways. Here, it is also relevant to mention in passing the stockpile of unserviceable debt of Air India, though the losses in this case are being funded by the sovereign.

Approval of Resolution Plan by NCLT, Hope of Ray for Jet Airways

On 22 June 2021, after more than two years of filing for bankruptcy of Jet Airways, a resolution plan offered by the consortium of Jalan-Kalrock was approved by the National Company Law Tribunal (NCLT) after getting 99 per cent affirmative vote from the creditors. In this two-year period, the mood of all the stakeholders was alternating between hope and despair. There were multiple rounds of inviting Expression of Interest but could not progress to the Offer Stage for one reason or another till Committee of Creditors (CoC) took one more chance to invite offers in May 2020 and got two offers including Jalan-Kalrock consortium. Rajesh Prasad, who joined Jet Airways as Chief Strategy Officer only in the middle of crisis, and Ashish Chawcharia, the Resolution Professional appointed under IBC, have shown remarkable perseverance in bringing Jet Airways closer to a resolution and to avoiding liquidation.

While the plan has been approved, the allotment of slots at the airport is still causing uncertainty. It's a chicken or egg situation. The potential investor would not like to put money unless assured of slots at the airport. The civil aviation authorities have their own procedure for allotment of slots. This is the first case of insolvency of an airline being handled in the country and proving to be a big challenge for everyone, the potential investors, the lenders, the Tribunal, and the government.

We are today sitting on threshold of watching history being created if Jet 2.0 flies. The flyers loved Jet Airways and did not want it to go under. It was because of its employees, who stood out for their commitment and continued to provide the same quality of service to passengers in the midst of the crisis. Their willingness to make sacrifices and sustain hope of revival of the airline have, in fact, not waned even after nearly two years of the collapse of Jet Airways. A few weeks before my term ended, the staff of Jet Airways, including Ashish Mohanty, representing pilots, and the former flight attendant Nidhi Chaphekar, who had been injured in the terror attack at Brussels Airport on 22 March 2016 and had become the face of the Brussels attack with her bleeding face dominating headlines on the day of the attack, met me at SBI. It was a moment of both poignancy as well as helplessness for me as I had nothing much to offer at that stage. It's my desire to board the first flight of Jet 2.0. It would be my way of paying tribute to an airline which was once the pride of India, loved by flyers across the spectrum.

June 2021 proved to be lucky for lenders in respect of another airline. It was nine years after grounding of Kingfisher Airlines that a consortium led by SBI managed to recover around Rs 5,800 crore by selling shares pledged against loans as collateral security.

The civil aviation sector has huge growth potential in the country. However, since the opening of the sector for private participation, the failure of a large number of airlines, East-West Airlines, Deccan Airways, Sahara, Paramount Airways, Kingfisher, Jet Airways, to name a few, highlights the need for a thorough review of the policies governing aviation sector for ensuring commercial viability of the airlines. Otherwise, the potential will remain unrealized.

3

Non-Performing Loans: Are the Bankers Villains?

You Are Damned If You Do and Damned If You Don't

The Genesis of Non-Performing Loans

Arundhati Bhattacharya took over as Chairperson of the Bank in October 2013. Within a few days of her taking over, I was transferred as the Chief General Manager, Project Finance, because the new Chairperson felt that my skills would be best utilized in a credit-related role. I had a brief tenure of just 10 months there from October 2013 to August 2014. On my promotion as Deputy Managing Director, I was appointed as the Managing Director, SBI Capital Markets, where I remained till 26 May 2015.

This was the time when the RBI conducted an Asset Quality Review. The speech of Raghuram Rajan, then Governor of the RBI, at The Confederation of Indian Industry's (CII's) first Banking Summit on 11 February 2016, gives an inkling of what was going on in the minds of regulators:

> Over time, as you know, a number of large projects in the economy have run into difficulty. The reasons include poor

> project evaluation, extensive project delays, poor monitoring and cost over-runs, and the effects of global over-capacity on prices and imports. Loans to these projects have become overstressed.

Several articles and books have been published on the issue of non-performing loans (NPLs). Having worked in Project Finance, SBI Capital Markets, and with three years of my chairmanship of SBI coinciding with the peak of the NPL cycle, it would only be fair for me to present my perspective on the matter. While many claimants always rise to take credit for the success of any issue, no one wants to take any responsibility for failures. As regards NPLs, bankers have faced all the blame and flak for fomenting this crisis. It cannot be denied that many gaps pertaining to the quality of the underwriting, a weak or virtually non-existent monitoring mechanism, and the lack of requisite skills for performing risk appraisals associated with large projects were instrumental in creating the NPLs. However, the entire blame for the pandemonium or 'The Great Indian Banking Tragedy', as Tamal Bandyopadhyay christened the crisis, cannot be laid at the door of the bankers and the blame has to be collectively shared by many stakeholders.

In fact, it was amusing to see that a lot of blame for this state of affairs was being ascribed to SBI Capital Markets (SBI CAPS), the merchant banking arm of SBI, as if they were solely responsible for creating the non-performing loans in the country. The reality is that in the mid-1990s, country's financial horizon was also undergoing deep-rooted systemic changes. The demise of all-India financial institutions like IDBI and ICICI, and their conversion into universal banks had left a huge void in the system as far as project appraisal is concerned. The situation was aggravated by the decline of one of the oldest financial institutions, the Industrial Finance Corporation of India (IFCI), which was in a shambles and struggling for survival. In this situation, SBI and its subsidiary, SBI CAPS, stepped in to fill the vacuum and created the necessary skills and the infrastructure. SBI was the first bank to create a Project Finance SBU 25 years ago and has built up a formidable reputation in appraisal and financial closure of large projects.

Who Created World Class Airports, Highways and Made the Country Self-sufficient in Power Generation

No one can deny the veracity of what the RBI Governor said in his speech. But, what about the other side of the coin? Within 20 years of privatization, India has created many world-class airports. The country has almost forgotten days of power cuts, which is largely the result of private sector participation in power generation. As on 30 April 2021, the private sector has an installed power capacity of 181.3 GW, which accounts for almost 47 per cent of the total installed power generation capacity in the country, not a mean achievement by any standards. Thermal coal-based installed capacity is 206.4 GW, out of which 76 GW is being generated with private sector participation, involving an investment of more than Rs 3 lakh crore, while 25 GW comes from gas-based plants.

I recently had the opportunity to travel on the Meerut Expressway. The time taken to reach Meerut is only 60 minutes as against 3 hours to cover a distance of 70 kilometres. And this is just one example, among many. The face of the National Capital Region has changed beyond recognition in the last 20 years because of significantly improved connectivity of its highways. Today, India has the distinction of having the largest PPP programme globally. More than 560 road projects comprising a total length of 45,000 kilometres, with an estimated investment exceeding Rs 200,000 crore, have been awarded on a PPP basis by the Centre and State Governments.[1]

During my tenure at SBI, Mumbai, I had to travel extensively to Delhi. Most of the time, I took the Metro Airport Express to travel to Shivaji Park, always marvelling at its convenience. The experience is the same as that of travelling in the metro in London or Rome or Tokyo.

Would all this have been possible if public sector banks had not come forward to participate in the financing of these projects? This begs the question: Could the presence of a Development Finance Institution (DFI) have led to a different scenario? The answer is a resounding 'No' because the operating environment would have been the same. India Infrastructure Finance Corporation Limited (IIFCL) did not do any better. One of the reasons for the failure of many infrastructure financing companies like ILFS and of more than 40 Engineering, Procurement and Construction companies (EPCs) is the difficult environment in which companies have to operate.

Today, everyone talks about risk aversion amongst the bankers. That's why I say, 'You are damned if you do and damned if you don't.'

Other than the failure attributed to the bankers, what really happened? One needs to do an in-depth analysis here.

The Role of the Promoters and Their Declining Fortunes

To put it candidly, the promoters lack both equity capital and a vision. For a very long period of time, until the economy was liberalized in 1991, the system of government controls, licensing, and patronage, and the prevalence of tax policies encouraging tax evasion led to an economy which thrived on generation of unaccounted-for money. The policy makers too failed to distinguish between profit and profiteering, and a complex tax system characterized by exorbitantly high taxes left promoters with little money for re-investment. In such a scenario, the promoters often resorted to creative accounting and exploitation of the lax monitoring system of the banks, blithely diverting the bank funds, with a part of them coming back as equity. Existence of so many shell companies, till such time the Government came down heavily on these companies, points to this deep-rooted malaise. In the absence of an adequate financial stake, the burden of failure of any business is being borne by the banks, resulting in a situation of failed business enterprises that, however, have little impact on the flamboyant lifestyles of the failed promoters. All this becomes fodder for the TRP-hungry media and the self-appointed conscience-keepers, who just rake up the matter superciliously without acquiring any in-depth understanding of the real issues.

It may be pointed out that the liberalization of the economy in 1991, and the consequent evolution of the new-age economy and success of the information technology sector led to the rise of the neo-rich and many successful entrepreneurs like Narayan Murthy, Shiv Nadar, Azim Premji, Sunil Mittal, and Kiran Mazumdar-Shaw, to name just a few. This development not only ushered in new corporate governance standards but also gave wings to the dreams of many middle-class entrepreneurs in the country. The period 1995–2010 also witnessed the rise of many ambitious entrepreneurs aspiring to achieve the phenomenal success attained by business houses like the Ambanis.

During this phase of 'get-rich-quick' businesses, one of the most arresting tales is that of Dileep Jiwarajika of Alok Industries Ltd. He had appeared for the SBI probationary officer exam in 1979 but could not qualify for the post. Subsequently, he started trading in yarn and set up a small manufacturing facility in the mid-1980s. By the year 2005, his company had set up the most modern manufacturing facility and created a name in the overseas market in bed linen, with all the major stores in the USA and Europe gradually becoming customers of Alok Industries. However, Jiwarajika was still not satisfied with the scale of success he had achieved and started aiming for the heights and capacity created by China. Driven by the ambition to be the largest global player in its chosen field, the company continued borrowing, and the task proved easy as an endless queue of lenders were willing to lend to Alok Industries, which was an emerging blue-chip company. Jiwarajika not only raised more debt but raised equity also from investors, diluting his stake in the business. Meanwhile, Alok Industries derived the maximum advantage from the Textiles Upgradation Fund. Soon, however, the inexorable law of averages caught up with the company, and many of its acquisitions in Europe and the UK proved to be failures. The huge debt that the company had run into became unsustainable and led to the eventual downfall of Alok Industries. It was during this period that I met Dileep Jiwarajika after a gap of about eight years. In complete contrast to the company's heydays of 2009, he was now a totally shattered man, unable to come to terms with the failure of his company.

The stories of Prashant Agarwal of Bombay Rayon Fashions, and that of K.R. Thakur of Jyoti Structures are almost identical to that of Alok Industries. All of them exhibited the impatience to grow rapidly without adhering to the requisite checks and balances in their respective organizations, manifested in their desire to grow fast, failed overseas acquisitions, and lack of management bandwidth to handle the scale of the competitive global environment.

The fate of many secondary steel producers was no different. For instance, companies like Uttam Galva Steels and the Topworth Group all flourished during the first decade of the millennium, but their successes were short-lived and by the second decade of the millennium, either their enterprises had changed hands or they were facing liquidation. These are just a couple of examples of concomitant failures of wannabe high-flyers, and there is a long list of similar mid-level corporates that had to bite the dust due to their over-arching ambition. The experiences of these small and mid-level businesses clearly indicate that Indian industries suffer from lack of efficiency of scale and infrastructure bottlenecks, and often make insufficient investments in research and development that could help sustain them in the long run. Tight regulations and state monopolies on natural resources coupled with inconsistent high-level policies too cause hurdles for many private investors and banks, leaving them high and dry in the process of recovery of loans. The failure of so many mid-sized corporates is not a happy situation for a country like India with a huge population and widespread unemployment.

Faulty Allocation of Risk under Public–Private Partnership (PPP) Model

The pace of infrastructure development in India has always lagged behind the demand for such development. Neither the central nor the state governments have ever had sufficient resources to fund infrastructure projects. Many developed countries have been using the PPP model for developing their infrastructure. As per its definition, a PPP model is an arrangement between a government/statutory entity/government-owned entity on the one hand and a private sector entity on the other for the provision of public assets and/or public services, through any investments made and/or management undertaken by the private sector entity, for a specified period of time. This also entails a well-defined allocation of risk between the private sector and public entity, and the private entity receives performance-linked payments that conform to certain specified and pre-determined standards, measurable by the public entity or its representatives.

The PPP model started garnering the attention of policy makers in India only in the mid-1990s after the initiation of economic reforms in the country and its emergence out of the mindset of a socialistic economy. It is a strange coincidence that around the same time, development financial institutions, such as IDBI and ICICI, became universal banks and the commercial banks, like SBI, set up project finance verticals. A number of executives from IDBI shifted to SBI Capital Markets, the merchant banking arm of SBI. This was largely because a void was waiting to be filled in the bank, and within a short period of time, both SBI and SBI Capital Markets created a niche for the bank not only for funding of large projects but also for assisting the central and state governments in policy formulation. However, it is important to note that every project entails the involvement of several stakeholders and its success is thus dependent on the performance of each of these stakeholders. Merchant bankers also need to evaluate the commercial viability of the projects based on various assumptions, and to assess all the potential risks and risk mitigations. Non-performance by even a single stakeholder can lead to the failure of the project, making it go haywire. Here, it must also be pointed out that attributing NPLs entirely to crony capitalism or zombie lending only highlights the lack of an in-depth analysis of the situation, in turn causing resentment among the bankers.

Excepting airports, PPPs have not succeeded in other sectors like power because of the purported inability of the political establishment to affix commercial prices for power usage. Another prominent area where the PPP model has not met the expectations, is the road sector, which is plagued by issues related to delay in acquisition of land, approvals for construction and disputes between the contractors and National Highway Authority of India. The traffic projections on the basis of which commercial viability is assessed, also fell below the projections. The private sector companies, boosted by an unbeatable combination of excess liquidity in the banking system and political patronage, had believed that they were hitting a gold mine, but that was not to be so. To add to their woes, the pyramid-like financing structure adopted by many construction companies which enabled these companies to borrow excessively on a thin capital base of their own was bound to collapse, even if there was a trouble with any of the group companies. The failure of construction companies in Infrastructure led to trouble for the banks and non-banking financial companies.

Non-Performing Loans in the Power Sector, the Best Example of a Policy Flip-Flop

The PPP model was largely developed for power generation in thermal sector wherein some of the risks were structured to be shared by government agencies/procurers. This model was termed as 'Case II Bidding'. With the sharing of risks, this model was expected to result in a competitive tariff, in turn benefiting the end-users. Hence, the Government of India, in collaboration with various state governments, initiated implementation of the Case II Bidding model for thermal coal-based power projects. Under this model, various uncontrollable risks, such as fuel risk, tie-up risk, infrastructure availability, and government approval/clearance risks, were passed on to the government nodal agency, whereas the private sector developers were mandated to assume other controllable risk factors like implementation, cost over-runs, and operational risks.

It is not that at the time of bidding, the promoters or lenders were not aware of the risks. However, most of these projects became stressed because of non-fulfilment of obligations by both the parties—the governments and the procurers of power—as well as the tendency of the promoters to quote commercially unviable tariffs while also failing to take into account delays in the execution of the projects or foreign currency risks.

One of the leading challenges in the implementation of power projects across the country pertains to the availability of fuel, that is, coal and gas. Many of the projects have run into problems because of the cancellation of coal mines with a retrospective effect. In the case of imported coal, the depreciation in value of the rupee from Rs 45 to Rs 65 between 2011 and 2014 became a source of contention between the distribution companies and the power plants relying on imported coal at the Mundra plant owned by the Adanis and the Tatas. The depreciation in the value of the rupee not only impacted imported coal-based power plants but also led to a hike of almost 30 per cent in the capital costs of the power plants using imported plants and machinery from China. It is obvious that the power producers did not fully hedge the risks, and the absence of a pass-through mechanism of the increased capital cost adversely affected the commercial viability of these projects.

Another issue was the change in law in Indonesia regarding the tax liability for the coal mines owned by the companies that were supplying coal to these plants, and the consequential increase in tariff led to disputes, including Public Interest Litigation (PIL) before the Supreme Court of India.

The slower than expected growth of the Indian economy in the last six to seven years too has led to a surplus power supply situation, with India becoming a power-surplus country from a power-deficit one. This has led to an insufficient demand for power and the lack of long-term power purchase agreements. A big mistake made by the lenders was the financing of new power generation capacity without concluding long-term power purchase agreements, and the problem does not end with the non-availability of power purchase agreements. Policy flip-flops by many distribution companies and state governments in respect of the agreed tariff and the tendency to wriggle out of the contracts have, in turn, led to deterioration in the financial health of many independent power producers. The state of Andhra Pradesh represents a classic example of such a flip-flop, and even the orders of the Andhra Pradesh High Court have gone unimplemented.[2] Distribution companies owe huge sums of money to the power producers, who are under the obligation to service their debt. Several attempts to improve the financial position of state-owned distribution companies have also met with limited success. The last scheme in this direction was 'Uday', but four years after its implementation, we are again back to square one.

Further, delays in obtaining the requisite approvals and environment clearances as well as in achieving financial closures have led to time over-runs running into two to three years. The incidence of Interest during Construction (IDC) also inflates the project cost. The combined effect of IDC and currency depreciation caused an almost doubling of the project cost from Rs 4.50 crore per MW to Rs 7 to Rs 8 crore per MW, making the plants *ab initio* unviable. Many of these power plants thus had to be sold off at huge losses, with the average realization from the sale being less than Rs 3 crore per MW, which was the best price that could be realized given the currently prevalent tariffs.

Another such example is that of the creation of a power generation capacity of 22,000 MW on the basis of allocation of gas by the Ministry of Petroleum and Natural Gas (MoPNG), at an investment of more than Rs 1 lakh crore. This capacity is, however, languishing, as the Ministry withdrew the allocation of gas one fine morning as the anticipated production from the KG 6 basin did not materialize.

The viability of many coal-based thermal power plants and steel plants was based on the allocation of mines. The licences of these plants were cancelled retrospectively, causing huge damages to the power and steel sector. The mess in the once-flourishing telecom sector is also well known. It may be logical to auction the natural resources or spectrum through a transparent competitive bidding process but we cannot forget that the end-consumer will have to eventually pay the higher price. If this price realization is not aligned to the increase in the prices of the inputs, the enterprise is bound to suffer losses, leading to an erosion in the value of the investment made. This raises the following question: Who funds these losses? And the answer is, the banks, with the operational creditors, the Government, and the employees who lose their jobs bearbear the brunt of the suffering. While a part of the equity of the promoters may have come from the banks, the promoters bear the losses to the extent of loss of genuine equity put into a business. Since the public sector banks have the highest NPLs, the Government as owner has funded these losses by providing capital to the public sector banks. Any additional revenue that the Government may have earned through auction, irrespective of whether there has been a net gain or not, is also debatable considering the losses incurred by the public sector banks, revenue losses, writing off of government dues, and the enhanced burden of subsidies off liabilities resulting from the closure of many enterprises.

A minute analysis of the saga of NPLs in the power sector clearly demonstrates that actual factors that are responsible for this NPL mess among power companies are arbitrary changes in the regulatory regime, delays in the revision of tariffs, tendency of the distribution companies to contest or somehow delay the implementation of orders of the courts, misconceived notions about public interest, and inability of the distribution companies to recover a fair tariff from the end-consumers in order to avoid a political backlash.

A lesson that we in the bank learnt the hard way is that high tariffs or user charges cannot be passed on to the end-consumers, and any project that ignores this reality would ultimately end up in closure stemming from the non-recovery of tariff/charges. This eventually leaves lenders and promoters of the projects concerned with no choice but to accept substantial write-downs and bring down the debt burden to a serviceable level by implementing pragmatic tariffs that can be realized from the end-consumers. The replacement cost of a power plant is nearly Rs 7.5 crore per MW or higher, and the distress value realized has been in the range of Rs 3 crore per MW—these are phenomenal sums, which is why the solutions to the NPL crisis in the power sector need to be identified based on careful and rational thinking. In this case, the promoters and lenders ended up bearing the brunt of the financial losses through an indirect subsidy on the power produced by the projects.

The two case studies of Ratnagiri Gas and Power Plant (earlier known as Dabhol Power Company) and the power projects of

Essar, Tata Power, and Adani Power at Mundra corroborating my analysis are placed in the Appendix I.

Running Battle between Contractors and the National Highways Authority of India

The National Highways Authority of India (NHAI) has about 180 arbitration matters in several NHAI projects, wherein claims worth about Rs 70,000 crore are under adjudication.[3]

The disputes between NHAI and EPC contractors are primarily due to two reasons, as delineated below.

(i) *Right of Way*: There is generally a delay in obtaining the Right of Way, which is an obligation of NHAI, due to which there is a cascading delay in implementation of the project, achievement of milestones, and release of payments.
(ii) *Change in the Scope of Work*: NHAI generally delays approval of the Change of Scope, which impacts the liquidity of the contractor.

In order to resolve these issues, arbitration is provided as the mode of reconciliation between the parties. However, even if the arbitration panel rules in favour of the developer, the ruling is contested by NHAI in courts right up to the Supreme Court.

Spillover Effect of NPLs on the Construction Sector and on Financiers

The problems emanating from NPLs in the power and road construction sectors led to the failure of more than 40 companies in the construction sector. The closure of these EPC companies was a leading cause of the insolvency at ILFS, notwithstanding the numerous other governance issues that also contributed to its downfall.

Delay in the Execution of Projects

The delay in the execution of the major EPC projects that had already been commissioned was the result of various external factors, including pending land acquisition, non-approval of the construction plan by the client, and reduction in the scale of the project effected by the client. Slow progress in the execution of projects also led to piling up of an unbilled revenue as most of the projects had milestone billing parameters, thereby leading to a significant drop in the turnover and issues in cash flows.

Invocation of Bank Guarantees

The delays in project execution fostered a vicious cycle of financial losses, as they also compromised the existing performance of bank guarantees, which, in turn, caused further cash flow issues. This outcome also impaired the ability of the company to raise fresh bank guarantees, in future, and thus offer bids for new projects for maintaining their order books.

Stress in the Build–Operate–Transfer (BOT) Portfolio

Many companies had bid for BOT projects to ramp up their existing order books. However, due to their limited experience in this sphere, the stakeholders made aggressive bids for these BOT projects and the equity funding for those projects too was primarily done by raising corporate loans at the parent EPC company. Hence, delays in the execution of these projects due to various external factors, like pending land acquisition, pushed the companies concerned into further financial distress.

Increased Working Capital Cycle

Lower conversion from revenue to cash on account of the receivables led to a significant strain on cash flows. Slow progress in project execution due to cash flow issues further led to a piling up of the unbilled revenue and elongation of the working capital cycle.

Further, in the case of some of the EPC contracts, though the issue of cost escalation had been covered in the contract, the major portion of the actual escalated amount was paid only at the end of the project. Therefore, the company had to procure the inputs needed for implementation of the project at current market rates, leading to a mismatch in the cash flows and an increase in the unbilled revenue. The company also had to adjust its limited resources across all its projects to avoid bank guarantee invocations. This resulted in piling up of the unbilled revenue as the milestones for billing had not been achieved. Since several of the projects for which the company had already mobilized men and machinery got delayed, it had to incur establishment costs for those projects, as a result of which its operating margins were severely impacted.

Pending Realization of Claims

The cash flows of EPC companies that had to face project closures were also adversely affected by the non-realization of claims under arbitration awards from various public sector clients, and further contesting of these claims by the said counter parties.

NPLs in the Steel Sector

Apart from power, steel was another sector that contributed to a very high proportion of NPLs. Although the steel business is cyclical in nature, the problem this time became more severe due to declining demand caused by a number of internal and external developments. These included over-leveraging; cancellation of coal blocks; emergence of environmental issues pertaining to iron ore mines; the inability of indigenous steel companies to compete against cheap imports from China, South Korea, and Japan, with which India has free Trade Agreements; the alleged diversion of funds by many promoters; and downturn in the economy. However, despite these difficulties, steel is the only sector in which the lenders have succeeded in making a decent recovery from 30 per cent to 100 per cent, depending upon the quality and location of the plant.

Why Is the PPP Model Successful in Airports?

The following reasons can be attributed to the success of the PPP model in airports:

- *Economic Regulation*: The airport's aeronautical tariff is determined on a cost plus return principle, wherein some portion (30 per cent) of the non-aeronautical revenues is also used for cross-subsidization. As a result, the aeronautical revenues are more or less assured over the tenor of the concession agreements, which is consistent with the investment made by the airport operator on which an assured return is provided.
- *True Up*: As part of the tariff determination, there is a provision for true up, wherein the accumulated losses or gains emanating from the fluctuations in actual traffic, operating expenses, and asset additions vis-à-vis the estimates at the time of tariff determination are trued up along with the carrying cost. Consequently, the impact of any considerable dent in traffic is usually only short-term, which is deemed to be recovered in the next tariff determination exercise.
- *Non-aeronautical Revenue Upside*: As only 30 per cent of the non-aeronautical revenues go into cross-subsidization of the aeronautical tariff, the balance 70 per cent is always available for the airport operator to retain as an upside. The costs associated with earning these non-aeronautical revenues are also very minimal, as most of them are sub-concessioned

out, and the airport operator earns a considerable revenue share from these sub-concessions. Further, in the case of some of the airports, such as Mumbai and Delhi, the revenue from real estate land parcels (measuring close to 200 acres), leased as part of the Operation Management and Development Agreement (OMDA), is not reckoned for cross-subsidization by the regulator, as per the concession terms, thereby providing an additional upside to these airport operators.

- *Historic Traffic Growth*: There has been considerable traffic growth in most of the airports in the country over the last decade, with most of the major airports posting a ten-year Compound Annual Growth Rate (CAGR) in double digits in spite of the financial stress faced by the airlines. This has also contributed to a considerable upside in non-aeronautical revenues for these PPP airports, which now contribute roughly 50 per cent of the total revenues in most of the PPP airport projects.
- *Tenor of the Concession Agreements*: The tenors of the OMDA/ concession agreements in the earlier cases such as Bengaluru, Hyderabad, Mumbai, and Delhi have an initial concession period of 30 years extendable by another 30 years at the option of the concessionaire. On the other hand, the new concessions awarded in the case of the Navi Mumbai, Mopa, Jewar, and the six airports recently awarded to the Adani Group have a 40- or 50-year tenor. The presence of these long tenors provides considerable bandwidth for the airport operator to properly plan and implement the future expansion of the airport while also maximizing the non-aero potential of these airports.
- *Termination Payments/Substitution Agreement*: The concession agreements provide for substitution by the lenders or assured termination payments in the case of a financial event of default, thereby providing adequate comfort to the lenders/ financial institutions (FIs) that fund these projects.

The above incidences of financial distress and other developments and contingencies in various sectors of the economy clearly indicate that India needs huge private capital to fund its ambitious plan for building infrastructure. The experiences of the past decade regarding the challenges faced by the lenders can be used as stepping stones for addressing many unresolved issues in this sphere. Some of the solutions that need to be implemented urgently include the enforcement of contracts, a strong dispute resolution mechanism, and ensuring that committed cash flows get materialized to pay the debts and clear outstanding dues. In conclusion, it must be reiterated that treating bankers as villains does not help and cannot be part of the solution to the complex problem of NPLs.

Need to Restore Trust in Lending for Projects

I firmly believe that there is a need to restore the confidence of bankers and their vilification should stop. It is not my case that bankers are blameless, but as far as the situation leading to NPLs is concerned, the blame has to be shared by everyone including banks, the promoters, government authorities, the legal system, and regulators. The problem cannot be fixed by merely ascribing blame here and there. The bankers feel harassed and demoralized when they are called for an interrogation even after 10 or 15 years of retirement. If India has to regain its high-growth trajectory and attain the target of becoming a US$5 trillion economy in the next few years, it is imperative to restore the confidence of bankers and increase credit flow to the productive sectors of the economy. We must not overlook the fact that risk aversion amongst bankers and lack of flow of credit are often cited as primary reasons for the slowdown in the economy. The Gross Capital Formation (GCF) to Gross Domestic Product (GDP) ratio has declined from 34.3 per cent in 2011–12 to 27.1 per cent in 2020–21, which is a cause for worry.

Not everyone can be painted with the same brush as that can dampen the entrepreneurial spirit. At the same time, the need for stern action against financial frauds committed by the promoters or the management is equally important. The business of banking is based on trust apart from due diligence, and breach of trust should not be an accepted norm.

4

Non-Performing Loans: The Battle Continues

Insolvency and Bankruptcy Code: A Game Changer

The Insolvency and Bankruptcy Code (IBC) introduced in 2016 has brought about a paradigm shift in the creditor–debtor relationship. Until the advent of the IBC, many borrowers felt that an NPL is more of a problem for the lender, and it was not uncommon for the borrowers to warn the banks, 'Your loan account will become a non-performing loan', and then expect the bank to find a solution by giving additional support. The approach of the borrowers changed only after IBC came into being with the threat of losing their businesses looming large over the borrowers.

The So-Called Dirty Dozen

Initially, in June 2017, the RBI directed the banks to refer to 12 high-value NPLs for resolution under the newly introduced bankruptcy code. The intervention by the RBI had become necessary because of initial hesitancy on the part of lenders to enter into uncharted territory.

The 12 cases referred for resolution represent a mixed bag. Of the six cases that have been resolved within a period of 12–36 months, four are in the steel sector, including the high-profile cases of Essar Steel and Bhushan Steel Ltd. Further, three companies are in liquidation and the matter is pending before the Supreme Court in another three cases. Although almost four years have passed since the date of reference, the lenders, including the companies under liquidation, are yet to recover any money. While the best recovery has been achieved by companies in respect of the pending cases in the steel sector, the worst has been observed in the case of EPC companies.

Resolution of Essar Steel, a Milestone in Every Respect

As they say, all is well that ends well. The resolution of the Essar Steel case was another feather in the cap of SBI. It entailed very complex manoeuvring, and brought conflicting financial creditors together. However, there were many moments of despair and trepidation for SBI in this entire saga, precipitated by various developments. These included the fact that many banks had sold their assets to the Stressed Asset Funds and Asset Reconstruction Companies (ARCs), which adopted a different stand in the meeting of the CoC; frustrating delays in the legal process where for some inexplicable reasons, NCLT at Ahmedabad saw no urgency in hearing the resolution plan; the issuance of many confusing orders by NCLT and National Company Law Appellate Tribunal (NCLAT) with regard to the powers of the CoC; and a host of other provisions of the IBC. The most important beacon of light was the Supreme Court, which delivered a landmark decision, settling many important points of law and putting the IBC on a firm footing. (Refer Appendix II)

During this challenging period, I allowed my frustration to get the better of me on at least two occasions. One was at the time of the quarterly earnings call when I said, 'The Bank expects a recovery of Rs 16,000 crore from three NCLT accounts—Essar Steel, Bhushan Power, and Alok Industries. Every quarter I am looking towards the sky and to God, asking when all these decisions will be given and the amount recovered. Every morning I pray to God for this resolution.' This comment was definitely intended to draw the attention of the courts so that they would expedite the matter. The second occasion when I allowed my guard to slip was when after having failed to get the desired outcome, I made the announcement that SBI plans to sell the Essar Steel loan at a discount to an ARC. Fortunately, this announcement had the desired impact and things started moving. It was a bold gambit that paid off.

The fact that the Essar Steel plant was a state-of-the-art plant located near the port and could fetch good recoveries became clear to me because of the keen interest shown by Laxmi Mittal and Aditya Mittal in this project from the beginning. The Ruias, on their part, misread the situation and missed the opportunity on several occasions to retain an asset that they had built painstakingly and had, in fact, preferred to keep it while selling the oil refinery in Gujarat. They were obviously upset and could not digest the fact that the control of Essar Steel would slip from their hands. Lenders maintained complete neutrality in the matter and their sole interest was to get the best value of the enterprise.

The other steel manufacturers in the country were also not very excited about the entry of Arcelor Mittal in India and were willing to support the Ruias. The first resolution plan submitted by the Ruias would have given a recovery of only Rs 19,000 crore. Arcelor Mittal started by citing Rs 30,000 crore for the same asset. The entry of the Vedanta group into the fray fuelled more competition, as they had made a bid of around Rs 36,000 crore. Vedanta was encouraged by their success in acquiring another steel plant through the IBC process. Finally, Arcelor Mittal not only paid Rs 42,000 crore for Essar Steel but also paid another Rs 12,000 crore to settle the dues of Uttam Galva and KSS Petron.

Contrary to the general perception, there was no interference from the government in the entire process and from the beginning, it was clear that ultimately the matter would be settled by the Supreme Court. The lenders led by SBI maintained absolute neutrality but played their cards very well in maximizing the recovery which went beyond expectation, by creating enough competition amongst the bidders and by fighting the legal battle doggedly and unitedly. In retrospect, it can be said without doubt that the battle for Essar has forever changed the debtor–creditor relationship. Arcelor Mittal could finally make an entry into India after many failed attempts and probably bring about an unprecedented transformation in the steel industry in the country, by giving it one of the largest lenders and a full Foreign Direct Investment (FDI) value. I also presume that the promoters learnt many valuable lessons in the process, albeit by paying a very heavy price. However, the gains to the banking sector and the overall economy of the country would probably outweigh everything else.

Excluding the recoveries made in respect of a few large accounts, the recovery through resolution of corporate debt under IBC has given recovery of 24 per cent only. In many cases, the recovery has been as low as 5 per cent inviting public criticism. It's always a hard choice for the lenders, whether to accept the resolution at such a low value or press for liquidation of the enterprise which entails additional costs and delays. The recovery can be improved only if steps are taken to augment the bench strength of NCLT and NCLAT, appointing members having sound knowledge of commercial principles and timely reference of a distressed corporate debtor to NCLT for resolution of debt.

The values fetched by Essar Steel and Bhushan Steel for their stakes indicated that there was no issue with the quality of the steel plants set up by the Ruias and Neeraj Singhal. Many EPC companies, on the other hand, were able to borrow huge sums of money by creating Special Purpose Vehicles (SPVs) with high leverages at the holding companies. The money for the projects was not ring-fenced and was instead transferred from one project to another. These companies also had no tangible assets to fall upon and consequently, the banks lost heavily as far as the EPC companies are concerned.

The war on NPLs is not yet over. No doubt, the government has acted fast to amend the law whenever required. The various pronouncements of the Supreme Court have settled many issues around interpretation and implementation of the law. This is one of the most important laws today for preserving the economic value of an enterprise and India can be proud of its achievement. The immediate need is to remove the infrastructure bottleneck by appointing NCLT and NCLAT members with requisite knowledge of commercial principles. It is not a happy situation that the benches are working at less than 50 per cent strength leading to a pile-up of pending cases.

The low recovery in many of the NCLT cases has drawn public criticism. The preservation of assets during CIRP process, keeping the enterprise as a going concern by providing funding support, a competent and honest CIRP, an empowered Committee of Creditors, faster decision by the NCLT, a coordinated approach between various Government departments/agencies are some of the key elements needed for enhancing the value of the enterprise apart from the quality of the underlying assets and the industry scenario. Complete transparency in the discovery of the value of enterprise is a must to retain confidence in the CIRP process. The case of Essar Steel is clear proof and is a trailblazer as far as IBC is concerned.

PART TWO

The Giant Ship Sails through Rough Seas . . .

Dedicated to all members of the State Bank of India fraternity for their commitment and loyalty, making SBI one of the largest and most trustworthy institutions in the country.

5

Baptism by Fire

Two Major Events Preceded My Appointment as SBI Chairman

Even as the banking system was still fighting the war on NPLs, two other major events occurred that I had to handle as the Managing Director, Retail Banking. One was the merger of the five Associate Banks and Bharatiya Mahila Bank with the SBI, and the second—an even more momentous development—the demonetization of high-value currency announced by the Prime Minister on 8 November 2016. The brunt of the impact of both these events, particularly demonetization, was borne by the National Banking Group (NBG) at SBI, which I was heading as the Managing Director.

Demonetization: Testing of Nerves

One of the biggest challenges that came my way as Managing Director at SBI before I became Chairman was the impact and ramifications of demonetization. I heard the Prime Minister's announcement to demonetize Rs 1,000 and Rs 500 notes while having dinner at the residence of Anil Khandelwal, Ex-Chairman, Bank of Baroda. The SBI Chairperson, Arundhati Bhattacharya called me frantically, asking me to meet her at her residence immediately. I reached her home at around 10.30 p.m., and our anticipatory action started immediately. The first step was to disable all the Automated Teller Machines (ATMs) and Cash Deposit Machines (CDMs). The machines were also required to be reconfigured within the next two days to enable withdrawal of Rs 100 and Rs 50 notes, starting 11 November 2016. The details of notes in the denomination of Rs 1,000 and Rs 500, called Specified Bank Notes (SBNs) were to be furnished to the RBI and arrangements had to be made to deposit the SBNs with the RBI. Simultaneously, arrangements were also needed for the exchange of SBN up to Rs 4,000 at the bank counters. There was no limit for deposit of SBN in the accounts where the account was fully compliant with the Know Your Customer (KYC) guidelines, otherwise only SBNs up to Rs 50,000 could be accepted. Cash payment from a bank account over the counter was restricted to Rs 10,000 subject to an overall weekly limit of Rs 20,000.

Implementing all these instructions was going to be a nightmare for the bank as necessary modifications were required to be made in the accounting system to ensure compliance of the guidelines. The biggest worry was of course that of managing the crowds at the bank branches when they would open on the first day after the announcement, that is, on 10 November 2016.

The SBI is not new to managing crowds but this time we were entering into uncharted territory. Line managers were told to take care of both the public and staff conveniences adequately in view of the expected rush at branches for exchanging the notes. A warning memo was also issued that strict disciplinary action would be taken against any staff or officer engaging in any irregular practice. Having handled the return of almost 30 per cent of the demonetized currency notes, SBI won huge appreciation from the public and all government officials who visited SBI's branches during this period.

Considering that the decision had to be kept absolutely confidential till the last minute, it is apparent that even the RBI was caught by surprise and was totally unprepared to handle its fallout. I am not sure whether the learnings from this largest ever demonetization exercise have been documented. Hence, here I would like to mention a few things, which in my opinion could have helped avoid the chaos.

Firstly, the size of the new currency notes should have been kept identical to the demonetized ones in order to avoid the need for change of cassettes in more than two lakh ATMs in the country, which was a hugely time-consuming exercise. The service providers also did not have the requisite manpower and logistical support to finish this task quickly. Further, they were also looking at this opportunity to make some extra bucks. It was only through active intermediation by then Deputy Governor of the RBI, S.S. Mundra, between the service providers and the banks that the cassettes could eventually be replaced in a time-bound manner at a reasonable cost.

Since the focus was on quick re-monetization, the new currency note of Rs 2,000 was brought into circulation. This complicated the problem further as the currency notes of Rs 2,000 were of no use for small value cash transactions that common people needed to make. The next denomination was that of Rs 100 notes, which were not available in adequate quantity. The absence of lower denomination notes was one of the most critical problems emerging from the demonetization exercise. During one of the review meetings of the Secretary, DFS, and Secretary, Department of Economic Affairs (who is now the RBI Governor) with SBI, and a few other banks, including the Chairman of the Indian Banks' Association (IBA), the shortage of Rs 100 notes was a key point of discussion. It was apparent that there was a great deal of confusion about the availability of Rs 100 notes.

The SBI's assessment about the number of Rs 100 notes available was vastly different from the assessment of the RBI. The confusion apparently arose in the process of converting millions into lakhs—one or two zeroes simply went missing!

I kept insisting that Rs 100 notes were in short supply and there was an urgent need to augment the supply of 100 rupee notes while also rapidly bringing into circulation the proposed new Rs 500 notes. But this was easier said than done because all the note printing machines of the RBI were programmed for printing Rs 2,000 notes and required at least three weeks before the machines could print the new Rs 500 currency notes. The availability of currency paper posed another major bottleneck, and it had to be imported. Both the secretaries realized the problem and it was decided to immediately start printing the Rs 500 notes. It was only when the supply of the new Rs 500 notes started improving and the process of change of cassettes at the ATMs gathered momentum that the situation began limping back to normal.

The second issue was that remonetizing quickly by releasing the new currency notes was not the only problem to be tackled. There were several states like Telangana and some in the North-east, which had an insatiable requirement of cash, wherein managing the cash logistics posed a big challenge. There were frantic calls from currency chests across the country, and a round-the-clock war-room was set up by SBI to alleviate the hardship caused to the people and try to meet all their requirements. The storage and remittances of demonetized notes became another big headache because the RBI was not in a position to receive remittances from other banks and all the currency chests at the banks were getting choked. It took almost one year for the RBI to receive back all the discontinued currency notes and count the same with the help of high-speed processors lent to it by SBI.

The biggest problem in managing the whole exercise was the announcement that SBNs would be changed up to a value of only Rs 4,000. This measure was intended to take care of the common citizen, but the facility was grossly misused, as there was no restriction on the number of times one could exchange the bank notes. In a country where the number of poor people far exceeds the number of people who had SBNs, it became very easy to hire people to stand in the queue for a commission and exchange the notes. To deal with this problem, the RBI issued instructions that a person could change the notes only once, and to ensure compliance, it was decided that the indelible ink used in elections would be used for marking the finger of every person at the time of exchange of the SBN, in a similar manner as is done at the time of voting. Again, this decision did not take the crucial fact into account that there is only one supplier of the indelible ink, who is based in Mysore. The IBA was instructed to coordinate the effort of procuring and distributing the ink. The decision to use the ink and procure it urgently created so much panic that the IBA was reportedly given instructions by the Finance Ministry to airlift the ink from Mysore using a chartered plane. However, the need did not arise, as the indelible ink was arranged from the local offices of the Election Commission.

One of the ostensible solutions offered for all these problems was that of giving a big push to digital payments. However, the acceptance structure was inadequate and the country was dependent on the import of Point of Sale (POS) machines. A POS machine has to be tested thoroughly for security reasons and configured before deployment. Unfortunately, many officials were blissfully unaware of these limitations, and thought that millions of such machines could be distributed as easily as if they were like supplying steel utensils.

Meanwhile, the goalposts kept shifting and frequent changes in the limits for withdrawal and deposit of cash, as well as reporting requirements by the RBI became a nightmare for the IT departments of the banks. However, the RBI had little choice in the matter as it had to respond and react immediately to the issues being raised by the public.

Interestingly, and rather inexplicably, the first-hand experiences emerging from discussions with the people who were forced to wait in long queues to exchange their notes clearly indicate that contrary to the general perception, by and large, there was no resentment on the ground against the demonetization drive. The divide between the haves and have-nots, and the anger against the moneyed class is so deep-rooted in the country that people were apparently willing to bear any inconvenience that would bridge this divide in some way, and had the satisfaction that a decisive action against black money was being taken for the first time in the country, as a consequence of which rich people were suffering.

There were reports of instances of wrongdoing by a few banks in exchange for SBNs, which had a bearing on the reputation of the bank staff. Luckily such incidences were few and far between, and were limited to two or three banks. Considering that it was a mammoth exercise where currency notes worth approximately Rs 15 lakh crore were exchanged in a period of 45 days, the bank staff deserve all appreciation for their hard work and dedication while performing the critical exercise. How Indian people could achieve this humungous feat in such a short time is a subject matter for research.

Merger of Six Banks into SBI: An Unprecedented Bold Move

Five Associate banks of SBI and Bhartiya Mahila Bank were merged into SBI effective 1st April 2017. The decision to merge the banks in one go was not an easy one, and there was a huge debate about both the circumstances and the timing of this decision. The bank was grappling with asset quality issues in a big way, and the Board and the management were reluctant to initiate the complex merger exercise, which would require a huge management bandwidth and resources. However, prompting from the government led to an about-turn and the Board approved the merger of the banks. In retrospect, it seems like a wise decision and politically a bold one, considering the sensitivities prevalent around the regional character of these banks. The maximum political resistance against the merger came in respect of the State Bank of Travancore (SBT). Kerala was the only state where the Assembly had passed a resolution against the merger of the State Bank of Travancore with the SBI. The following is an excerpt from the protest registered on behalf of the State Bank of Travancore against the proposed merger:

> Sir, State Bank of Travancore is part of Kerala's heritage. It is a bank which belongs to all Malayalees. Delusion about history is a serious matter or it can affect the history that is about to be made . . . Through this merger, we are trying to create banks which are too big to fail. But Alan Greenspan himself said, 'If they are too big to fail, they are too big . . .'

The fervent plea, almost akin to an emotional outpouring, was voiced by a young Member of the Legislative Assembly (MLA) of Kerala, G. Sabarinathan, an engineer with a postgraduate degree in management, while he was speaking on a motion under Rule 130 in the Kerala Assembly on 18 July 2016. The Kerala Assembly was considering submitting a motion of representation against the merger to both the Centre and the RBI. The associate banks, owned by SBI, had developed deep local roots and identities in the geographies where they were working and nowhere was this more pronounced than in the politically sensitive State of Kerala, where the Government in power was under the control of the Left Democratic Front led by the Communist Party of India (Marxist). The State Bank of Travancore was more well-entrenched in Kerala than its parent bank and had a 75-year-long connection with the state.

Sabarinathan's was not a lone voice. Reports received from the Kerala Assembly indicated that member after member except the only MLA representing the Bharatiya Janata Party (BJP) had spoken out against the merger of the State Bank of Travancore with SBI. It reflected the concern felt by various political parties that the merger would affect the prospects of the state as a bank headquartered at Thiruvananthapuram was being targeted for the merger.

In a way, these protests also represented a vote of confidence for the manner in which SBI, the parent bank, had managed its subsidiaries and allowed them to flourish and grow, imbibing the spirit of the areas in which they operated. The overall mood was not against SBI *per se* but reflected a general fear among regional banks of being overwhelmed by the dominant partner. While participating in these discussions, the Chief Minister, Pinarayi Vijayan himself said that he recognized the role and stature of SBI. He said in the Assembly, 'Sir, the State Bank of India does not face any problems in its growth now. Its existence and future are safe. SBI stands now as the best bank in the country . . . our objection is to the merger of a Kerala-based major bank.'[1]

We were completely focused only on the business and re-organizational aspects of the merger, and paying attention to the politics surrounding this reorganization was the least of our priorities. However, the protests and tumult following the announcement of the mergers forewarned us of the potential irritants and challenges we would have to negotiate before completing the process of the first major merger of banks in India's history.

Around this time, the Kerala High Court admitted a public interest writ petition filed by the Save SBT Forum under Article 226 of the Indian Constitution. The petition, filed by about a dozen customers of the State Bank of Travancore, inter alia, made a case against mergers per se. After flagging the possible loss of jobs and opportunities resulting from the merger, the petition also said,[2]

> Studies have revealed that the large-scale mergers and acquisitions all over the world had resulted in huge failures in most of the cases and the surviving conglomerates are trying

for decentralization of their management and operations, with a participative management approach. Many of them have stopped operations in some jurisdictions. There is empirical evidence that one consequence of the merger and acquisition wave in the US banking system during the 1990s has been that loan approvals for racial minorities and low-income applicants have fallen and the extent of this decline was more severe for large banks.

'The consolidated Banks are found to shift their portfolios towards higher risk-return investments. Any approach in favour of mergers and acquisitions for creation of large conglomerate organizations beyond the optimal level will be a disaster and in the case of a public sector bank like SBI, such disaster will be at the cost of the nation and the general public. After acquisition, the businesses of the merged entity will be approximately 20 per cent of our country's GDP and any systemic weakness will result in a huge drain of Government resources for providing financial support and additional capital.

'Now, SBI is functioning at more than optimal level and hence, the plans for acquisition of associate banks including the State Bank of Travancore are unwarranted and will lead to lack of proper control, increased systemic risk and risk in lending huge loans, chance for malpractices and misappropriations of funds through falsification of accounts or otherwise, etc. The consolidation could also result in less competition, which will result in fewer choices to the customers and arbitrary pricing of products.

After long-winding statements against the merger of the State Bank of Travancore, the petitioners concluded that the

proposed acquisition is without having any research, analysis, study, discussions on merits and demerits, pros and cons, etc., on the effect of the acquisition based on financial

> and feasibility factors. If the respondents are not withdrawn from the proposed acquisition, it will cause irreparable damage and loss to the stakeholders of the State Bank of Travancore, especially minority shareholders, customers and the employees. Hence, the acquisition of State Bank of Travancore by the SBI will cause severe hardship, irreparable damage and loss to the petitioners and the general public at large.

Looking back today at these developments, one can say that the way in which SBI dealt with the political controversies surrounding the merger and other efforts made through legal means to stall or at least delay the merger process sent out the message loud and clear that such attempts would not be successful. SBI's legal team got down to business immediately. While the bank's internal work was not at all affected by these protests and arguments, coordinated efforts were required at all levels to ensure that no hurdles emerged to stall the process of the merger. Attempts were made to initiate direct and open communication with staff at all levels to allay apprehensions about the merger among the naysayers.

Meanwhile, court proceedings had also been going on in parallel but the writ petitions were finally dismissed in the Kerala High Court by a Bench consisting of its Chief Justice Navniti Prasad Singh and Justice Antony Dominic. In their unanimous judgment, delivered on 23 March 2017, the judges stated,

> We have heard the parties at length. We must note that initially these writ petitions were to be taken up for urgent interim orders. But with consent of the parties, we heard the parties at length for final disposal of the writ petitions itself, at this stage.
>
> To begin with, we would note that we are not involving ourselves in emotional issues which are apparently quite high

> and significant. A court is concerned only with legal issues leading to legality of the transaction or illegality therein.[3]

The judges thus found no merit in the PIL and dismissed the petitions just a week before the actual date of the merger.

Other than the fact that the associate banks of SBI had their origin in the erstwhile princely States before they were made subsidiaries of SBI and had maintained some regional identity, they had lost their relevance and were overshadowed by the presence of SBI. The asset quality and corporate governance as well as the processes followed in these banks were relatively weaker than those in SBI. The cost of funds in these banks was also higher as compared to that of SBI, and their lending portfolios carried a relatively higher risk. Many loan accounts and corporates from which SBI had kept away were able to secure credit facilities from the associate banks. The latter had also not been able to carve a niche or build a distinct identity for themselves. Further, SBI had to shoulder an additional burden of providing capital from time to time. While the preparation for the merger was going on in full swing, on 8 November 2016, the Prime Minister made the unprecedented announcement of demonetization of high-value currency notes. This created some uncertainty and at one stage, it seemed that the merger would not happen. However, better sense prevailed and though the merger date was pushed back to 1 April 2017, it proved to be a blessing in disguise as the transition team got more time to plan the actual task. There were many factors which led to the successful merger of six banks with SBI in one go, in the shortest period of time. The balance sheet merger happened on 1 April 2017, and the data merger was achieved within eight weeks. In the months of April and May 2017, every weekend, one bank was taken up for data merger as soon as the statutory audit was over. This was possible only because of meticulous planning by a multi-disciplinary team that covered all the dimensions of the proposed merger. Neeraj Vyas, who was leading the team, had the requisite experience stemming from his erstwhile membership of the core team that had handled the merger of the State Bank of Indore. There was perfect coordination between the teams at the Global IT Centre and Tata Consultancy Services (TCS), who did the gap analysis at a very granular level. Although all the banks other than Mahila Bank were on the same platform, many gaps still remained, as not all the banks had achieved the same level of implementation of technology or business processes.

Apart from the financial impact of the merger on the balance sheet, and profit and loss account of the merged entity, the most critical challenges in such a case have to do with the cultural and technological integration. There is also the danger of loss of business, unless general fears surrounding the merger are alleviated through a strong communication strategy.

It was easier to deal with the staff-related policy issues regarding fitment, retirement benefits, and promotion, among other things, as precedents had been created by the merger of two associate banks earlier. The biggest problems pertained to rationalization of the branch, and of administrative offices, and the consequent transfer of staff. The two pillars on the basis of which the entire exercise needed to be carried out were transparency and speed of execution. The branches were identified on the basis of certain well-defined parameters. However, a degree of resistance was anticipated from the landlords and their ability to bring in political pressures. The only way to deal with the situation was to put forth a strong rationale for the merger of branches and avoid a strategy of randomly picking and choosing any branch. The Global IT Centre at SBI developed a capability of doing data mergers of 400 to 500 branches every weekend. The entire exercise was carried out within a span of three months and there were barely 10-odd branches, that too only in rural and semi urban centres, where the decision to merge had to be put on hold due to strong political resistance. Given the magnitude of the entire exercise, we were mentally prepared to give some concessions here or there, as adoption of a very rigid stand could have derailed the entire process. On the staff front, a very clear message was disseminated to all the controllers to minimize the friction points and ensure that the incoming staff and officers of the merged banks did not encounter or even perceive any discrimination in matters of posting. Town-hall meetings of customers and staff were held in all the district headquarters and the general atmosphere had become conducive for a smooth merger process by the time the official date of 1 April 2017 dawned.

The successful and relatively painless merger of the associate banks and the Bharatiya Mahila Bank into the SBI encouraged the Government of India to carry out mergers of other public sector banks and eventually rationalize the number of Government-owned banks from 26 to 12. From the beginning, it was clear that though SBI had shown the way, the merger of other public sector banks would be a much more difficult exercise. However, the decision for other such mergers would have to be taken at some time in the future. It goes to the credit of then Secretary, Rajiv Kumar, that he decided to bite the bullet with strong political backing. There is no rationale for having too many Government-owned banks without having any differentiated business strategy, and there is no right or wrong time for such decisions. The idea of bank consolidation had been mooted by the Narasimham Committee in 1994. If no right time could be found for implementation of this idea in 24 years, there was no guarantee that the right time would ever come in the immediate future. Mergers, however, are not by themselves expected to solve the issue of poor corporate governance, and the banking sector continues to be a weak link in the growth of the economy, with the target of achieving a US$5 trillion economy in the next four to five years likely to remain a pipe dream. I strongly feel that the dual control of public sector banks needs to be done away with and the responsibility of regulation and control should lie only with the RBI. The governance of the banks should be left to the respective boards and management while ensuring their accountability.

6

Challenges of Captaining a Large Ship

It was in the backdrop of demonetization, mergers, Asset Quality Review, and the all-pervasive problem of NPLs that I took over as Chairman of SBI on 6 October 2017.

The date of 6 October has become a special day for the State Bank of India. The Government ushered in a major change in the rules regarding the appointment of SBI chairpersons, by fixing their tenure for a period of three years. Arundhati Bhattacharya, who was the first to be subjected to this rule was appointed for three years starting 6 October 2013. Subsequently, her term was extended by another year, and she demitted office on 6 October 2017 after crossing 60 years of age and devoting four years to the service of the bank. The two subsequent appointments of chairman, SBI, have been on the same date.

Over the years, there have been several changes in the rules pertaining to the appointment of Chairpersons of SBI. When the bank was created in 1955 under a special Act of Parliament, John Mathai, who had served as Finance Minister in Prime Minister Nehru's Cabinet, was appointed as Chairman at the age of 69 years. For a long time, the SBI Chairman used to be a civil servant, and it was only in 1969 that R.K. Talwar was appointed from among the cadres of SBI, as he was employed in the Imperial Bank of India, a precursor of SBI. Talwar achieved this accolade at a very young age of 45 years, and continued on his post for eight years until he was forced to quit the bank following differences with Sanjay Gandhi, who exercised tremendous power during the era of Emergency imposed by his mother, Prime Minister Indira Gandhi in 1975. Subsequently, there have been only two other occasions when the Chairman of the bank was an outsider. The concerned gentlemen in these cases were D.N. Ghosh, a civil servant who was appointed for four years in 1984, and M.N. Goiparia, who was appointed in 1991 but had to unfortunately exit in 1992 because of the Harshad Mehta scam that shook the financial markets across the country.

Until the year 2000, the practice was to appoint the senior-most MD as the Chairman, which implied short tenures for the incumbent, often not even exceeding six months. However, realizing that the phenomenon of short stays of such senior functionaries was hampering both the growth of the bank and its ability to compete with the new-generation private sector banks, a major policy decision was taken by the government to stipulate a requirement of two years of residual service for the chairman from the date of appointment. In case none of the managing directors had residual service, one of the deputy managing directors could be appointed as the chairman. Under the new policy, Janki Ballabh became the first SBI chairman at the turn of the century, much to the discomfiture of the two managing directors, who were senior to him in terms of the number of years of service but who did not have the requisite residual service. Later, one of them was appointed as the Deputy Governor of the RBI. This policy continued till the appointment of Pratip Chaudhary in 2011.

Meanwhile, the policy of directly appointing a deputy managing director as the chairman, ignoring the seniority of managing directors, was causing lot of resentment within the bank. Consequently, governance was becoming a casualty because of the issues of *inter se* seniority and lack of cooperation from the managing directors as their reaction to being superseded in the chairman's appointment as they did not have the required residual service. This was a serious flaw in the policy for a public sector bank where seniority is of critical importance in allocation of positions. Eventually, this policy was amended in 2013, mandating thereafter that only the managing directors would be considered for the chairman's post irrespective of residual service. It was this change in policy in 2013 that gave me an opportunity to become the Chairman of SBI, even though I had only 3 months of service left before my due date of retirement in January 2018. I consider it to be another stroke of luck. Being selected for this highly coveted position in the Indian financial sector was like a dream come true for me, a dream that everyone joining the bank as a probationary officer, as I had done, was bound to nurture. But the elation on reaching the top was tempered with a realization of all the hurdles and uphill battles I had to confront while undertaking this arduous journey.

Facing Internal and External Challenges

Many observers have commented that my tenure as the Chairman of SBI coincided with one of the most challenging periods for the banking industry in the country. I dare say that this was true as these three years witnessed a host of unprecedented events and decisions at the highest level. Some of the prominent occurrences included demonetization, the merger of six banks in the State Bank of India, Asset Quality Review by the RBI, the introduction of IBC, turmoil in debt markets resulting from the failure of ILFS and Dewan Housing Corporation, the bankruptcy of Jet Airways, and the crisis at YES Bank, to name a few. The icing on this unwelcome cake was the arrival of COVID-19 during the last six months of my term, which posed a huge challenge not just to the economy and banking system in India but to every economy across the globe.

How could SBI emerge as a winner amidst all these crises? What could I do to optimally utilize the bank's inherently strong systems and foundations to combat these upheavals? And how could I harness all my personal energies into dealing with these overarching challenges and taking the right decisions at the right time? I strongly believed then and do so now that repeated emphasis on the values propagated by the organization and its alignment with the personal values of its staff, both in the lead roles and among the rank and file, are a key to its success. My first communication to the staff immediately on joining as the Chairman, which is reproduced below, outlined my vision for the bank.

Rajnish Kumar
7 October 2017
Chairman

My dear colleagues,
After taking charge of this great institution, I, first of all, thank all my worthy and admirable predecessors who headed SBI and have made it what it is today. I also take this opportunity to express my special gratitude to Arundhati Bhattacharya from whom I have taken over a sterling legacy and a host of path-breaking initiatives. This is a humbling moment for me and I really feel blessed to get the honour of leading a dedicated team of 2,68,705 associates, eager and keen to take forward the unmatched legacy of SBI.

We are a 211-year-old organization. We have relentlessly gone from strength to strength. We have faced challenges. We have enjoyed glories. But during all these long years, we have shone and continually preserved our position of being the Best Bank in the country. This fact gives huge satisfaction to each of us, who are committed to make a difference—each in his or her unique way.

The nation banks on us. We have always been the proud custodians of our people, their trust, and their financial dreams. But let's face it, right now, the banking industry is passing through very tough times. This is happening worldwide. India has also not escaped the tremors. Despite our grit, fortitude, hard work and resilience, we also could not stay insulated from the unfavourable macro conditions, more so, in a highly interconnected world and economic environment.

But challenges inspire us. We are wired that way. Our history tells us this. The recent merger proves this. A few years ago, we were perceived as a traditional bank. Today we stand out as a technology-savvy, modern and forward-looking bank. Be it on the delivery channels, new cutting technologies, banking products and services, and other less tapped customer segments, we are offering a slew of new age banking services to meet the financial needs of one and all Indians. This is our new persona. This is our ethos of optimism and inclusion. With this essential core of our strengths, I have no doubt that our bank will overcome the current challenges soon. Still, we should not forget that the crown position in the industry bequeaths greater responsibilities on us to push ourselves extra hard.

In this background, I would like to share with you a few points which strike me on this occasion:

I read somewhere that a man without a smiling face must not open a shop. This is the finest expression of the spirit of a service organization that I have ever come across. A bank is as good as its frontline people. They are the face of the bank. They make what the SBI brand stands for. Being polite to your customers is the best way to grow your community of loyal customers. Customers prefer to bank with the people who treat them well. We may have the best of products, technology, ambience, but if we are not courteous and polite to our customers, our business will not endure. We will not progress. Politeness is what builds a Great Bank.

We are living in a time when technology is changing the way we do banking. A hallmark of these technologies is that only a few realise at first, how transformative they will be, going forward. This situation brings us to confront the new challenge of assimilating technology in our operational culture. Bare adoption of digital platforms for delivery is not going to serve us. We need to educate and functionally update ourselves on the tech-front continually for providing easy-to-navigate and seamless digital services, especially for millennials and Gen-X customers. Only then will technology provide us with a sustainable, competitive advantage. Only then would we be able to efficiently deliver new-age banking for new India.

Each of our employees makes our backbone. SBI has always been and continues to be a great place to work in. We believe in the total welfare of our people, including their families, and form a lifelong bond even when they are not actively serving us. We also care for the aspirations of our staff members by constantly trying to enrich their lives and job experiences. The fact that the global #1 job site 'Indeed.com' recently named SBI among the Top Three Best places to work in India only attests to that fact. You will agree with me that a 'Healthy Mind in a Healthy Body' is applicable not only to individuals but also to organisations. While performance and productivity are non-negotiables, they are not achievable if the employees are not healthy and happy. We have been taking a number of new initiatives focused towards achieving a work–life balance for employees by introducing facilities like sabbatical and work-from-home, and refining some of the existing ones. I urge all my colleagues to ensure that they and their co-workers pay attention to their health and maintain a proper work–life balance.

Learning is another important aspect for our individual and organisational growth. Our ability to expand our minds and quest for ceaseless learning is critical for upholding our lead position in new India. We have begun an ambitious journey for empowering our 2,68,705 employees for facing the challenges of the future through 'Saksham'. 'Saksham' leverages the power of technology to help each employee realize his or her full potential. On one hand, it supports a data-driven and objective performance management system for identifying and rewarding achievers. On the other, it helps provide guidance and constructive inputs for improvement to those colleagues who lag behind. The 'Right Person in the Right Job' is vital for achieving the best results. We also need to groom future leaders of the Bank. 'Saksham' is designed to achieve all this in a structured and holistic way as a main pillar of future HR. It is important that we continue this journey, making course corrections, where necessary.

I strongly believe that ethics matters in a fiduciary setting like a commercial bank. Banking must stick to strong ethical standards. To ensure this, our conduct must be absolutely clean. But clean conduct requires that we follow the rules of governance and principles of strong ethics. SBI has always stood for the highest ethical standards in the country. We are the first in the Indian public sector to start an independent 'Ethics and Business Conduct Vertical' to weave our trademark ethos into our operational fabric. Today, there is also a severe trust deficit amongst the various stakeholders in the financial ecosystem. I believe that Ethics is the only way out to bridge this gap. Therefore, I urge you all to promote moral and ethical grandeur unconditionally in your daily actions and decisions.

Let us keep in mind the values of STEPS, which stands for Strong Ethics; Transparent and High Standards of Corporate Governance; Empathy and Compassion for Colleagues, Customers and Communities around; Politeness in Dealing with Customers, Peers, Seniors and Junior

Colleagues; and Sincerity. Let us ensure that this STEPS spirit passionately persists with us till the end.[1]

I shall close by saying that I am proud to lead Team SBI and I wish that with the determined STEPS and untiring efforts of each of you, Team SBI will transform SBI into **Divya** and **Bhavya,** making SBI a proxy for Grand and Divine India.

Thank you all.
Rajnish Kumar
Chairman

The paragraph on work–life balance in my note touched the emotional chord of the staff the most. I was constantly getting feedback about the staff facing pressure and anxiety due to the long hours they were required to put in. Thus, reducing the anxiety and tension levels in the organization had assumed great importance. When the union leaders came to congratulate me on my appointment, I told them clearly not to worry about anything. The only message they needed to carry to the rank and file was for them to provide efficient and courteous service to the customers.

The Bane of Non-Performing Loans

One of the major bottlenecks to growth that the bank constantly faced was NPLs that acted as a huge drag on its performance. The proportion of NPLs in the corporate accounts segment was as high as 25 per cent,[2] and unless there was a recovery in the large accounts, there was no way that banks could improve their performance. Circumstances were thus ripe for accelerating the process of resolution and recovery of NPLs from corporates. In this direction, the introduction of IBC in November 2016 can be considered as a watershed moment in the history of the creditor–debtor relationship in India. It was anticipated that the implementation of IBC would lead to legal challenges going forward, as the law was new and all its provisions would be tested in practice. The general perception was that the existing promoters would not let go of their business easily and would prefer to fight till the end rather than giving up. Banks had their own reasons for scepticism and apprehensions about the success of the process mandated under IBC. The RBI had to initially force banks to take recourse to the bankruptcy code if the amount of NPLs exceeded Rs 2,000 crore. Further, 12 cases, the so-called 'Dirty Dozen', as labelled by CNBC,[3] were referred to the NCLT. However, even after four years of their emergence, the resolution of these 12 cases has not fully been achieved. I had objected to CNBC putting the tag of 'dirty dozen' on these cases. Nowhere in the world is such stigma attached to business failures. There are enough provisions in the law to deal with wrongdoing by the promoters under both the Companies Act and the Prevention of Money Laundering Act (PMLA) as well as the Criminal Procedure Code (CrPC).

The approach of the RBI in respect of recognition of NPLs and provisioning on these loans was hardening and it was no longer willing to offer any forbearance. The pendulum had, in fact, swung to the other extreme and the bank officials felt that many accounts that had been performing well currently were classified as 'non-performing' by the supervisors on technical grounds. Even a bank like HDFC Bank which did not have the problem of NPLs in the corporate segment was not spared the embarrassment of declaring an account NPL the day after the announcement of its quarterly results. Nevertheless, the word of the regulator was the final word. This led to huge divergences in the numbers reported by the banks and the RBI assessment as there was a time lag between the finalization of the RBI report that was released nine to ten months after the closure of the financial year and declaration of results. Immediately after my appointment as Chairman, I met the then RBI Governor, Urjit Patel, who had earlier served on the board of SBI. This was my first and last meeting with him. As the RBI Governor, Patel had decided to close the doors for all communication with the banks. Even the heads of large international banks were denied an audience with him on one pretext or the other. This gave me strong insights into what was going on in the minds of regulators. With its image as a regulator having taken a huge beating due to the chaos on the NPL front, the RBI was now determined to rebuild its reputation as a tough supervisor. It felt that it had given a long rope to the banks and it was now time to crack the whip. While no one can question the authority of the RBI as a regulator, it was quite likely that in many cases, supervisors would go overboard without realizing the negative consequences of their over-zealous actions. Once an account is tagged as 'non-performing', the flow of funds to it stops immediately, though, in theory, banks can lend additional funding that would be treated as a standard procedure. Mercifully, many such companies are doing well and have been able to avoid the tag of a Non-Performing Account (NPA). But it goes to the credit of the RBI supervisors that in a majority of the cases, their assessment proved to be right, and their categorization of NPAs was justified. On my part, however, I had decided that under no circumstances would SBI go to seek any forbearance from the RBI, even if it meant declaring losses for a few quarters. The strategy was to align the provision for loan losses with the estimated recovery and even go beyond the regulatory provisions. In line with the above change in the approach, the bank did not even take the benefit of spreading the provision in four quarters of the 'mark to market' losses on the bonds, even though the RBI had allowed it. The bank consequently declared losses continuously for three quarters starting from December 2018. I had sounded Rajiv Kumar, Secretary, DFS as well as the then Finance Minister, Arun Jaitley, who, in his typical style, showed his agreement with the strategy by nodding his head. His exact words were, '*Aur kya kar sakte hain, Rajnishji?*' ('What else can be done, Rajnish?') It was a shock to many people including my Chief Financial Officer, Anshula Kant, as well as many senior serving and retired officers of the bank, that SBI could actually ever declare a loss. Anshula took some time to adjust to the new approach but once the bank declared a loss in the December 2017 quarter, she was emboldened and stopped worrying about the quarterly profit and loss statement. The corporate accounts group team led by Sriram, Managing Director, was completely aligned from the beginning with the goal of upfront recognition of stress and raising the provision cover on the NPLs.

Meanwhile, the NPLs increased by more than Rs 1 lakh crore during the financial year 2017–18. The RBI, however, still assessed a divergence of Rs 12,000 crore in the reporting of NPLs. It is not as if there was any deliberate attempt by the banks to under-report their NPLs but it was the overall regulatory approach and the forbearance given by the RBI in the past that led to the occurrence of such a large accumulation. SBI did not generate NPLs of more than Rs 1 lakh crore in 12 months. As they say, 'Better late than never'. The Asset Quality Review and the change in the RBI's approach towards the recognition and handling of NPLs, as manifested in the February 2018 framework for the resolution of stressed assets (which was replaced by the June 2019 framework after the Hon'ble Supreme Court set aside the February 2018 framework[4]) was bound to cause huge distress to the banking system and the economy, though the hope that both would eventually emerge stronger lingered on.

My impromptu remark during the earnings call after the March 2018 results was, 'The year 2018 was a year of despair, 2019 is a year of hope, and 2020 will be a year of happiness.' This statement attracted huge media attention, and subsequently, all the efforts and energy of the bank management were directed towards achieving this goal.

The immediate step that was taken was the transfer of all the NPLs to the Stressed Assets Resolution Group and strengthening it through placement of most competent officers who had a profound knowledge of credit. For handling large corporates, it was important to build a consensus amongst lenders, for which the State Bank Bhawan at Nariman Point, Mumbai, became the hub of high-level meetings and coordinated action by the major lenders, including private sector banks, mainly ICICI Bank and Axis Bank and financial institutions like the Power Finance Corporation and REC Ltd. It was natural for every institution to be guided by self-interest, but all the lenders were willing to accommodate each other in the larger interest of the industry. Fortunately, the outcome of these efforts has been very positive for the industry, with notable successes like those of Binani Cement, Essar Steel, Bhushan Steel, and Prayagraj Power and Ruchi Soya to name a few.

Focus on Operating Profit Growth

It was equally important to augment the operating profit of the bank, which was not sufficient to meet the loan loss provisions. Although the bank had been able to control overheads, the Net Interest Income could be improved only by bringing down the cost of deposits. The interest rates were softening and there was a huge criticism that banks were not passing the benefit of the lower interest rate to the borrowers. Here, it is pertinent to point out that banks in India are hugely dependent on retail deposits and without a drastic cut in the deposits rate, there is no way that banks can reduce the lending rate in tandem with changes in the REPO rate by the RBI, which is used as one of the main tools for the rate transmission by the RBI. Significantly, 45 per cent of the deposits in SBI are savings and current account deposits. The rate of interest on savings remained unchanged and was almost fixed at 3.5 per cent for several years. Since the RBI was moving in the direction of introducing an external benchmark for lending rates, despite a high degree of reservation amongst the bankers, it became clear to me that unless the bank brought in variability in the savings rate, there would be high pressure on the margins. When there was a proposal to make the savings bank interest rate a variable rate, members of the Asset Liability Committee (ALCO) were clearly not ready to give their approval for it. After a huge debate, eventually ALCO decided to bite the bullet and linked the savings bank rate to the REPO Rate, which helped the bank in improving its Net Interest Income, and also in implementing the external benchmark-linked lending rates.

In parallel, the emphasis on risk-based pricing of loans and resisting the temptation faced by relationship managers to book high-value loans at uneconomical rates of interest helped in improving the net interest margins. This, in turn, helped the bank create headroom to aggressively deal with the losses from loans. It may be concluded that the notable change in approach, wherein the emphasis shifted from managing the quarterly Profit and Loss to strengthening the balance sheet, has started paying rich dividends for the bank. Finally, the bank's outstanding performance during the COVID pandemic has catapulted SBI's share on the buy list of all analysts, including the likes of Macquarie and Morgan Stanley, who had been bearish on SBI.

These ruminations at the end of my career at SBI, and what I can humbly call some of my accomplishments as the head of the bank, invoke a sense of satisfaction in the way we have handled many of the challenges faced by the bank during both the normal times and the COVID-affected times

While most of my time was being spent on handling the legacy issues, I did not lose sight of the need for strengthening the risk management in the bank so as to ensure that the learnings from the past don't go to waste and the bank does not find itself in similar situation.

Strengthening Credit Approval Processes

Traditionally, SBI had robust credit approval skills and underwriting processes, which not only augmented its credit strengths in the corporate space but also undoubtedly made it a benchmark in Indian banking. However, the growth binge fuelled by debt, which carried on among a large portion of Indian corporates after the global financial crisis of 2008, led to significant challenges for both businesses as well as their bankers.

The credit situation at SBI deepened the NPL crisis. Hence, even while facing an overall challenging macro-economic scenario, the bank had also lost some of its credit skills that had always been a matter of pride for all of us. Conventionally, the credit committees of the bank took all the credit decisions after debating them extensively. But in view of the large number of credit proposals they had to consider, it was impossible for the committee members to minutely assess all details of every proposal, as a result of which some of the specific nuances of each industry would get missed out at times. Further, despite the existence of a strong risk department at the bank, the role of staff working in this department was largely limited to providing an industry perspective; the actual decision on each individual credit proposal was left to the credit committees, wherein the number of people from the business world often outnumbered those dealing with credit and risk. We also realized that while banks took a backward-looking view of risk, usually trying to examine balance sheets that were often three to six months old by the time they were submitted to us, the equity markets took a much more forward-looking view of risk management, and priced in the risk into the daily moving share prices. This discrepancy in risk assessment between the bank and the corporate world was another key hurdle in addressing the

NPLs. One solution to this problem was to access the vast external data beyond the client's balance sheets that was available to us and that could be incorporated into the credit underwriting process of the bank to make it more robust.

Setting up the Credit Review Department

An analysis of the above challenges clearly indicated that we needed some additional support for our credit committees to enable them to comprehensively examine each credit proposal. For this purpose, the conceptualization and structure of the proposed department, referred to as the Credit Review Department (CRD), had to be fleshed out. My initial suggestion was that we should have a separate team to assess the infrastructure proposals and sift them out from those pertaining to loan requests for non-infrastructural purposes, as the NPLs were largely from the infrastructure sector. However, given the fact that several Indian corporates were engaged in both types of businesses, it was not easy to make clear distinctions between the two, and consequently to isolate the proposals associated only with infrastructural development. In an effort to address this challenge, I constituted a team to design both the structure and processes of the department, and also brought in McKinsey & Co to help with the entire restructuring.

First and foremost, we needed to answer the following questions to set the ball rolling:

1. How should this department be organized, and what would be the extent of its authority and autonomy? This was a key question, as the department obviously had to have some teeth to be able to wield power but this power had to be exercised prudently to prevent it from becoming a roadblock for business development.
2. How should we allocate clients within this group—geographically or by sector or in some other way?

3. How could we incorporate a forward-looking perspective on risk management into our risk processes?

We spent nearly three months debating each of the elements that would determine the composition and conduct of the department, and evolved a set of design principles, which we piloted and subsequently rolled out. The entire project took shape through implementation of the following plan of action:

1. The CRD was set up as a separate group under the Chief Credit Officer (CCO), with the objective of reviewing each credit proposal before it was sent to the credit committee concerned with final decision-making. The role of the CRD had been spelt out unambiguously—it had to review the proposal and identify the areas of risk, thereafter liaise with the business team on how best to address the concerns. After much debate, we agreed that the CRD would not have any veto power. It could point out the risk and send the proposal back, but in case the business owners felt that they had done everything possible to mitigate risk and still wanted to put up their proposal before the credit committee to seek its decision on the matter, they had the right to do so.
2. It was decided to organize the CRD by sector. This was done based on the realization that it was critical to ensure access to expertise in the right sector for thoroughly analysing the risks inherent in each credit proposal and for integrating the risk trends within each sector into the credit underwriting process. While evaluating our portfolio, we found that over 80 per cent of our clients were engaged in one of eight sectors, which led us to choose these specific sectors for our project.
3. We hired external resources and obtained access to market data in order to attain forward-looking perspectives. The sector teams within the CRD included a mix of internal and

external resources to ensure that we got the best of both worlds in terms of talent.

4. The structure of the credit committee itself was also revamped to include peers in all the committees within the bank. This was particularly important because past experience had shown that if committees comprised people at different levels of hierarchy, it was typically the view of the senior-most person that held sway. All the committees had equal representation from the risk and business functions so that neither could override the other.

Reorganizing Client Coverage

After reorganizing the credit structure, we also realized the need to review our corporate banking client coverage architecture. Historically, the bank had two separate client coverage groups—the Corporate Accounts Group (CAG), which was meant to focus on the largest and higher quality clients, and the Mid-Corporate Group (MCG), for engaging with mid-sized clients, who potentially symbolized a higher risk of defaulting in loan payments. However, over the years, the distinction between these two groups had disappeared both within the country as well as in the bank. The sweep of delinquencies among large corporates had shown that the big corporate groups were no longer safer to lend to as compared to the smaller ones. Since the bank's portfolio was a reflection of the country's economic environment, we had large and risky clients within both the CAG and MCG, and the NPL levels in both the groups were similar. As a result, the leadership in both CAG and MCG had to focus on resolving the issue of stressed assets and had little time to assess the new business. Even within each group, the client coverage model was highly distributed, often with little coordination across the different groups. For instance, a conglomerate like L&T could have one Regional Manager (RM) in Mumbai and a separate one in Chennai, with differential product pricing and very little coordination between the two coverage teams. Another drawback in the bank was that we had been overly focused on lending to the exclusion of almost any other product. The ramification of this skewed policy was our lack of focus on and appropriate attention to a number of large non-borrowing corporates.

In view of the above limitations, we decided to make some fundamental changes to our coverage model going forward. While we would retain two separate client coverage groups, the CAG would concentrate solely on clients that were both large and enjoyed a particular high credit rating. This would enable the RMs within the CAG to focus singularly on growing the business. As these were also among the most exclusive clients in the country, competition was exceptionally stiff in this segment and margins were extremely thin, we had to deliver the entire bank to the clients in order to meet the cost of capital. The newly formed Commercial Clients Group (CCG), on the other hand, would focus on clients who were below either a certain size, or a certain credit rating. This brought some of SBI's largest and most important clients into the ambit of the CCG. The objective of the CCG was to facilitate growth of business while at the same time keeping an appropriate focus on risk. The inherently more risky nature of this portfolio meant that we could get better yields but only by keeping risk costs firmly under control.

We also introduced the concept of a Group Relationship Manager (GRM) for the largest conglomerates in the country to streamline coverage and make it consistent across the country. The GRMs, who were hierarchically at the same level as that of the Chief General Manager (CGM), were mandated to maintain our relationships at the levels of the Chief Experience Officers (CXOs), and oversee the RMs who were leading the individual relationships at the company and geography levels. This helped us upgrade our relationships as our senior folks were interacting at peer levels with the CXOs of the largest conglomerates.

We also decided to streamline the number of branches for both the CAG and CCG. Our erstwhile ambitious plans had resulted in over-expansion in too many locations, which constrained us from providing either the level of client service or the risk management expertise that was needed for our corporate clients, particularly in the smaller locations. We, therefore, created a separate Credit Light Group (CLG) to focus on non-borrowing clients, which included some of the largest corporates in the country, even though they had no need for borrowing from us.

The CLG focused on providing the entire suite of the bank's products to these clients. SBI was the largest lender to many corporates but since HDFC Bank was deeply entrenched in the lucrative cash management business of the corporates, when it came to cash management, HDFC got obvious preference over SBI. This was not without reason. HDFC and other new-generation private sector banks had built highly efficient technology platforms and were proactive in canvassing fee-based business and capturing cash flows of the corporates, which gave them a huge advantage in terms of income on float funds. To put this in perspective, the current accounts in the three large new-generation private sector banks amounts to 15 per cent of their deposits as compared to less than half, at just 7 per cent for SBI. Realizing this, albeit a bit late, we set to work on creating one of the best cash management products. The next challenge was to market it aggressively. The board of SBI also pushed very hard and in many of the high-value credit proposals coming before the Executive Committee of the board, the major point of discussion was centred around the other business being captured by the bank from the corporates. As in other ventures, I decided to lead from the front in this case too. Interestingly, and perhaps deliberately, my first port of call after taking over as Chairman of SBI was the office of Hindustan Unilever Limited (HUL) in the western suburbs of Mumbai. This came as a pleasant surprise for Sanjiv Mehta, the CEO of HUL, and also served as a clairvoyant message to the CAG team that the focus at the bank now would have to shift from fund-based to fee-based business, which was not an easy shift by any standards.

The Outcome

As with any path-breaking endeavours, the implementation of this new structure at SBI also posed new and seemingly insurmountable challenges. There was expectedly some friction between the CRD and business teams, to begin with, but this was soon resolved by the entire senior management team, which started focusing on both the business and risk parameters, while working diligently to resolve the friction points. I appointed one of our best CGMs, Ashwini Bhatia (now MD in charge of Corporate Banking), to oversee the implementation of the project, and he, along with his team proved equal to the task by tirelessly fleshing out all the details and the potential failure points, and also involving me in the exercise as and when required. I was often asked to intermediate between business and risk, which also gave me the opportunity to gently remind both sides that the bank is actually in the business of taking appropriate risks. This meant that we had to walk the tightrope between the twin realizations that we could not do only risk-free business, nor could we sacrifice growth of business because of risks! After overcoming teething troubles, the entire structure settled down into a smooth functioning unit in about six months, and has been working quite well since then.

On the client side, the reorganization of the coverage groups created its own set of challenges. Many clients raised questions about why they were being moved from one group to another, and in a few of the smaller locations where we shut down branches, some of our clients threatened to move away. However, we managed the situation by executing a detailed client outreach programme. We spoke to every single client who was in any way affected by the reorganization, and educated them about the concomitant benefits of the new structure. We had to convince them that we would now be able to respond faster to them, and also have a more coordinated coverage model. In the rare circumstances, when we shut down branches in some locations, we made sure that the servicing was taken care of by a designated branch in that location, while the responsibility for coverage was assigned to the RMs stationed in the nearest CCG locations. These efforts brought rewards as overall, we did not lose any clients in this process, and our wallet share with our largest clients only grew, as we ended up doing substantially higher and innovative businesses with our CAG clients. Thanks to the CLG, we also managed to do some businesses that we had not focused on in the past, fulfilling the entire spectrum of our clients' needs.

Our efforts in terms of both strengthening credit underwriting (through the CRD) and resolution of the stressed assets have borne fruit over the years. The gross non-performing assets (GNPAs) reduced from 10.35 per cent in the third quarter (3Q) of 2017 (when I took over) to 4.98 per cent as on 31 March 2021. In absolute terms, the GNPAs have come down from Rs 1.99 lakh crore to 1.35 lakh crore, whereas the total advances have grown from Rs 19 lakh crore to 25.5 lakh crore.[5] More importantly, the market has also begun to recognize this, as reflected in the recent analyst reports raising the target price for SBI, all of which commented on the significant strengthening of risk management and underwriting in the bank, and reposed greater faith in the bank's ability to contain credit costs. In some ways, this has been one of my most satisfying and enduring contributions to the bank, and I believe that it has built the foundation for a much stronger SBI.

The CLG also achieved many successes and opened new vistas in supply chain financing by providing holistic solutions to meet the entire array of needs of large conglomerates. One of its biggest successes was the conclusion of a comprehensive Memorandum of Understanding (MoU) between HUL and SBI. According to this arrangement, nearly a million outlets of HUL (*kirana* shops) that would otherwise find it difficult to get any credit line, now became eligible for a credit limit if they approached a bank branch in the traditional method of lending, symbolizing the power of technology in collaboration between two corporate giants. In fact, technology and collaboration have become the buzz words for the CLG, which led me to rename it as the Corporate Solutions Group to project the new solutions-oriented approach of SBI. In conclusion, I would like to point out that the collaboration between large corporates and banks has the power of transforming millions of lives, particularly small businesses which are part of supply chains. I can also derive immense satisfaction from the personal rapport I built with Sanjiv Mehta of HUL during my very first visit to his company, which came very handy later in driving the extremely fruitful relationship between the two most respected companies in their respective domains.

7

From a Legacy Bank to a Tech-Savvy Bank—The YONO Vision

> 'SBI's retail positioning, along with value unlocking potential from its Digital App YONO, which could also be hived off into a separate subsidiary, are key growth triggers. YONO is expected to be worth between $20–$50 billion for SBI.'
>
> —Goldman Sachs[1]

The Genesis of the Idea

The concept of the digital application You Only Need One (YONO), devised by SBI, started off as a germ of an idea, emerging from the bank's decision to create an 'Online Marketplace' in order to attract the millennial generation. It was widely felt that SBI, while successfully projecting itself as the 'banker to every Indian', was actually lagging behind in its ability to acquire the younger generation of customers. It was felt that this gap could be bridged by creating an e-commerce marketplace which would attract young and new customers into the SBI fold. In its original form, therefore, YONO (or 'Project Lotus', as it was initially called) was a finite concept with a limited shelf life—it would help the bank attract new customers through the marketplace with the hope of converting some of them into SBI customers; and this would entail an added benefit of embellishing the digital credentials of SBI.

After taking over as MD, NBG, however, I started wondering if we were underestimating the transformational potential of YONO. SBI had already made significant progress on digitization, with its well-established and stable platforms of Internet banking and mobile banking. Since both these platforms offered most, if not all, the services that other leading banks were offering on digital platforms, and had achieved reasonably good ratings on performance, there was no urgent need for ushering in a change or creating a new platform. But my aspirations as the head of the leading bank in the country went beyond creating 'me-too' products that did little for the bank's image as a trendsetter in fulfilling people's financial requirements. This raised a couple of seminal questions: Should we be content with a well-functioning platform offering an add-on service that would hopefully attract a larger number of younger customers? Or should we take the bull by the horns and plunge headlong into the wave of digitization that was sweeping the financial sector, along with other sectors, across the globe? How could we optimize our digitization campaign, and efforts to participate in the Digital India programme for creating innovative digital infrastructure that would transform banking in the country and firmly establish SBI's credentials as a market leader in the digital space?

In order to help us think through on how to shape the programme, we invited a number of consultants and external thinkers to make presentations to identify the potential objectives for Project Lotus. While all the presentations provided rich insights, one of them, in particular, stood out—this was the presentation by McKinsey & Co, which incorporated three key elements, comprehensively suggesting what SBI could do differently from other banks in projecting itself as a digital icon. These elements were delineated as follows:

- *Create an omni-channel and a seamless customer experience for all customers*: Instead of only trying to attract new millennial customers, we should focus on the entire 450 million-strong customer base of SBI, providing them differentiated customer experiences, which was as important (if not more) as trying to acquire new customers.
- *Drive disproportionate growth through digital achievements*: While SBI's digital platform was well established as a servicing channel for the bank, we wanted to shift the focus towards making it an acquisition channel, achieving 30–40 per cent of our sales through digital means. We wanted to ensure the sales of both our core banking products as well as our joint venture/subsidiary products through this platform, while also providing an online marketplace for meeting the 'beyond the financial services' needs of our customers. Hence, from purely an online marketplace, the concept would evolve into a 'one-stop platform for all banking, financial, and lifestyle needs of our customers'. It was this element that subsequently gave rise to the tagline YONO (You Only Need One)—the idea was to offer each SBI customer everything s/he needed on a single platform.
- *Improve productivity and reduce cost–income ratios through customer journey redesign*: The new platform would provide us an opportunity to fundamentally redesign our customer journeys for both improving the customer experience and augmenting productivity, thereby eliminating several redundant steps in the banking process. This model could also be replicated on the branch platform, which would be akin to offering an in-branch experience to customers that was similar to the digital experience.

The McKinsey & Co presentation set me thinking hard and deep. It was increasingly becoming clear to me that we had to do something remarkably different from the run-of-the-mill apps to catapult SBI as a leader in the digital space as well. None of the other Indian banks had taken such an expansive view of their digital aspirations—for me, at some level, it was an aspiration to win the 'Only SBI can do it' tag.

My dreams for taking the bank to new heights were, however, dampened by the over-cautious members of the bank's top team, who were full of scepticism about the success of an advanced digital application promoted by a bank that catered to all classes of society, including those with limited digital literacy. So, I had my task cut out in trying to convince my reluctant colleagues to go digital in a big way. But this resistance from senior officials at the bank also made me wonder if we were biting off more than we could chew. The contrarian argument was that we already had decently functioning digital platforms, so there was no pressing need for us to set in motion a huge transformation when we could simply add a few capabilities, and fill in some gaps. Finally, we also had to negotiate a complex technology landscape, which would pose major challenges of navigation for any technology provider. There were several intense debates on the topic in the bank—the discussions culminated with an obvious question from the bank's Chairperson, Arundhati Bhattacharya: 'Are you sure we are not taking on too much?' However, I managed to reassure her that while this was a big programme, we would try to prioritize and sequence it in a way to make the transition manageable for all customers, and that I would personally oversee the implementation of the programme to ensure its success. Thus was born the vision for YONO, which would soon become a critical part of my life for the next four years, first as the MD and then as the Chairman of the bank.

Setting Off on the YONO Journey

Having laid out the vision for launching YONO, we decided to move forward with the plan, appointing McKinsey & Co as our consultant and IBM as the technology partner, both of which were selected through a detailed Request for Proposal (RfP) process as required for all Public Sector Units (PSUs). Before initiating the programme, however, I was clear that this would not be just another 'traditional' technology application. We would instead build not merely a unique digital platform, but also a different operating model, so that it could form the kernel of a programme that would unleash a chain of innovations in the bank. Following were some of the key changes we made to the standard operating model:

1. *A separate operating environment*: We hired a separate building for the YONO team, with the SBI team, the consultants, and the IT developers associated with the project stationed in the same office. The meeting rooms in the office were converted into 'garages' with digital whiteboards and videoconferencing facilities, and were painted in bright colours to convey the impression of a typical start-up.
2. *A separate team*: From the beginning, we knew that the team had to be a mix of internal and external talent. While we ran an internal selection process to identify the best among our in-house resources, we also recruited a number of talented youngsters who had aspirations to create an impact in the technological space at a scale that would only be possible in a large organization like SBI.
3. *Different style of working*: The garage model of working, with all the various stakeholders placed in the same room and operating in two-week sessions, signified a completely new model. Gone were the days of sending out notes or memos across departments and waiting for comments—the teams would lay out the process

flows, and debate and discuss the suggested changes; and at the end of two weeks, they would create a redesigned process flow integrating inputs from all the stakeholders. Albeit, there were several other necessary steps in the process. Each of the redesigned technological innovations had to undergo a formal process of risk and compliance approval, but the path to receipt of the final approval was significantly shortened due to the new ways of working that we had facilitated.

All this was new to the bank, as we had always been a very traditional bank that prided itself on its extensive compliance and risk processes. Thus, without meddling too much with the bank's traditional strengths, we retained the focus on risk and compliance, but ushered in a change by expediting decision-making. And the only way to do this was to become a role model for this myself. So, I decided to invest my personal time and effort in attaining our goal in the right way. We set up fast-track approval processes, which I oversaw personally to ensure that we were following a different operating model. This necessitated a significant effort upfront, and hence, for the first six months, I ended up spending nearly eight to ten hours a week on the project. The rewards lay in the new way of working that was visible at the bank and the opportunity to bring about an exciting transformation in the bank. The effort was well worth the gains.

The Initial Challenges

We started the YONO journey on 6 September 2016 with ambitious targets—we wanted to build and launch the first version of the platform in six months! The all-round consensus in the bank was that this was too ambitious a target and virtually unachievable—while I privately agreed with the naysayers, I also knew that unless we reached for the stars, we would not be able to achieve even our potential goals.

As we started with the first set of redesigns for the app, the entire team started behaving like the proverbial kid in a candy store. All the journeys to be navigated on the app showed significant scope for rationalization. For instance, the previous account opening journey at the bank branches took about 60–70 minutes, and required the customer and branch staff to fill in 58 fields. Leveraging Aadhaar, we designed the journey on the app to perform this entire task in eight to ten minutes, and reduce the number of manual fields to 14. Likewise, for payments, what earlier would take more than ten clicks to complete a payment was now designed to be done in three clicks. My advice to the team was to ensure that none of the tasks should take more than three clicks by the customers to get done, and we found that in most cases, this was actually possible. We also spent a lot of time challenging the existing orthodoxies. For instance, if we got the client data validated through the Unique Identification Authority of India (UIDAI), why would we need someone to check it? We had a huge group of people who were focused on checking documents that had been submitted by the frontline—this arrangement made sense when there was a possibility of manual errors, but why did we need to check if the data was already validated?

Some other decisions were more complicated. For example, while we were underwriting the customers on the basis of machine learning-driven analytical models, we needed to assess the limit to which we could comfortably do away with the traditional credit underwriting models and rely purely on analytics-based underwriting. All these discussions were debated by a cross-functional team from different parts of the bank, and the risks and mitigating factors were discussed threadbare. Ultimately, however, the final decision regarding the level of risk that was acceptable had to be taken by us as the leadership of the bank.

There were also some more debates about the technology architecture itself, leading to a fundamental question: Should this just be a nice front-end, building on the existing Account

Information and Payment Initiation (APIs) portals and the platforms that the bank had, or should we redesign the journeys end-to-end, including introduction of changes in the core processes? After some intense discussions, we agreed to do a full redesign of the key journeys to achieve a consistent customer experience. We wanted just a basic front-end, not a really fancy one, but which offered an optimal experience to the customer. We also agreed to have a differentiated front-end stack, which facilitated agility, while retaining our existing core banking platform that already provided us a technologically robust and secure back-end platform. Simultaneously, the team was acutely conscious of the fact that the bar on any SBI digital platform, especially in terms of information security and customer safety, had to be extremely high, and all our processes and decisions were geared towards attaining this objective.

The Hills and Troughs

After the initial excitement of the first three to four months, as we got closer to our initial target of six months for the launch, we started realizing the depth of the challenge we had set for ourselves. The heady initial period wherein all the teams had worked day and night to hone the customer experience was followed by a reality check when our aspirations suddenly seemed beyond reach. These were the most difficult moments, as the team endeavoured to create a world-class technological infrastructure at the front-end and to integrate it with the existing technological platforms of the bank, while at the same time provide a stable and safe platform for digital users. The fact that nothing of this scale and size had been attempted by any financial institution in India before also weighed heavily on our minds. As the above challenges mounted, delays began to set in. The launch deadline of April came and went, and with every week of delay in the launch, we witnessed frayed tempers among the key staff. There were multiple reasons for failures, both major and minor. Sometimes the redesigned journeys would not perform as they were supposed to, at other times, the APIs connecting the front-end to the Core Banking System (CBS) failed to respond. Often, we noticed flaws in the design journey itself, compelling the entire team to go back to the drawing board, and leading to a complete waste of the time and effort spent in the development of the journey. To add to the complications, we were also dealing with regulatory changes. Suddenly, there were unprecedented dislocations, like opening of the Aadhaar-based digital account being disallowed, and then we had to redesign the entire journey from scratch. These roadblocks had an obvious adverse impact on staff morale, with a number of my colleagues now questioning both the logic and logistics of the project, and whether we would be able to deliver the app as envisaged. I soon found myself frequently defending Project Lotus and responding to the sceptics in the Central Management Committee (CENMAC).

In addition to resolving the technological challenges, we were also trying to stitch together a set of partnerships with a broad range of marketplace partners. Although we were not going to charge the merchants for being on our platform (the Banking Regulations Act did not allow us to charge for this), we did want them to create a differentiated offer for SBI customers. The concept was clear—while the merchants got access to the 450-million strong customer base of the bank, our customers got access to special discounts and offers which attracted them to the platform. However, in order to set this up, we needed to not only get the merchants on board, but also to ensure technological integration with their platform, while meeting all the information security guidelines. The positive outcome was that a number of the largest merchants were ready to partner with us, and we were slowly but surely making progress on the technology integrations.

The most critical task for me at this stage was to make sure that the morale of the team continued to remain high. We had weekly meetings with all the teams, and while we dispassionately analysed the reasons for the delay and tried to fix them, it was important to retain the focus on moving forward and fixing the challenges, rather than focusing on what went wrong. This was one of the hardest times for me personally, but I trusted the team and our partners to do what was right. This, I believe, is the most critical role of the leader—when things are down, you need to stay calm and not transmit the stress to the team, but support them in resolving the issues.

Finally, the Launch: November 2017

After several months devoted to resolving the build and performance journey, application stability, and issues pertaining to information security and data privacy, the month for launch was finally set as November 2017. The entire project had taken us more than double the anticipated time—13 months instead of the originally planned six months, but as our consultants never failed to remind us, what we were aspiring for was a much more ambitious project than anything attempted by any bank prior to this.

In the meantime, I was appointed Chairman of the bank in October 2017, which meant that I could continue to drive and supervise Project Lotus even more closely in my new position. Everyone in the bank was well aware how much the project meant to the new Chairman, so the all-round focus on the project only increased. Finally, we were able to fix the launch date—17 November 2017. In the run-up to the launch, the overwhelming discussion was around selection of a name for the app. Clearly, it could not be called Project Lotus, which sounded a bit pedantic, nor could we christen it as an SBI mobile banking or Internet banking channel. So, we resorted to detailed market research and tested a few names. There was a great deal of resonance with the name, 'YONO', which was the brainchild of our marketing team.

The name—You Only Need One—was simple and yet highly suggestive. It was also easy on the diction and could be understood by all customers. Having finalized the name, we moved next to fixing the right colour scheme and the 'look and feel' of the app, with the mandate being that it should project a youthful and contemporary image. Things were slowly falling into place!

The YONO launch was done by the then Finance Minister, Arun Jaitley, at the Taj Palace Hotel in New Delhi. It was a grand event, with the Finance Minister acknowledging the vital role played by SBI in providing overall leadership, in general, and technological leadership, in particular, to the banking sector in India. Much to our pleasure, all those present seemed quite mesmerized by the new-age features as well as the entire ecosystem symbolized by YONO. We were also delighted at the widespread appreciation for the name of the app among the audience. Meanwhile, the bank had to convey the message that YONO was much more than just an app—its aim was to really provide a seamless multi-channel experience to all our customers. Indeed, for the SBI customer, YONO was the complete bank itself at the tip of the fingers!

The Scale-up

Notwithstanding the highly successful launch of YONO, it was merely the first step for us. Our real work actually began the day after the launch. The focus now shifted to the twin objectives of scaling up the customer base and driving adoption of the app, while at the same time adding new customer journeys on YONO.

Having launched a number of digital platforms earlier with mixed success, we were clear about the efforts needed to drive adoption. In the first place, we needed a very simple and attractive user interface, and a set of key journeys that were intuitive. We felt that we had achieved this aim even if we had not been able to put all the journeys that we had wanted on the app. The core journeys around account opening, fixed deposits, payments, credit cards, consumer loans, and products like mutual funds and life insurance were available on the app, and in a simplified format. However, we also needed to get our 150,000 employees on board the digital platform. I knew from past experience that if our employees were convinced about YONO, they would act as our biggest ambassadors, and the connection and interaction they had with the customers could make the app a huge success.

In order to motivate our customers to join the YONO bandwagon, we started by identifying the journeys that would really make a big difference, both for the customers and the staff. Account opening was one such journey—what earlier entailed a long waiting time before the counter staff could now be mostly done on the mobile, though customers still needed to visit the bank physically to share the original KYC and sign on the documents for regulatory reasons. Likewise, the Pre-Approved Personal Loan (PAPL) section was a major hit with both our customers and staff. While we had always had a pre-approved customer base derived from analytical models, YONO offered us the platform to provide loans to these customers in three to four clicks. I experienced the ease of accessing loans myself when I went to Gorakhpur, a remote Tier-3 town in India, where I saw customers taking a pre-approved loan on their own, being assisted by the branch staff only on a few occasions, for urgent reasons like a marriage in the family, and their relief at the speed and ease with which they could access funds was apparent. Customers were also excited about the different offers they could get from the likes of online sellers like Amazon (which partnered with us from day one) and other large merchants.

In order to promote staff enthusiasm and participation, we arranged for training sessions for our entire staff. Over 100,000 employees were trained on how to use YONO for simplifying the banking experience both for themselves and their customers. Since it made transactions easier, employees were obviously excited about using it—what had earlier taken them 30 minutes to complete in the premises of the bank could now be done in 5 minutes without visiting the bank. And they could communicate this effectively to their customers.

Over time, the number of YONO registrations started growing. The figure of the first million customers was crossed in February 2018, and the first 10 million customers in June 2019. Today, we have over 35 million YONO customers, making it the largest digital bank in the world! What was even more interesting and linked to investments was the business generation—from offering virtually zero personal loans digitally, we eventually became one of the largest digital lenders in the country, generating an average of 1,500–2,000 crore loans per month through the YONO platform. Likewise, 70 per cent of our accounts were opened on YONO, either through the app or through the assisted platform. Consequently, YONO became the first digital bank in the world to break even in less than two years, and thereafter started generating significant profits for the bank.

At the same time, the customer engagement with the platform continued to increase—60 per cent of the YONO customers logged in monthly, and each customer logged in five times per month, on an average. We also noted that the average active YONO client spends 25 minutes per month on the platform, thereby creating a highly engaged customer base.

Expansion into New Areas

After two long years of initiating the app, its success had laid to rest all doubts about whether YONO had added value to the bank. The debate was now instead centred on how much we could add to the YONO platform, and how fast we could scale it up. While this was already happening on the retail side, we decided to extend YONO into two new areas: YONO Business and YONO Global.

YONO Business was aimed at creating an innovative offering for our corporate customers, with a single client interface, and streamlined journeys around foreign exchange, trade, and cash management. While YONO Business is still evolving, we have already scaled this up to over one million corporate and small and medium enterprise (SME) clients. Today, nearly 90 per cent of the import Letters of Credit (LC) transactions for corporate customers of the bank, for instance, are being done on the YONO Business platform. SBI is well ahead of both Indian and global leaders on this metric, for whom this metric ranges from 20–40 per cent. Similarly, over 1,000 customers have been given access to book foreign exchange on the platform; and nearly 60 per cent of their forex transactions now take place on YONO Business. The adoption of YONO by customers was also significantly helped by the COVID-19 pandemic—the number of customers using the platform jumped from 15 per cent pre-COVID to 95 per cent post-COVID!

YONO Global was intended to provide a world-class experience for our global customers, starting with the UK, and then on to other markets where we had local retail presence. It was launched in the UK in September 2019, and quickly scaled up to 40,000 customers, accounting for about 500 transactions daily. YONO Global also has a significantly higher level of engagement as compared to the earlier platform with over 5,000 daily logins; this, in turn, has led to a higher share of wallet of consumers with remittances multiplying twofold and more than 25 per cent higher deposit balances for YONO customers.

We developed YONO Krishi in parallel as a means to reach out to rural consumers and farmers. Through YONO Krishi, the farmers among SBI account holders are able to gain access to all banking services, including applying for agriculture loans, transferring funds, and opening accounts instantly and securely from the convenience of their homes. The power and reach of YONO Krishi does not stop at banking. The true pain point for the farmer is obtaining a precise agricultural advisory and farm inputs on time. With YONO Krishi, farmers can secure all information at their fingertips, learn about newer farming techniques, talk to agri-experts, get quick weather updates, get to know real-time crop prices, and much more. They can also buy farm inputs online with cash on delivery (CoD) options. We, at SBI, understand the rich diversity of farmers in India and have localized the app in multiple regional languages to provide them State-specific solutions. Since its launch in July 2019, YONO Krishi has seen a highly positive response, with more than four million farmers registered and more than two million loans being disbursed on the platform till date.

YONO Is Still Evolving . . .

As I mentioned earlier, YONO is still 'work in progress', as even after four years of its launch, we are continuing to add more journeys to the platform. Very recently, a set of home loans and other journeys were added on the app. However, the platform also still encounters some of the challenges faced by digital platforms in India, such as lack of stability of connections and delays in logins. But the team is fully motivated and hands-on, persisting with its troubleshooting efforts every single day since the launch of the platform in order to make it a greater success with time. Thus, it is both inspiration and perspiration that have made YONO SBI the unique digital app that it is, enabling it to stand out in comparison to the plethora of other digital banking applications across the country. I cannot help but feel pride at this achievement for both my team and the bank's vision at capitalizing the virtually (*pun intended*) limitless opportunities that YONO has set in motion.

The online marketplace has proved to be a hook for the younger generation. It was an exciting moment for the YONO team when Mercedes agreed to sell their cars on the platform.

8

Nurturing the People at SBI: A Journey with a Human Touch

I have always believed that individuals build institutions and that their toil, commitment, and sincere efforts at a collective level drive an organization forward. My experiences over several years in both my personal and professional life have taught me that people should always come first—before institutions, work, and our mundane responsibilities. It is thus imperative to invest in the welfare and well-being of one's team, at home and in the workplace. If you are able to foster a high level of motivation and contentment among your team members, you automatically inspire confidence and commitment, which, in turn, creates synergies for enabling greater trust and better performance. To win in the marketplace, you must first win in the workplace.

As these ideas moulded my thinking during my long and enriching tenure at SBI, I kept trying to devise ways of improving outcomes and achieving loftier goals with the cooperation of my valued colleagues at every stage. By the time I became MD, I knew without doubt that a well-cared for employee is the best contributor to an organization's progress, and SBI is a living example of this adage. Its glorious past, irradiant present, and the promise of an equally effulgent future are testimony to the respect for its human capital ingrained in the philosophy of SBI—a philosophy that has engendered selfless contributions from its workforce, making the bank a mammoth financial powerhouse and a highly admired institution across sectors.

Since I was so deeply committed to and passionate about my work, time just flew by as I kept climbing the corporate ladder. This reality came home to me, unbidden as it were, when I was appointed to be the Chairman of SBI on 7 October 2017, and I realized how far I had come on this long road, starting out as a humble employee of the bank. Looking back from the seemingly exalted position I had reached, I also became acutely conscious of the enormity of the task that lay ahead. Now, the entire burden of carrying forward the legacy of the bank was on my shoulders. In a passing moment of apprehension and self-doubt, I wondered if I would be able to do justice to this challenge that life had offered. But deep down I also knew that this was my moment of reckoning, an opportunity to translate my dreams and plans for the bank into reality, to bring to fruition all the blueprints for the success of the bank that had been at the back of my mind for years. Now was the time to dust off the cobwebs and refine these goals into a cogent framework for action. And at the heart of this endeavour would lie my aspiration to nurture the human resources at SBI, and make them grow exponentially with every milestone achieved by the bank. But where was I going to start?

Family at the Centre of Staff Welfare: Promoting Work–Life Balance

The response to the above existential question lay in the very ecosystem of the bank, and how it had been evolving over the past few years. The only way forward was to continue, with all guns blazing, on the path of reforms in the financial sector, meeting head-on the flurry of new players dotting an already dense banking landscape. This cocktail of challenges in the banking sector was fuelled by the emergence of several fintech entities and rising customer expectations, as also by the piling up of NPLs that had especially shaken the bank to its very core, imposing a huge stress not only on all SBI employees but also on their families and social lives. It goes to the credit of the resilience of the bank staff that SBI had been faring much better than its peers in dealing with these multiple crises. However, something needed to be done urgently to reduce the stress quotient at the bank to prevent the very real possibility of burn-out among the staff. Ostensibly, the bank had been doing fine, it seemed to be very much alive and kicking from the outside, but deep down, sentiments were worn out and frayed. For ensuring sustained growth, the people at the heart of this effort needed care and compassion, which could only be provided by a work environment that promoted a *good work–life balance,* where recreation and rejuvenation went hand in hand with roles and responsibilities.

Keeping people both happy and productive at the same time is one of the biggest challenges faced by the Human Resources (HR) department of any organization. Often, we conflate employee welfare with the provision of facilities, monetary or otherwise. But this is tantamount to just scratching the surface. We need to go deeper to address the issue of work satisfaction, making it a more wide-ranging and comprehensive effort. This should translate into a healthy work environment and mutual respect and empathy in the workplace. Employees should also have adequate time to devote to their personal and family needs. It was with this perspective that my journey of putting life into the 'H' (the human element) of 'HR' at SBI kicked off. I launched the first HR initiative in the bank in October 2017 itself, the very month that I took over as Chairman, integrating the concept of work–life balance into the bank's corporate philosophy. This initiative was a sort of overt signal to the employees, reiterating the message that the bank valued them not just as employees but also as human beings, and that their personal well-being was just as important as the success of the bank's work plan.

The initiative kicked off with a bang. Positive vibes began to circulate in the bank, manifested by an effusive response from the staff. All of a sudden, everyone felt uplifted and energized. We could clearly see a paradigm shift in employee attitude and conduct. For the first time in their work-lives, people at the bank felt that they were being looked after and taken care of. I must admit that putting in long hours has been the bane of SBI's work ethic. Sitting up late in office is often seen as evidence of an employee's hard work and commitment. But I couldn't disagree more with this perception. If you had the occasion to meet me in a C-suite during my tenure as Chairman, you would never have found any file or paper pending for action on my table. This was just my way of recapitulating Peter's principle—efficiency is not a function of how many hours you spend in office, it is the by-product of many other variables.

Old habits, however, die hard. When I came to know that even after the roll-out of SBI's work–life initiative, a few CGMs in some bank circles were sitting as late as up to 9 p.m. in the office, and their subordinates had to wait for them to leave before calling it a day, I knew it was time for me to step in. I personally called up all these overzealous bosses to put an end to this practice of over-time and over-work. My intervention worked and the idea of completing work and leaving office on time spread like wild fire. It also brought a welcome collateral—in many instances, the staff, without being asked or instructed, went beyond the call of duty to ensure the best interests of the bank. This was clearly an affirmation of the Biblical idiom that goodness and mercy rebound, bringing as much benefit to the giver as to the recipient.

Voyaging Together in Happiness and Sorrow

After putting in about three-and-a-half years of service at SBI, including two years of probation, I was placed in the personnel department (the erstwhile nomenclature for the HR department), Local Head Office, Lucknow. My four-year-long stay here laid the foundation for my ideas of what the HR department in a bank should be doing. Here, I would like to share an incident that occurred about six months after I had joined the Lucknow office. One day at office, at around 12 p.m., I came to know that the father of one of my colleagues had just passed away. We all rushed to offer our condolences to this gentleman, who was in the office at that time. But even in his moment of grief, he was deeply worried about having to resort to leave without pay for performing the last rites and rituals of his father extending over 13 days, as he had run out of the stipulated leave. I was greatly moved by his predicament, realizing how he felt as taking leave without pay in the bank has seniority implications.

This was the pre-reforms period in India. Organizations were still trying hard to unshackle their workplaces and work regimens from colonial legacies, which included antiquated, often harsh, leave rules. The leave-related facilities in SBI also symbolized a continuation of the Imperial Bank era, with little provision for personal contingencies in an employee's life. I felt that there should be the option for allowing staff special leave when they face the unfortunate loss of a close family member. They should be allowed to stay long enough with their families during these periods of loss and emotional crises while also being given adequate time for attending to the final rites and their social obligations. The bank needed to demonstrate the intent that it shares the sorrows faced by its people, standing by them in the darkest hours of their lives.

It was in this backdrop that in December 2017, I asked the Deputy Managing Director and Corporate Development Officer, who is responsible for managing the HR in the bank, to introduce the provision of *bereavement leave*. This provision included seven days of paid leave and was applicable to all categories of permanent or contractual employees and officers in the bank. In a sense, it was a reiteration of the fact that SBI is not just another organization but akin to a big family that stands by its staff through thick and thin. In this context, the statement of Richard Branson seems quite apt—'Train people well enough so they can leave. Treat them well enough so they don't have to.'

Amongst the big bang initiatives that heralded the beginning of the new year, one small initiative taken in February 2019 is particularly dear to me. It pertained to the transfer/posting guidelines regarding the employees who were caregivers for a dependent family member. We exempted them from the routine requirements of transfer/rotational transfer. Apart from highlighting the bank's profile as a caring employer, this compassionate step was also intended to reach out to the employees beset with genuine family problems.

Hand-Holding Employees for Life and Beyond Life

Through the various innovations I have mentioned, SBI has been setting a benchmark for the banking industry with respect to its HR policies, best practices and other employee-friendly measures. During the initial phase of this transformation in the bank, we had tried to offer some comfort and solace to any employee who had lost a near and dear one by way of the Bereavement Leave facility. However, there was no provision to help the family in the event of the unfortunate demise of an SBI employee. Hence, in order to fortify our long-term relationship with our employees, we realized the need for nurturing in them a sense of belonging and assurance that the bank was committed to take care of them and their family members, while they served in the bank and also after it. For this purpose, a scheme called Atoot (translated in English as 'Unbreakable') was introduced in November 2019 for offering immediate support to the family on the death of an employee while in service. The scheme was applicable to all regular and contractual employees of the bank, irrespective of cadre, and also covered suspended employees. Under Atoot, while a lump-sum amount was immediately payable to the next of kin of the deceased employee, additional support was provided for transportation of the mortal remains of the deceased employee at the bank's cost in case the employee's death had occurred outside of the place where s/he had been enrolled.

Next, we focused on those who had provided yeoman's service to the bank for decades and now needed the bank's support in the twilight years of their careers. As an ode to their selfless service, and as a commitment to the bank's philosophy of being there in times of need, I overhauled the medical benefit schemes for the retirees. Medical expenses are the biggest source of worry for a retired person. The existing medical insurance schemes were thus recast to provide good health care to the retirees at an affordable cost, by instituting new health care plans and subsidization of a part of the health expenditure. A tie-up with a pharmacy was also concluded for the doorstep delivery of medicines to retirees.

Two-Way Communication: Key to success

What is Your Vision?

For me, the demand side of HR, that is, its perception by the employees assumes more significance than its evaluation from the supply side, or the management's view. This is also part of the bank's efforts to link the functioning of its HR with all round employee well-being. Meanwhile, I was also deeply involved in the exercise of articulating a *new vision, mission, and value statements* (VMVSs) for the bank. The bank had first espoused the concept of the VMVSs in 2007. During the past 10 years, the bank had undergone a lot of transformation, and the existing VMVSs did not resonate in any way with the bank's new persona. Instead of being simple but lucid, these were lengthy and difficult to recall. In the bank, people mostly remembered them only at the time of promotions or interviews. Off the cuff, none of them would have been able to delineate the bank's vision and mission statement. It was this gap between the vision envisaged by the bank and employee perception of this vision that compelled me to intervene and re-design the VMVSs of SBI and integrate them into the bank's consciousness so that they could energize the people and enable them to live up to the high standards set before them.

Post the merger phase, the bank was evolving well but in view of certain peculiarities of the corporate world, adjusting to the new ecosystem would take its own time. SBI was inarguably a modern, progressive, and tech-savvy brand by now. If we could make values the centre of the way we think about the bank, it would help in harnessing the enormous potential of the post-merger organization in the coming days. It was with this idea that we formulated a long recalibration exercise, and a new vision, mission and value statement for the bank. It was a massive endeavour and one that was initiated and completed in-house throughout. More than 30,000 staff-members shared their inputs for this exercise. And I unveiled the new VMVSs of the bank during the first Top Management Summit held at our Institute of Leadership at Kolkata in January 2018, just three months after I had taken over.

The bank's new vision was to 'Be the Bank of Choice for a Transforming India'. To make our vision come true, our new mission or action framework was to be 'Committed to Providing Simple, Responsive and Innovative Financial Solutions'. The bank opted that our values of *STEPS* shall guide us in our daily actions and decisions for accomplishing this mission and would, in turn, translate our vision into a reality. STEPS stood for the five core values of — Service, Transparency, Ethics, Politeness, and Sustainability.

The next challenge was the internalization of the new VMVSs in the rank and file of the bank. A tutorial was developed and hosted on the intrasite. Display boards of the new VMVSs were installed on all the floors, lift lobbies, meeting rooms, dining areas, and the cabins of senior officials in the corporate centre and other offices. The soft copies of the new VMVSs were sent to all the Circles/Verticals for further propagation at their end. To ensure their 100 per cent internalization and absorption among the staff members, a quiz on the VMVSs was hosted on SBI Times. A certificate would be generated upon successful completion of the quiz by each employee. I completed the quiz on the first day itself and the completion certificate mentioning the Chairman's name was shared with all others to motivate them to follow suit. We leveraged all the communication channels like email broadcasts, lift displays, public address systems, and tele-calls to the Circles/Verticals to reach out to most of the staff members, exhorting them to take and complete the quiz. Through persistent follow-up, the bank was able to ensure 100 per cent internalization of the new VMVSs by June 2018.

Internalization of values is, however, not a one-step course. It is always work-in-progress. The full power of the VMVSs could be optimized only when it became an integral part of the action framework at an individual level all across the bank. Various programmes were initiated to sustain all-round awareness about the newly adopted VMVSs. For example, an email quiz series titled, 'Test your Knowledge: Our VMVSs' was launched and broadcast to all the employees on a regular basis.

Meanwhile, the Chief Ethics Officer was working on a *Code of Ethics* structured around the values of STEPS. The Code listed the key ethical principles for each value of the STEPS. Every principle was then broken down to behavioural norms required to achieve the stated objective of the principle. These norms were then further spelt out in terms of the expected practices to be followed by the employees while discharging their roles and responsibilities. The Code was packed with several practical examples of desired practices and actions to provide an understanding of what was acceptable and what was not. It had been composed to help employees face real workplace situations that would throw challenges and dilemmas at them. The Dos and Don'ts and Q&As had been incorporated throughout the Code to help participants decide what was the right thing to do in workplace. Thus, a broad-spectrum guidance had been provided about the bank's expectations from its employees, highlighting situations that may require particular attention, and referencing the additional resources available. The entire exercise of formulation of the Code of Ethics was conducted in-house and was made public during the Strategy Retreat at SBIL Kolkata in July 2018. And not to mention, with this, SBI became the first public sector institution to have its own Code of Ethics.

Offering a Sympathetic Ear: Sanjeevani

When we talk of family at SBI, it also stands for the creation of an environment that encourages free and frank conversations. The bank has traditionally had channels, both official and otherwise, to communicate effectively with its employees. But I observed over the years that the channel of reverse communication, of employees sharing their personal thoughts and concerns with the bank, was missing completely. This necessitated the creation of a formal system for offering quick but heartfelt solutions for employee grievances. Such issues generally lay under the domain of HR. How can we talk of being a 'people first' organization if we do not listen to and resolve the problems of our colleagues with fairness and empathy? This prompted me to urge HR to ascribe a new tone and identity to the bank's existing grievance redressal mechanism to synchronize it with contemporary workplace realities.

In February 2018, almost after four months after my taking over as Chairman, we decided to launch *Sanjeevani,* SBI's HR helpline. It was a highly efficient, multi-modal, and integrated platform designed to handle all staff grievances and HR-related queries. Both current and retired SBI employees could reach this helpline through IVR, e-mail, and SMS. The concept of Sanjeevani was not something new. It had just been languishing in the bank for more than 13 years in its manual form, calling out for energization and digitization. So we recalibrated, redesigned, and re-launched it. Sanjeevani received a hearty reception at the bank in its digital avatar. We soon witnessed speedier and more efficient grievance resolutions, inspiring employee confidence in the system. The bank also engaged the services of trained counsellors at Sanjeevani. Staff were encouraged to contact the counsellors to share their issues and concerns while seeking help in easing stress, coping with work and societal pressures, and enabling a positive approach to dealing with both real and perceived problems.

The Sanjeevani initiative had a definite calming effect on the workforce. The message we wanted to send out was clear and simple—if any employee was experiencing feelings of despair and distress for any reason, the bank would not ignore or brush it away. Each grievance would be heard and resolved within the shortest possible time. This was the first step toward keeping our employees happy so that they could, in turn, keep our customers happy. In the knowledge economy, the workplace relies heavily on trust and mutual engagement. Sanjeevani helped to strengthen this mutual trust between the Bank and its workforce. Encouraged by the success of Sanjeevani, we launched Sanjeevani-II in July 2019.

Testing and Expressing Ourselves: Abhivyakti

By the time my tenure as Chairman was nearing 18 months, the bank had rolled out many new HR initiatives that I have discussed above. But the key question was whether they had made an actual impact on the ground, and whether they had brought about a positive change in the lives of the bank's employees. Our quest for a response to this question led to the advent of a detailed impact analysis exercise. In February 2019, we conducted an employee engagement survey called Abhivyakti, which ended up becoming one of the largest surveys conducted by the bank to collate employee feedback.

The objective of Abhivyakti was to read the pulse of the people in terms of what drives them to perform at their best as also to identify the factors that limit their performance. The survey also aimed to obtain employee feedback on the different HR policies, work culture, and support systems created by the HR department of SBI to promote managerial control, leadership quality, and training and development within the bank.

The survey had wide-ranging questions relating to the most important workplace values, job satisfaction, culture, internalization of vision of the bank, and employee dedication. A record number of 191,881 employees participated in the survey, and 63 per cent of the staff were assessed as being engaged and contributing to the bank's growth and finding satisfaction in their work. This surpassed the overall Banking and Financial Services domain average of 62 per cent. Most of the respondents stated that they felt a sense of pride in working for SBI. However, one of the areas of concern that emerged from the survey was the low level of mentoring by the middle-level managers. The survey, therefore, helped us understand the effectiveness of employee reward and recognition programmes, incentive schemes and other employee welfare measures. It also enabled the bank to identify areas of improvement for manpower planning, transfer processes, and employee grievance redressal mechanisms. This valuable feedback was utilized for redesigning the extant policies and procedures. Thereafter, an appropriate one-year action plan was worked out and implemented based on the employee feedback.

Talent Matters: Capacity Building

The Onboarding Process for Establishing Linkages and Improving Skills

Empowerment is a ceaseless process and should ideally begin from the moment of onboarding of a new employee. It adds value not only for the employee concerned, but also to the organization as a whole. Realizing that the bank's onboarding pedagogy was a little obsolete, I asked our Strategic Training Unit (STU) team to alter the onboarding design and make it relevant for the bank's new GenY entrants, or boys and girls born between 1990 and 1996. Digitally savvy and passionate about their work, these young professionals were already changing the bank's demographics in many important ways. Unless the onboarding scheme was made highly engaging in both content and delivery, it was not possible to connect these youngsters to the bank's throbbing heartbeat. We also had to acclimatize our staff, especially the younger members, with both the hard and soft sides of onboarding for ensuring the proper integration of new recruits into the bank's work culture.

The onboarding process was accordingly redesigned and personalized to a great extent. The day an officer or an associate reported at work, they were welcomed with a small cake cutting ceremony to make them feel at home and a part of the team. If they were coming from outstation, they were received by their future colleagues at the railway station or airport with sweets and a bouquet. Such small but vital gestures encouraged the social integration of all new staff members even before their formal reporting. Three main training programmes—mandatory, specialized, and electives for the pull factor—were devised and delivered to them. Simultaneously, a fair and holistic evaluation was also included in the entire process to facilitate immediate in-person feedback. The one-time confirmation test at the end of an employee's probation period was thus effectively replaced with a continuous assessment mechanism. More than 6,000 Probationary Officers and Trainee Officers (POs/TOs) were eventually groomed under the new policy. Similarly, the training curricula and approach for Junior Associates was redesigned as a two-tier institutional training curriculum, incorporating basic banking with a greater emphasis on developing a digital mindset.

Aligning of Training Infrastructure with the Current Needs

After setting the backdrop for psychological changes in the functioning of HR at SBI, I turned my attention to the promotion of skills and professional growth of the bank's employees through capacity building. The bank management had always realized that a competent and motivated workforce is critical for accomplishing sustainable results. The exponential growth of the banking industry in recent times made it essential for employees to constantly upgrade their knowledge and skills. The transition from analogue to digital was also causing a lot of uncertainties in the minds of employees. And the bank had a pivotal role to play in tackling these feelings of uncertainty and the consequent ambivalence and insecurity.

I was well aware of the strengths and weaknesses of our training functions. The bank had an extensive training infrastructure in place, supervised and guided by a STU at CC. I was, however, quite unsure about the strategic elements of the STU. The template of its trainings was generic in nature, and largely without any strategic orientation. The training modules at the bank did not address the actual knowledge needs of a changing SBI. I suggested that unless each Administrative Training Institutes (ATI) did not become a vehicle for the creation and dispensation of specialized knowledge and training content, we would not be able to meet the needs of our multi-generational workforce. Domain speciality was increasingly becoming a key for dealing with competitive streams regularly emerging in the banking workspace. This called for a comprehensive relook at and revamping of the bank's training architecture by prioritizing the growth of key priority areas to create an oasis of excellence. I therefore asked the STU officers to develop an actionable plan for amplifying the strengths, bridging the skill gaps, and optimizing the potential of our workforce. The training system needed to evolve systematically in order to adapt to an increasingly volatile financial ecosystem, rapid digital progress, and changing customer demographics amidst the growing competition. Several initiatives were thus later conceptualized with the objective of up-skilling as well as reskilling the employees to make them future-ready through the adoption of a four-pillar approach—resource optimization, capacity building, focused training, and research.

The six ATIs, equipped with world-class amenities, were repositioned as *centres of excellence offering high quality, domain-specific trainings*. Each ATI was a think tank focused on a specific area. The name itself signalled its domain. The State Bank Institute of Management (SBIM), Kolkata, was rechristened as the State Bank Institute of Leadership (SBIL), with a focus on leadership. It was also mandated to be a leading institute for training senior executives in the Banking, Financial Services, and Insurance (BFSI) sector in India and the neighbouring countries. Similarly, the State Bank Academy (SBA), Gurgaon, was renamed as the State Bank Institute of Credit and Risk Management (SBICRM), focusing on risk, foreign exchange, and credit. Likewise, the State Bank Staff College (SBSC), Hyderabad, was renamed as the State Bank Institute of Consumer Banking (SBICB), with consumer markets and retail banking as its key focus areas. The State Bank Institute of Rural Development (SBIRD), Hyderabad, was rechristened as the State Bank Institute of Rural Banking (SBIRB), to offer specialized knowledge in the area of rural banking and financial inclusion. The State Bank Institute of Information and Communication Management (SBIICM), Hyderabad, became the State Bank Institute of Innovation and Technology (SBIIT), with a core focus on IT innovation and technological products. Last but not the least, the State Bank Foundation Institute (SBFI), Indore, was renamed as the State Bank Institute of Human Resource Development (SBIHRD), with on-boarding, and the orientation and induction of new officers and lateral recruits being its key areas of specialization.

We were perhaps the first bank in the country to introduce role-based certification programmes for promoting thorough capacity building across all the business functions. In addition to the classroom to desktop training—the *e-Gyanshala* initiative—the bank developed a search engine that provided online access to various Standard Operating Procedures (SOPs). Providing access to these documents helped improve the workplace effectiveness of the employees. The objective of all these efforts was to harness the best practices that we could find all around us by collaborating with other leading institutions, academia, and industry experts both in India and overseas for helping design and impart in-depth training to our people.

We started conducting certified capacity building workshops in association with external accredited agencies such as IIBF for Forex Operations, Treasury Operations and Risk Management; Moody's for Credit Management; and NIBM for Accounts and Audit. Further, role-based graded certifications were started for the employees with the content being designed in consultation with the respective business units. This was aimed at ensuring the relevance of trainings for the day-to-day workplace needs of employees. The staff receiving these trainings were also evaluated through a common, pan-India exam at periodic intervals.

Redesigning the Training Template

Change is the only constant, and hence the need to regularly update the training modules at SBI. The quality of base resources determines the outcomes of the learnings but there was a lacuna in the bank on this issue. As a perfectionist, I was always in search of better ways of achieving our desired results, and knew that there was a lot of scope to bolster the knowledge and resources at the bank. This thinking paved the way for several new learning initiatives in the bank, some of which were also pioneering efforts in the Indian banking sector as a whole.

For example, in order to benchmark competency, 47 critical roles were identified which required precise skills to enable a holistic customer service, create a digital mindset, and reduce operational and other risks. Hence for each role, mandatory in-house certification courses and comprehensive role manuals were developed and implemented. This was over and above the external certifications mandated by the RBI. Likewise, for linking knowledge to performance and the end-goal of exemplary customer service, all employees, from award staff to the deputy managing directors, were asked to obtain internal/external certifications from institutions like edX active in executive education within a stipulated time frame. Almost all the top executives, including deputy general managers and those above them completed their mandatory learnings within a year. Certifications were also linked to performance appraisal and, for officials up to the assistant general manager grade, obtaining these certifications was a condition for eligibility for promotion. This prompted more than 96 per cent of the officers to complete their role-relevant certifications.

Adaptation is the key to survival. And in a professional context, with the prevalence of cut-throat competition, it was imperative to leverage the potential of our workforce to enable them to keep pace with the changing products, processes, and operational archetypes. An up-to-date and empowered employee is a key factor in driving a knowledge-based versatile organization so that it can stay ahead of the curve. This, in turn, necessitates upskilling or constant honing and renewal of the existing skills. Accordingly, a course on 'Digital Transformation and Leadership Development', was conceived for honing the skills of all officials due for promotions in middle management. Nearly 75 per cent of the eligible employees underwent this certification. An Online Assessment Centre was also created for assessing the competency of the bank's top executives.

In order to shore up the cross-functional readiness of employees and prepare a leadership pipeline, a Personalized Managerial and Leadership Development Plan, that is, Individual Development Plans (IDPs) charting the relevant areas of strength and development, was made available to each participant. Based on these IDPs, as many as 1,142 top functionaries in the grade of deputy general manager and above were imparted high-end/focused external trainings to internalize and adopt the latest concepts and best practices within the organization. This was an important move as the views, styles of functioning, and ethos of the top executives have a significant impact for the bank.

Here, it is also important to distinguish between active and passive learners, as, like every other organization, SBI too had its share of both types of learners. While active learners thrive on self-induced motivation for quenching their thirst for knowledge, passive learners in an organizational context, on the other hand, need to be nudged into action for innovation and reinvention. I found that this passivity was not on account of any mindset that resisted knowledge stimulation but that people were mostly bogged down at work and burdened by family and societal commitments. What could be the solution to this impasse? I recalled the answer from my childhood—don't make learning a boring chore. Make it interesting, interactive, innovative, and self-paced. And in this lay the genesis of the gamification App 'Play2Learn'. It was developed to supplement the traditional learning tools for fostering a better learning experience and retention among the staff.

Similarly, a real-time collaborative platform, 'Ask SBI', was released on a pilot basis, which served as a one-stop knowledge repository for all employees, through which they could access over 23,000 documents related to operational instructions and guidelines at their workstations. We received more than four lakh queries within the first two weeks of its launch, highlighting the potential for this kind of an application among employees keen to expand their knowledge. All we needed to do was plug-in the gaps to exploit this potential. A regular quiz platform, 'My Quest', was also introduced as a brief knowledge refresher on subjects such as credit, emerging areas, and the bank's guidelines.

An app on the mobile platform was unveiled for content delivery and assessment, wherein learners were assigned learning 'milestones', followed by quizzes for evaluation. Being simple, fast, and easy to use, this app was hugely successful among employees. We also created a digital repository of 754 e-lessons, 477 e-capsules, and 739 mobile nuggets along with a question bank for self-assessment. This enabled staff to access all e-lessons on a new cloud-based learning management system (LMS) called Meghdoot, which had user-friendly features. A total of 1,329 thought-provoking case studies were listed and made available to employees to help them acquire practical inputs. These case studies were based on real-life banking scenarios and experiences of account-holders. Further, in order to build a virtual community of domain experts and to promote peer group learning among employees, the bank initiated a Discussion Board Forum that presented real-life case studies. This Discussion Board was platform-agnostic and could be accessed through multiple devices. The Forum witnessed more than 350,000 site visits within a few months of its launch. Thus, the potential of technology was leveraged to offer digital learning tools to employees who could use them at their own pace and convenience.

We also signed an MoU with the National Banking Institute (NBI) of Nepal to establish a mutually beneficial strategic alliance for the development of NBI's human resources in the critical areas of education, training, and research. Various conclaves and workshops, such as the HR Heads Conclave on Re-Vitalising Our Human Capital, and the PSB Heads Workshop on

Corporate Governance and Media Management were organized at SBIL, Kolkata, to initiate discussions on these key issues within the industry. A workshop on 'Navigating Disruption and Managing Innovation in the New Economy' was organized in collaboration with Wharton University, with the objective of bringing together established players and young professionals on a common platform to facilitate a meaningful exchange of ideas and perspectives.

A journey of a thousand miles begins with a single step. And we consistently took each step to move collectively towards a paradigmatic change in our functioning. The fact that our efforts at innovation and progressive ideas were being noticed and appreciated came home to us when the bank was awarded the prestigious Business World Award for 'Excellence in Learning and Development'. In HR, the bank had consistently made substantial efforts to identify potential leaders and develop their skills through customized training programmes aimed at creating a leadership pipeline. Consequently, in 2018–19, the bank was ranked at the top among the Public Sector Banks in the Enhanced Access Service Excellence (EASE) Index for 'Developing Personnel for Brand PSBs'.

With each such accomplishment, I felt pride and gratification at the positive changes they had brought about in the learning culture in the bank. Our capacity utilization also rose phenomenally to cross the 100 per cent mark, manifested in an increase of over two lakhs in the number of employees receiving training every year. The average training man-hours per employee too rose to 54 hours. All the ATIs were now equipped to conduct online webinars on niche topics without causing any workplace disruption. Above all, these developments not only converted passive learners into active ones but also made the already active learners hyperactive achievers. Spare capacity at all the training outfits was also freed up due to the shift to a new pedagogy wherein non-traditional teaching techniques were utilized for revenue generation through the designing and marketing of BFSI-sector specific paid programmes. Meanwhile, the bank also licensed the use of its LMS and e-content to select external organizations.

Mindset Transformation: Nayi Disha

The last month of 2018 occupies a distinctive place in my heart. I had always envisioned touching base with each and every employee in the bank for adopting a mindset of collective and inclusive growth in the bank. This idea had engaged my mind for quite some time. It finally came to fruition in December 2018, with the launch of a pan-Bank level employee engagement programme that we labelled Nayi Disha. It aimed to make the senior managers and employees embrace new and agile ways of thinking, understand the big picture in context, stay relevant to their roles, and manage challenges within the moral compass of core values of STEPS. It represented another transformational journey from a fixed mindset to a growth mindset for meeting the organizational expectations head-on. The programme was conceptualized in two stages. While Phase I was employee-centric and self-reflective, inspiring employees to align with the values of the bank, Phase II was customer-centric. It was tool-kit-driven and equipped the employees with the requisite skill sets to provide excellent customer service at every stage of the banking service cycle. It thus focused on the translation of the organizational vision into action.

Themed as 'Vision 2030', Phase I of the Nayi Disha programme saw the coverage of a staggering 2.5 lakh employees in a span of just 90 days. Phase II was launched in the financial year 2020 and by March 2020, all the employees in the bank had attended the programme, which, therefore, had a momentous positive impact. It re-ignited a strong sense of pride among employees for being a part of an institution like SBI. It also reinforced my understanding that only great customer service makes a great bank.

The icing on the cake was that for this well-timed intervention initiative, the bank won three Brandon Hall Excellence Awards, also known as the Academy Awards of Learning and Development. The award recognized the best organizations that had successfully deployed programmes, strategies, modalities, processes, systems, and tools to achieve measurable results. SBI won these awards in three categories: the Best Learning Programme Supporting a Change Transformation Business Strategy, Best Use of Blended Learning, and Best Unique or Innovative Learning and Development Programme.

Accountability and Discipline Management

Another intriguing incident occurred when I was heading a zone. During the routine exercise of annual transfers and postings, two managers reported to the module. My CM (HR) briefed me about their history. A couple of years ago, both of them had to undergo an investigation and they were subsequently awarded minor penalties. I posted them in two different retail branches. In the ensuing months, while one of the two officers received a number of appreciation letters from customers, the situation was the exact opposite for the other officer, who was the butt of a heap of complaints. I was quite taken aback when I learnt this. The past records of both these officers had been more or less similar. Both of them had also endured an almost equal number of professional shocks. Then, why was one of them performing and the other was seemingly so incompetent? Digging a bit deeper into this conundrum, I asked the CM (HR) to bring me the personal files of both the officers. As I went through the files, the picture suddenly became clear to me. In one case, the disciplinary process had been concluded within four months while in the other, it had dragged on for an inordinately long time. Consequently, the first officer was functioning with a constructive frame of mind while the other was still bogged down with disenchantment. The management that had disciplined the two had unwittingly made one of the culprits into a complete non-performer by over-stretching the punishment. And then I discovered an insight from this incident that has stayed with me since then—it is not punishment that breaks a will but endless waiting and dark suspense accompanying that punishment which breaks a person.

I used this insight to bring in reforms in the area of discipline management in the bank. While we had taken care of grievance redressal, in general, discipline management had hitherto remained a neglected area in the bank and needed urgent action. The primary purpose of discipline management is to foster orderly conduct amongst perpetrators of some transgression or crime, not to push them into the brink of despair and bitterness by punishing them disproportionately to their misdeed or misdemeanour.

The reasons for such delay was also known. While working as Chief General Manager, Guwahati Circle, I had noticed that the senior functionaries had to spend a lot of time in trying to understand the crux of disciplinary matters and taking the right decisions. This adversely affected their managerial bandwidth, as the various committee meetings and personal hearings associated with such motions demanded investments of time and effort, taking away the officers concerned from their other priorities of business growth. I was of the view that business functionaries should solely focus on business and all non-business-related undertakings or maintenance functions should be away from their domain to enable them to focus on their business priorities. With this thought in mind, I proposed the centralization of the Internal Advisory Committees (IACs). These committees scrutinize the disciplinary cases arising in the bank to determine if there is a vigilance angle to the alleged case of indiscipline. A two-tiered structure was put in place for such committees, with one IAC posted at the corporate centre for officers in executive grades, and one IAC each at every circle (taking the total number of IACs to 17) to oversee cases pertaining to other officers and staff members at the circle. Within two months, the IACs were centralized and two committees were formed at the corporate centre to examine all cases, thereby helping save significant amount of time for the business functionaries in the circles.

The centralization of IACs was one part of the process aimed at attaining an exclusive business focus, with the other part being the centralization of the disciplinary authorities. Prior to this decision, more than 1600 officers were functioning as the disciplinary authorities in the bank, and centralization brought down the number of disciplinary authority to just 30. For the circles, four discipline management hubs (representing the North, South, East, and West, respectively) were established at Delhi, Chennai, Kolkata, and Mumbai, and four to five circles were linked to each hub headed by a dedicated GM-level officer who handled the disciplinary cases of officers up to the grade of Assistant General Manager. The structures of the Appellate Authority (AA) and Reviewing Authority (RA) were also reconfigured in line with the changes made in the DA structure. These initiatives altered the character of discipline management in the bank and were bound to travel a long way in facilitating a shared sense of urgency and uniformity in the bank's discipline management ecosystem.

The period 2012–19 was a choppy phase due to the NPLS. In this monumental mess up, even as the bank was working in a mission mode to get things under control, one trend caught my eye. As the battle against NPLs intensified, so did the number of cases being filed against the officials of the bank, both serving and retired. Although the bank had various guidelines and provisions when it came to extending legal and financial support to such officials, these were scattered and at times, ambiguous, which also resulted in unnecessary confusion and delay in helping out the needy officials. It was distressing to see sincere retired officials being subjected to legal harassment because they had sanctioned some loans during their active service and were now struggling to get support from the bank. Hence, in July 2018, we decided to introduce a single comprehensive *policy for extending legal and financial support to serving/retired employees* and officers, and present/previous directors of the bank and their family members against cases arising out of their bona fide work during their service/tenure. It goes without saying that this policy instilled deep confidence and a sense of security in the minds of the not only retired officials but also the serving ones.

New Policy for Acceptance of Gifts

Taking the liberty of digressing here, I would like to point out that at times interesting and dynamic ideas can also emanate from seemingly pedantic situations or statements. In fact, I recall one such case that was the consequence of a rather amusing incident. During an interaction with my senior executives at one of the bank's leadership conclaves, one of my MDs made an innocent remark, with a very plain face, that left all of us in splits. I could not have agreed more with him when he complained that with a ceiling of Rs 500 on SBI executives for acceptance of gifts on occasions like marriages, anniversaries, religious functions, or official farewells, he was too scared to even host his marriage anniversary party. Like other organizations, we too had a set of rules regarding gifts to be accepted by the employees. However, there was a glitch in these rules.

The monetary ceilings for acceptance of gifts were framed in the year 1992. These limits had remained unchanged even 26 years later despite the multi-fold rise in prices all around. Today, even 1 kg of sweets or a decent book would not cost less than Rs 800–1,000. Jokes apart, this important aspect of inflation had somehow been overlooked at the bank, and ironically in an institution that constantly dealt with money! Any such guidelines should be in tune with the times. So, we soon undertook a quick upward revision of the gift-related guidelines. After taking into account the prevailing economic scenario, we modified the monetary ceilings in July 2018. When this was done, I personally called my MD to inform him about it, following it up with the one cheeky question, 'When are you scheduling your marriage anniversary party?'

Other initiatives

The Digital Transformation of HR at SBI

Digital processes have virtually taken over the entire financial sector over the last few years, leading to upgradation of technology, products and workflow on a scale never seen before. The traditional workplace at SBI was not immune to this digital churn. We thus implemented a slew of measures to foster a digital culture within the organization. After all, without synchronizing its internal HR workflows in the HR department with the rapid external digital changes, SBI could never fulfil its dream of becoming the bank of first choice for transforming India. It is apt here to reiterate Steve Wynne's observation that 'human resources isn't a thing we do, it's the thing that runs our business'.

To return to the significance of human capital, every employee's experience with HR, whether offline or online, should be comfortable and interactive. We therefore decided to fully automate and streamline our HR processes. The virtual platform of Human Resources Management System (HRMS), which is used by the bank for performing almost all its employee-related activities, was made more comprehensive and inclusive. Manpower planning was also shifted to a data-driven model to ensure objective and optimal utilization of human resources. In addition, manpower requests from various units were validated on the basis of a footfall study undertaken by the Analytics Department. The promotion and transfer process was also streamlined to enable its completion in the first quarter of the financial year. Initially when I urged HR to conclude all the promotions and transfers by the end of the second month of the first quarter (Q1), I had my doubts if this feat could actually be achieved as the bank had not taken any steps in this direction in its 35-year-old history. Hence, when this goal was achieved in reality, I felt an inexplicable sense of both awe and pride. And the process has been sustained since then. This re-affirms the innate quality of SBI that its people always deliver in response to any demand. The swiftness in promotions and transfers also accorded stability in the various units and branches of the bank, allowing them to actively focus on business activities during the major part of the year.

From an organizational perspective, SBI's endeavour to encourage and reward well-performing employees has fostered the rise of talented and meritorious staff. This effort has been accompanied by the accurate recording of individual performance metrics through an exhaustive objective appraisal system known as the Career Development System (CDS). However, I insisted on regularly upgrading not only this system but also the style of functioning of the bank's employees and its operational frameworks.

Meanwhile, banking was undergoing an all-round transformation across regions, spurred by the rapid and seamless integration of digital technology with traditional banking systems. In this state of flux, the appraisal parameters too needed a thorough review and reconstruction so as to correctly capture employee performance in these dynamic prevailing conditions. An employee *opinion survey on CDS* was, therefore, held during the year to understand the perceptions, reach, acceptance, familiarity, and expectations of the employees, and modifications were implemented based on the feedback. Moreover, this move helped bring refinement and transparency into the system. A structured feedback mechanism was also introduced as a part of performance evaluation process.

In order to bring in greater objectivity, the weightage of Key Result Areas (KRAs) was increased and discretionary scores were reduced. Increments were made in the equivalent marks corresponding to the CDS grades to motivate employees to augment their efficiency. Further, it was decided to consider the average performance of the best 9 out of 12 months in the budgetary/measurable roles in case an employee performed the same role throughout the year. These major changes, along with others, ensured synchronization of the appraisal system with the changing times while also factoring in the employee expectations and enhancing the value of their own assessment of their work in the overall scoring. Additionally, the CDS system became more robust by operating through the five functional levers of 'Strategic alignment', 'Stakeholder Commitment', 'SMART goals', 'At least one role per employee', and 'Constant Evaluation'. All these small steps signified big strides on the road to digital transformation, thereby helping promote a healthy culture of business orientation in the bank.

Steps to Sustainability

As a responsible corporate entity, SBI has always believed in adopting environment-friendly work practices. We had set ourselves the goal of becoming the first carbon-neutral Indian bank in the public sector. It was in this context that I instituted a slew of innovative practices to minimize the impact of our commercial activities on mother nature. A sustainability cell was set up and became operational at the corporate centre. I made it a part of the HR vertical to promote synergy and make it a focal point for all activities related to business responsibility. 'Carbon neutrality' implies all actions taken by businesses and individuals to remove an equal volume of carbon dioxide from the atmosphere, as they keep on continuously contributing to it. We conceived a pan-India carbon neutrality strategy, and accordingly prepared a comprehensive greenhouse gas (GHG) inventory for SBI's domestic operations, encompassing more than 22,000 branches. These steps were essential to counter the significant infrastructural footprint of SBI due to the total volume of energy consumed by the bank across the country. The bank thus rolled out several steps in a phased manner in order to control its energy consumption. Some of the key initiatives in this direction included the installation of thermal sensors, LED lights, energy-efficient air conditioners, and power management tools across large offices in India. The bank also invested in a number of rooftop solar power plants. It was expected that, going forward, increasing its renewable energy capacity to 25 MW would enable the bank to save approximately Rs 30 crores annually.

Another area in which I tried to usher in sustainability was in positioning the bank as a paperless entity. Throughout my stint at the bank at various branch offices, and finally in the top deck, I had witnessed that the movement of a paper moved the cogs of the bank wheels. However, this needed to change after we started positioning ourselves as a digital bank and came out with multiple digital initiatives for the customers. Could we conceive and deliver something on the same lines for our internal customers, thus going completely paperless? In an effort to establish paperless offices at different sites, we introduced 'Easy Approval', a customized solution for approval of notes, on cloud. Through this solution, the bank tried to replicate all the user-friendly features of the current paper-based system in addition to some new features. This paper-saving initiative had the added benefits of conserving resources, reducing costs, and improving work efficiency within the bank. By migrating our substantial paper flow to a digital mode, I succeeded in ticking off one more item from my to-do bucket list, with a great deal of personal satisfaction.

Safeguarding the Garima *of the Bank's Female Workforce*

Early in October 2017, following the exposure of the widespread allegations of sexual abuse against Harvey Weinstein, the 'Me Too' movement began to spread virally as a hashtag on social media. Gathering a sharp momentum, it had reverberations in India too. It was a welcome development as it brought into sharp focus the importance of gender sensitivity and inclusivity. In today's times, both women and men work together to contribute towards the growth of their organization. In SBI, at that point of time, 24 per cent of the total work force of 253,000-plus employees were women. Besides, close to 2,400 of our 22,400-plus branches were headed by women officers. We took pride in the fact that women employees were spread across all hierarchies as well as geographies in the bank.

Inclusiveness has always been the cornerstone of SBI culture. The bank also promoted unbiased behaviour towards all employees regardless of their gender. The number of women joining the bank from among the new generation was also steadily going up. This segment of employees was more aware and expressive, and believed in equality in the workplace. Being more articulate and social media savvy, it was also ushering in a different set of cultural aspirations and expectations in the bank. Hence, from an organizational perspective, it was important to identify and handle the existing and emerging concerns affecting this segment. The fact that Indian society was witnessing a broad shift in attitude towards working women and reshaping its gender narrative for workplace behaviour only reinforced the need to assure our women staff that others would always be more sensitive and respectful while dealing or working with them and with customers. It was for this reason, in general, and for sensitizing all our employees, especially women colleagues, in particular, that we brought out a detailed document offering guidance on 'Workplace Behaviour: Promoting Inclusiveness', in November 2018.

We named our Prevention of Sexual Harassment of Women (POSH) programme Garima, which is a Hindi word with several nuances. While the exact English translation for the word is dignity, it falls short of capturing the depth and range of the Hindi word. We named it Garima to convey the message that the dignity of a woman colleague represents the dignity of the entire workplace, the dignity of the bank, the dignity of the society, and the dignity of the nation, in one word. For creating a better understanding among the people regarding the basic tenets of Garima-POSH, the bank published not only a detailed Standard Operating Procedures (SOP) document for the employees and the Internal Committees, but also a lucid and informative FAQs document. In the first month of Financial Year 2019, with the same objective, an online certification on Garima-POSH was hosted on the bank's intra site, which was mandatory for all the clerical and supervising staff. I cannot help but assert that it was no mean achievement for us to achieve a 100 per cent completion and success rate. In the month of October 2019, the bank participated in a pan-India survey 'Safe Places to Work' conducted by M/S Rainmaker, in which more than 4,000 women employees of SBI participated. As per the survey, SBI was adjudged one of the top 10 safe places to work for women employees in India, again a source of pride for me to be associated with such an organization.

Earlier, if an aggrieved woman wanted to file a complaint related to sexual harassment before the internal committee, she had to do so manually and everyone around her came to know about it. For rectifying this situation, a real-time online portal for escalating the POSH concerns was ideated and operationalized in January 2020. The portal, named GARIMA, not only enabled any aggrieved woman to file an online complaint with complete confidentiality, but also provided her a convenient option to track the status of the complaint. The portal led to effective monitoring, follow-up, and disposal of complaints and also for generating reports for statutory reporting.

Braving the Pandemic

I had envisaged that of the three significant years of my tenure as Chairman, 2018 would be the year of hope; 2019, the year of happiness; and 2020 as a year of delight. How wrong I was about 2020! It will forever be etched in our memories as the year of the pandemic that let loose a virus of monstrous proportions on the entire humanity. Undoubtedly one of the biggest crises faced by humankind since World War II, the Coronavirus pandemic assumed the visage of a savage storm devastating everything in its path. Be it individuals, institutions, communities, or countries, all had to bear the brunt of the catastrophe, at varying levels.

As the entire world grappled with the menace of COVID-19, India too was making efforts to contain the rapidly spreading virus. In this hour of calamity, organizations contributed in various ways to the nation's efforts towards providing basic commodities and medical facilities to the needy. When the Prime Minister appealed to all individuals and organizations to contribute wholeheartedly to support the government in its fight against COVID-19, SBI and its employees rose to the occasion by contributing one day's salary and encashment of one day's privilege leave to the 'PM CARES Fund'. SBI thus *donated a total amount of Rs 100 crores to the fund.* This was in addition to the 0.25 per cent of its annual profit for 2019–20 that the bank offered for fighting COVID-19.

In those testing times, the importance of conducting business in a responsible manner became more evident than ever. SBI recognized that its employees' health was directly related to the well-being of the communities within which it functioned. One of the ways in which the bank worked to strengthen these two parameters was by providing them with the financial support needed to purchase essentials such as masks and sanitisers. It also promoted further digitization to minimize physical contact without compromising its operations. Simultaneously, the bank also kept raising awareness among its employees about ways of dealing with the pandemic and staying safe through its various communication channels, screening of staff and visitors, prioritizing hygiene and disinfection, and offering staff to work with flexibility, wherever possible.

Since banking is classified as an essential service, the employees had to physically attend office regularly. Thus, the bank staff continued to serve the public while facing a high degree of risk during the pandemic. We took all possible steps and implemented various support measures to support our dedicated workforce, either by offering them extra monetary assistance or extending coverage of other facilities like providing accommodation and staff loans. At the very onset of the pandemic, it was decided that the period of self-quarantine would be treated as sick leave. While our commitment towards the nation and communities at large was unquestioned, we had an immense responsibility towards our workforce, which had the onerous responsibility of keeping the financial wheels of the nation moving through this grave crisis.

Despite taking required precautions, many employees at SBI tested COVID-positive and there were even cases of unfortunate deaths of employees. The treatment for COVID-19 included hospitalization/quarantine and post-discharge management, which involved considerable expenses. Hence, we offered a monetary package to our staff members to meet these expenses. Other relief measures included extending insurance coverage, providing additional monetary benefits, and tie-ups with hospitals and hotels.

I also take this opportunity to salute our Corona Warriors, that is, the health and frontline workers, who lost their precious lives while serving their communities. And as head of my organization during this challenging time, my gratitude goes out to all the employees of the bank who have helped us in tiding over the unprecedented pandemic without giving up hope and sincere commitment to their work. It is this devotion of our staff and the importance accorded to human capital at SBI that makes it one of the most distinguished and celebrated organizations to work for, keeping it head and shoulders above all others in the industry. I will close this part of my story by emphasizing that HR had slowly and steadily ushered in a culture of care for employees at SBI, and I can take credit for owning and building this department. By the time I left the bank, I prided in and loved this culture, nurturing the hope that it would achieve greater heights in the years to come.

PART THREE

My Journey with SBI

Dedicated to my immediate family, including my parents, my wife, my daughter, and other members of my extended family, as well as to all my dear friends, whose encouragement motivated me to initiate and fructify this ambitious venture.

9

The Pre-SBI Years: Strife and Struggle

Today as I remember all the incidents that shaped my life and career—personal developments, professional accomplishments and many more milestones—many years down the line the date 18 November 1980 flashes clearly before my mind. I most vividly remember that when I boarded the Sangam Express at Meerut station to travel to Auraiya where I was slated to join SBI as a probationary officer (PO), my heart missed a beat and tears almost started rolling down my cheeks. I kept waving to my entire family standing at the platform till they became specks in the distance as the train gathered speed. Settling into my seat on the train, I mulled over the special relationship I enjoyed with each one of them—relationships that have endured and remained unchanged throughout my entire eventful life and career—with my elderly parents, my eldest sister who is 20 years older to me, her children who have been more like siblings and childhood friends as they are closer to my age, and four of my closest school and college friends. This train journey, symbolizing the advent of the most significant phase of my life, in fact, became a metaphor for a larger journey of the mind, swathed in Wordsworthian memories, with reminiscences of the past and speculations about an unknown future looming ahead.

Meerut, a Historic City, Where I Was Born

My thoughts took me back to my birth in Meerut in 1958 and the subsequent faint but choate memories of my early life. I was the youngest in the family, with my eldest sister already being married since as far as I can recollect. We lived in a modest house in one of the narrow lanes of the old city of Meerut. The city is associated with many legends and interesting tales. Its most famous identity is as the launching site of India's first war of independence against British rule in 1857. Not far from where I was born stands the statue of sepoy Mangal Pandey, the hero who signalled the start of the war at the Barrackpore ground near Kolkata, on the afternoon of 29 March 1857, by attacking and injuring his British sergeant and wounding an adjutant. Thereafter, the proper war of independence began in Meerut on 10 May 1857, when 85 members of the 3rd Bengal Light Cavalry, who had been jailed for refusing to use the new Enfield rifle cartridges greased in the fat of pigs and cows, were released from prison by their comrades. They rampaged the streets of the city, where they ransacked the military station and killed any Europeans they encountered.

Apart from this militaristic history, Meerut also has a prominent religious association with the *Ramayana*, and Ravana, the king of Lanka, who was vanquished by Lord Rama. According to this legend, Meerut was originally known as 'Mayarashtra' or the home of Maya, who was the father of Mandodari, depicted as the sensible and devoted wife of Ravana. Mandodari's wise counsel was ignored by her arrogant husband, who dared to kidnap Lord Rama's wife, Sita, ultimately leading to his defeat and death at the hands of Lord Rama.

Another version is that Maya(sura), being a distinguished architect, received from King Yudhishthira the land on which the city of Meerut stands.

The religious connotations about the city of my parental home resonated in my mother's daily routine, which began with recitations from the *Ramayana* and *Bhagavad Gita*, early every morning, without a single day's break. Being early risers themselves, my parents did not allow any of us to either sleep or wake up late. So, we had to perforce listen to my mother's morning discourse. In fact, she would become so emotional during these readings that we would listen to her in fascination, absorbing and learning from the morality of the story that has lasted with us through life. According to the tale, Ravana was the wisest, richest, and most powerful king not just on earth but in the entire universe, but his arrogance became the reason for his downfall. It was this vital message that I assimilated from my mother's daily ritual, which has also influenced my behaviour and shaped my character.

Both my parents were strict disciplinarians. However, this was the only common characteristic in their otherwise sharply contrasting personalities. My mother was very outgoing, and loved mingling with people, while flaunting her excellent culinary skills. She also had an eagle's eye, and nothing could escape her attention, right till she passed away at the age of 92. I daresay that I too have imbibed some of her qualities, especially her sharp eye for detail. My father, in contrast, did not have many friends and was somewhat of a loner. He was also very frugal, determined to live within his means and could not tolerate even the smallest financial loss. Both of them had an infamous temper but I was lucky to escape their anger most of the time both because of being the youngest in the family and because of my childhood illness. Mother would, however, scold me roundly whenever she caught me indulging in a game of marbles, my childhood passion. My father, on the other hand, scolded me only on two occasions in my entire life—once when, much against his wishes, I carried my sister-in-law's precious fountain pen to school and it got stolen on the very first day; and the second time when I had to return home barefoot after my friends mischievously stole my slippers. On both the occasions, my sister-in-law came to my rescue, without uttering a single word of remonstrance or rebuke on losing her expensive fountain pen.

My childhood illness, which I briefly mentioned earlier, raised its head when I was only two years old. It began with problems in my kidneys and was manifested in swelling up of my entire body. This forced restriction in my diet and I was not allowed to consume salt for four years. My mother recounted how the period from 1959 to 1962 was the toughest for the family. My father, who was employed in the irrigation department of the Uttar Pradesh government, was transferred from Meerut to Lucknow, and had to leave behind my mother and 18-year-old brother with the responsibility of looking after my ailing grandmother, a two-year-old sickly child (that is, me), and two young school-going daughters. This incident left such an empathetic imprint on my mind that whenever someone in office requested for a transfer or cancellation of a transfer on compassionate grounds due to compelling family circumstances, it would melt my heart, reminding me of my own family's struggle. My brother shouldered the responsibility adroitly despite his youth and inexperience, coupled with the pressure of studies. Although he did not do well in his Intermediate examination, he later went on to top in his post-graduation at Agra University. My mother also courageously fought a lone battle to save my life, frequenting all the renowned doctors of Meerut at the time, including Dr Karauli, Dr Laxmi Pandey, and Dr Sen. I was told that there were many anxious moments when my life was ostensibly hanging by a thread and these doctors, though unable to cure me fully, were able to ensure my survival.

Dehradun, Saviour of My Life

Things changed for the better when my father was transferred to Dehradun and the entire family moved there with him in 1962. Although Dehradun is located only 200 km north of Meerut, culturally the two cities are vastly different from each other. Yamuna Colony in Dehradun, where we shifted, was a new residential colony built exclusively for employees of the irrigation department, and therefore all the families like ours were the first occupants of the colony. Our house was spacious and luxurious, especially in comparison to the much more modest house in Meerut where I was born. The colony too was very expansive, well laid out, and verdant, with the seasonal Bindal River flowing alongside it. My treatment continued in Dehradun's Civil Hospital, under the care of its head of the Paediatrics division, Dr Chandra, who succeeded in curing me completely. In fact, I believe that the change of environment, along with his sustained treatment, did the trick, and within six months of my arrival at Dehradun, I was up and about on my feet. I can never forget the first steps I took at the age of four years, with the help of my brother. It was nothing short of a miracle. My brother continued to be my biggest source of support till he left for his first job in Pune and subsequently got married in 1965. The period after his departure from Dehradun signified a sad and poignant phase in my life.

—

I was fortunate to acquire my early education in Dehradun, which has some of the best educational institutions in India, including the hugely famous and elite Doon School for boys and Welham for girls. However, I could not enrol in any of the prestigious schools as the family's financial position made them unaffordable. So, my first alma mater was a small primary school, Bharti Shishu Mandir, which was ironically situated right across Doon School, and was also accessible through a shortcut in the Doon School grounds. Blithely ignoring the sign against trespassers, we would race into our school through this shortcut though there were moments of trepidation about being caught and punished for our transgression. But the risk was worth taking because the alternative was a long walk of an extra half mile.

My first day at school was an embarrassing one, as unaware of any of the morning protocols, I was subjected to a lot of teasing and light-hearted mockery by the other children, but it was a happy beginning. I did well in my studies, also becoming my teachers' favourite because of my good behaviour and discipline. My classmates were much naughtier than me and also more talented in other disciplines like drama, singing, and sports. My first experience at acting was not very pleasant, as the play was about a bride selecting her groom, and I had to play the role of a suitor who is rejected by her due to his dark complexion. This so-called handicap stayed with me, leading to other unsavoury incidents later in life, especially during my school years in Dehradun, where most of my classmates were fair-skinned, and there was a natural bias towards fair complexion. However, I did not let this affect my studies, and not only did I became a bright student but also managed to acquire acting skills along the way. In fact, my excellence in academics brought a lot of attention from the teachers and parents of many of my school friends, who encouraged their children to be in my company. This did wonders for my self-confidence.

I soon became an accomplished child actor and participated actively in many school functions, which helped me overcome any stage fright and reticence very early in childhood. My most memorable role is that of Narada, one of the most popular mythological figures, who used to pass on information about events on earth to Lord Vishnu, one of the three leading celestial figures in Hindu mythology. Hindus believe that Lord Vishnu appears on earth every time there is rule of *adharma* or evil. In one of his incarnations, he appeared as half lion and half man (Narsingh avatar) to kill Hiranyakashyap, who refuted the idea of God. Hiranyakashyap's son Prahlad, however, was a devotee of Lord Vishnu and when Hiranyakashyap wanted to murder his own son for believing in God, Lord Vishnu appeared on the earth in the form of Narsingh and eliminated Hiranyakashyap. One of the popular books for children at the time had this play in which Lord Vishnu was tried in a court of law for murdering

Hiranyakashyap and Narada was his defence lawyer. I played this role of Narada to perfection a couple of times.

I shifted to another school in class five and studied there till class eight when my father retired. The school, which was run by a Mahant (leader of a Mutt), was part of a chain of schools. Mahantji was a very generous and caring person, and took a lot of interest in the all-round development of students, encouraging them to participate actively in sports and cultural activities. Aware of my family's frugal financial situation, he would quietly pay my tuition fee and perhaps that of one more boy in my class, without any of the other children getting to know of this. The school also had some outstanding teachers, particularly for English and Mathematics. I always scored full marks in mathematics.

Back to Meerut

My family returned to Meerut in 1970 post my father's retirement. After our stint in Dehradun, Meerut was a cultural shock. My father had not been able to buy a house for the family to move in after his retirement. So my maternal uncle generously offered to host us in a portion of his house, which he had bought a few years back. It was a very old property and he had been living there for decades. It was a double-storeyed house with eight rooms on the ground floor and around twelve on the first floor. A total of three families were living on the first floor and we were given two rooms on the ground floor. The building had a common toilet shared by at least 20 people. Adjusting to this new environment in the crowded house while at the same time having to focus on my studies was a huge challenge, and I started missing Dehradun acutely.

In 1971, I joined class nine in BAV Inter College. I was accustomed to a very small class of only 10–12 students till class eight in Dehradun. But here the classroom was crammed with as many as 60 students. Even the teachers here, though competent, lacked the sophistication and accessible demeanour of my teachers in Dehradun, and would often shout at the students. However, my academic acumen was noticed here too, and within a few days, the teachers asked me to shift to a front seat, and as in Dehradun, the other boys started seeking me out to become friends. One of them was Gopal, a quiet and decent boy. I began spending most of my time either at his place or at my sister's home nearby. As I had mentioned earlier, her children were about my age and we had always been quite close.

The family's financial position continued to be precarious with my father earning only a meagre pension. However, the situation improved somewhat after the marriage in 1972 of my second sister, who was eight years older than me. Meanwhile, my father also managed to find a full-time job as an accountant in a local transformer manufacturing firm. Now, the only liability for the family was my education which, in any case, did not cost much. I remember an extremely long discussion spanning several hours about whether we should buy an LPG gas connection and cooker, before we finally got them. The discussion mirrored the family's concern as to whether the potential taste of the food would remain unchanged if it were cooked in a pressure cooker over a gas burner instead of the traditional gas stove. What a contrast with the purchase decisions of today, especially our erstwhile excitement at such small things, which is completely missing now! We went through the same gamut of emotions on purchase of a Philips transistor the same year. The invaluable transistor became the only source of news and cricket commentary for the family. This was the era of legendary cricketers like our very own Sunil Gavaskar and Gundappa Vishwanath, and the 'hurricane' West Indian fast bowler duo of Andy Roberts and Vivian Richards, among others. And since very few test matches were played in those days, compared to the almost endless barrage of matches today, everyone remained glued to the cricket commentary whenever there was a match.

The transistor was also the most important source of entertainment as only one or two families owned a black and white television set, on which the only channel available was Doordarshan. Children from the entire locality would troop in to the houses of these families to watch two trademark programmes, the Sunday Hindi movie and the melange of Hindi songs on the weekly Chitrahaar, telecast every Wednesday evening, as part of what literally became a community television event. The families always welcomed the children and never objected to their presence. Colour television was launched much later, coinciding with the Asian Games held in India in 1982.

Coming back to my education, the principal of my college was a strict disciplinarian, insisting on the closure of all the gates of the college at a set hour to prevent any of the students from venturing out. The college was affiliated to the UP Board. I cannot forget the palpable excitement we all felt when the results of the class 10 board examinations were published in the local newspaper. I secured a first division with 66 per cent marks though the score was way below my expectation. Even in the subsequent board examination for class 12, I barely managed a first division again, scraping through with just a 60 per cent score. Both my teachers and I were sorely disappointed at my below par performance.

In complete contrast to my years at BAV Inter College, life at DN Degree College was a lark. Here, I tasted virtually unfettered freedom for the first time in my academic career though my parents kept a sharp eye on me and continued to enforce strict discipline at home, never allowing me to stay out beyond 9 p.m. I wistfully watched many of my friends who were not subjected to a curfew at home. However, we made full use of the liberty in college, watching almost every movie screened in the two cinema halls located nearby, by bunking classes at least once a week. The iconic movies of Amitabh Bachchan, *Sholay* and *Deewaar*, were released during those years, and as we watched each of them many times over, this movie experience became an intrinsic part of my college days. It also fuelled in me an unending passion for Hindi cinema, which has remained with me till today.

Search for a Dream Job

From DN Degree College, I moved to Meerut College, where I post-graduated in Physics in 1979. As was the norm among children belonging to non-business families, I too started preparing for and took various competitive examinations around this time. Unlike our peers from business families, who were keen to join their family businesses after graduation, we aspired to become doctors, engineers or chartered accountants. For others who were not interested in these 'staid' professions, there were a host of options, including examinations for the state civil services, administrative officers in insurance companies, excise inspectors, bank clerks, bank probationary officers, and the most coveted Indian Administrative Service (IAS). The job of a PO at SBI was very much on the list. Even the post of a bank clerk was seen as a respectable job, as it entailed a handsome four-figure salary. In a lighter vein, the financial worth of each of these jobs was unofficially determined by the dowry market. While marriage to an IAS officer commanded a hefty premium, intriguingly, a Junior Engineer's job was superior in perceived value than a bank officer's job. In fact, much to my chagrin, a bank job has consistently been one of the worst performers on the dowry index!

As I waded through these employment options, I started selecting my prospective occupation by elimination. Becoming a doctor was definitely not on my list, and I found the examination for becoming a chartered accountant (CA) a tough nut to crack even though I had been teaching mathematics to CA aspirants. This also applied to entrance examinations for engineering. Private colleges mushroomed much later, and even if they had existed, I would not have been able to afford studying in them. Also, starting my own business was out of question.

Hence, I began the long haul of appearing for competitive examinations. The first exam I took was for Special Class Railway Apprentices. The tough question paper provided me a flavour of what to expect in competitive examinations. We had access to a number of 'guides' for preparing for these exams, such as *Competition Master, Competition Success Review*, *Malayala Manorama* (knowledge compendium), and the NCERT-mandated history books for class 10. I soon mastered the art of clearing the written tests but always baulked at the interview stage, succumbing to nervousness. One of my most notable experiences was that of appearing for the Services Selection Board (SSB) examination, followed by the physical fitness test at Allahabad, and a personal interview. The SSB process was very structured, and posed questions that were markedly different from the routine ones asked in other interviews.

Many of my classmates at Meerut College were seriously preparing for IAS and bank PO exams. The Meerut College library was full of IAS aspirants, with history being the most widely chosen subject for the IAS preliminary and main examinations. I found it easy to clear the preliminaries but the mains were difficult to crack, particularly for those opting for Physics as the primary subject. Consequently, I started veering towards the bank PO exams, which seemed relatively easy to clear because of my science background coupled with a good command over the English language. I soon cleared three bank PO exams, for SBI, Bank of Baroda, and the State Bank of Bikaner and Jaipur. My interview for the SBI position was held on the twelfth floor of the SBI branch in New Delhi's Parliament Street, which houses the camp offices of the Chairman and Managing Directors of the bank. As I appeared for the interview, I could not have envisaged in my wildest dreams that I would one day be occupying the Chairman's room. This is also one of the reasons why I am overcome with nostalgia every time I visit my Delhi SBI office—it symbolizes my long and momentous journey from a small branch at Auraiya in UP's Etawah district to the top position of the bank.

In the meantime, I also travelled to Mumbai to appear for an interview at the Bhabha Atomic Research Centre (BARC), where the relatives of at least two of my friends were employed. Both these friends also generously offered to arrange for my stay in Mumbai, and partaking of the hospitality exhibited by both the families was an unmitigated pleasure. Today, such warmth and geniality have sadly become hallmarks of a distant past. The emotions and reminiscences of those initial years of my career and education sneak in unbidden into the narrative, and I hope the reader will forgive these digressions, but I would not be doing justice to my story without recounting those evocative remembrances.

The tale of my travel to Mumbai would be incomplete without touching upon my first experience of the Mumbai suburban trains, which are literally bursting at the seams at any time of the day. In my attempt to avoid the crowded coaches, I inadvertently jumped on to a first class coach. When I deboarded at Sion Station, I was asked to pay a hefty penalty of Rs 10 by the ticket checker. My plea of ignorance fell on deaf ears, and I had to eventually shell out the fine with a heavy heart. Since I had no reservation for the return journey, I had to rely on *coolies* (porters) for buying space for Rs 20 on the luggage shelf, which was spacious enough for stretching one's legs and catching a wink. Even this was not so easy to get but I managed to secure a luggage berth in the Frontier Mail. My host in Mumbai warned me that during training at BARC, I would be able to live in the Centre's hostel, but on completion of the training, I would have to live in paying guest accommodation for at least 12 years before being allotted one of the luxurious, sea-facing apartments in the BARC Campus. Little did I know then that I was destined to occupy one of the most expensive houses in Mumbai 40 years later.

My odyssey in SBI commenced when I received a cyclostyled appointment letter in September 1980, instructing me to join the Auraiya branch office on 3 November. Even though I belong to UP, I had never heard of this place. But my family exploded in excitement on learning that I had actually secured the coveted job of a PO at SBI. The occasion demanded some indulgence, and we ended up shopping for an expensive VIP suitcase, Bombay Dyeing bedsheets, a few utensils, and some new clothes, and the excitement of acquiring this limited inventory was akin to that of buying a new car. Such purchases are routinely made by youngsters today but they were indeed exceptional for a middle-class family in the pre-liberalization India of the 1970s and 1980s, when poverty was very real and shortages and rationing even of essential items were the order of the day. Very few households could afford a telephone, TV set, or a cooler, and air conditioners and refrigerators were really owned by the crème de la crème.

Since there was a clash between the dates for the IAS main examination and my joining date at SBI, I took an extension of 15 days, and left Meerut on 18 November 1980, setting out for my first job at SBI, Auraiya.

10

Journey with SBI, First Sixteen Years of Learning

Auraiya was a small start to my momentous career, soon catapulting me to bigger horizons and distant shores. As my mind races ahead another 16 years from this humble beginning, I find myself ready to set off on yet another journey, this time not from one town to another but from my beloved country to another. Again the date is clearly imprinted on my mind—28 September 1996, the day I boarded an Air India flight for Toronto from Indira Gandhi International Airport at Delhi, along with my wife and two daughters. And again, my entire family was there to bid me goodbye—my mother, my brother with his wife and children, and my three sisters. It was the first time that someone from their midst was going abroad for as long as four years. Prior to this, only my brother had been lucky enough to travel abroad and that too for about three months to New York. At the time I had come to Delhi from Lucknow to see him off. And here he was, returning the gesture, I thought with a sense of déjà vu, and a twist in my heart.

The angst of separation was most evident on my mother's visage, who had been living with us since my father's death in 1991, and had become deeply attached to my daughters. Albeit, my brother would take care of her but she was not particularly keen to stay with him as his children were married and had left the nest. Her life had revolved around my daughters, and feeling guilty at whisking them away from her for four years, I promised her that I would call her to Canada after settling down there. But she was apprehensive about whether she would live to see us again. Her mournful and unconvinced look, when I reiterated my commitment to return under all circumstances, was the last image I carried as I boarded the flight to Toronto.

First Branch, Auraiya in Ravines of Yamuna and Chambal

But what was taking me to Toronto after all? The answer to this question carried me back to my initial days as a PO at SBI 16 years ago. It seems that I landed in Auraiya only yesterday, when I deboarded the train at Etah station at 4.30 a.m. and boarded the bus to Auraiya at 6 a.m. on a chilly winter morning, spending the interim period between the two journeys in a waiting room infested with mosquitoes. And then the ride on the rickety bus was an even bigger ordeal, with the driver stopping to pick up every stray passenger who waved at the bus in the middle of nowhere.

Since I had not yet found a place to stay at my port of call, I straightaway proceeded to the bank branch from the bus station, using its changing room for guards to freshen up. Auraiya was a small town with a population of just about 20,000. My colleagues at the bank included another probationer, who subsequently joined the provincial civil services as a Sales Tax Officer; the Branch Manager, a senior but languid probationer who lacked control over the branch affairs; and about 20 staff members, including officers, clerks, and messenger staff.

There was no orientation procedure for newcomers at the bank, and I was left to fend for myself from day one. On the very first day, the accountant allotted me a day book for manually recording all debit and credit transactions, which, in view of my science background, seemed like Greek and Latin to me. Soon, I also learnt the colour codes of banking, something I had never expected to encounter in a bank—debit vouchers were white in colour, savings account credit pay-in slips were yellow, and current account pay-in slips were orange! I was firmly told that all the debit transactions were to be written in the left column of the book and credit transactions in the right column. I ended the first day with a huge mix up, writing many entries in the wrong column, and erroneous totalling of the columns, for which I received the firing of my life from the accountant next day. Gradually, however, I learnt the nuances of recording transactions. I remember glowing with pride when within a few days of my joining, the Branch Manager complimented me for being a fast learner. The staff were also friendly, going out of the way to make me feel at home, and surprisingly, the most memorable and useful lessons came not from the senior officers but from the clerical and messenger staff. Of course, I had to pay them *guru dakshina* in the form of pitching in for them when they wanted to leave early, or treating them to a meal or a glass of *lassi* at the local *dhaba*. They also arranged a single room accommodation for me in the town. However, despite my new-found friends at the bank, I was severely homesick, rushing back home on the very first weekend after joining, caring little about the tortuous journey between Auraiya and Meerut. My parents were taken aback on seeing me back so soon, worriedly asking if I had quit the job. But my dash between home and office soon became a much anticipated event both for them and me, as I made this commute a fortnightly ritual.

My tenure at Auraiya was also tinged with unexpected drama, quite unrelated to my personal or professional life. Etawah, the parent district of the town where I was stationed, was notorious for hosting *baghi*s or rebels along the entire stretch with the neighbouring districts of Etah and Mainpuri in Uttar Pradesh, and the Chambal ravines on the Madhya Pradesh State border. The place was also infamous for its inter-caste rivalry and the antics of several dacoit gangs that were active in the area at the time. I still recall the fear and anxiety which gripped the entire town when the news of killing of 12 Thakurs by the dacoit Phoolan Devi spread like wild fire. She was the leader of one of the dacoit gangs and was reportedly bent on taking revenge for her harassment by the Thakurs, who routinely exploited her both for her gender and her inferior social status. On the evening of 14 February 1981, Phoolan and her gang marched into Behmai village dressed as police officers, gate crashing a wedding in the village, in a bid to find her tormentors, Sri Ram and Lala Ram, who had earlier been instrumental in her molestation, and were allegedly hiding in the vicinity. When the two men could not be produced before her, she lined up all the young men of the village before a local river, shooting each one mercilessly, before departing as rapidly as she had come with her brigands, leaving behind 22 corpses and turning the marriage into a mass funeral. The Behmai massacre, Phoolan's subsequent surrender in 1993, and her election as a Member of Parliament from the Mirzapur constituency in UP in 1996, have been immortalized in the popular biopic, *Bandit Queen*, by the famous film-maker, Shekhar Kapur. Her deeds eventually caught up with her and she was assassinated in front of her home by three masked gunmen in 2001. But the night when she had entered Behmai village and left a trail of death behind her, was a night of dread that I could not forget easily.

The first instance of relief from the drudgery at Auraiya came for me when as part of a team of 30 officers, I was sent to participate in a three-week orientation programme at the Apex Training Institute in Hyderabad Staff College. The institute, with its exquisite French architecture and sprawling campus in the heart of Hyderabad, was the first such Apex Institute of SBI, followed by the establishment of four others later. This was the first time that I really felt like a 'bank officer'. Each room assigned to a delegate in the training programme had an orderly attached to it to take care of housekeeping, and the college had very well-planned infrastructure. The experience was akin to the *joie de vivre* of our college days, and we took the opportunity to explore Abids, the posh main market of Hyderabad, and the famous night club, Three Aces, which was a novelty for most of the officers coming from the hinterland. The coordinator of the programme was one Rajeshwar Rao, who always had a mischievous smile on his face, but was otherwise very affectionate and friendly. The advice he gave us during our stay in Hyderabad proved to be very valuable. He told us, 'At times you will feel important in the bank, and at times you will not, but you should never get disheartened.' This gem from an experienced person stood me in good stead throughout my tenure at the bank, never letting me feel demoralized even on occasions that warranted pessimism.

Auraiya offered very limited opportunities of entertainment. While the town suffered frequent power cuts, it had only one makeshift cinema hall operating from a tent with a few benches lined up for the audience. Most of the bank staff were not even based in the city and would commute every weekend from their homes in Kanpur. This total absence of any extracurricular activity made the weekends when I was not visiting Meerut extremely boring, and playing cards became the only way to pass time, and I started indulging in this pastime regularly. Initially, I was overcome with pangs of guilt whenever I thought of my father's cautionary advice, to me as I was leaving for Auraiya, that I should never give in to temptations like playing cards or having drinks with friends. Being a strict disciplinarian, my father was convinced that these vices would be the harbingers of trouble and spell doom for my integrity. However, I soon realized that I had to ignore this advice to some extent in order to survive in a place like Auraiya. But I did not deviate from the one cardinal principle that I resolutely believed in, that excess of everything is bad, and accordingly always consciously kept my enjoyment and indulgences under check. I consider this as a very practical approach to life, as it prevents us from succumbing to dogma or rigid adherence to principles, allowing for a balanced life. I also came across many officers in the course of my career who were either very shrewd or very naïve, or very lax or very rigid in attitudes and habits, which prevented them from achieving professional success.

Rampur, a New Chapter in Life Begins

After completion of six months of training at Auraiya, I was transferred to a relatively better bank branch at Rampur, which is a district headquarters and well connected to Meerut. Now it was possible for me to visit home every weekend. In complete contrast to the branch manager at Auraiya, the branch head at Rampur, Janki Ballabh, was a dashing young doer and achiever. He was considered to be a star performer and a potential chairman, in bank circles. This assessment proved to be true as he eventually became Chairman for two years in the year 2000. I considered myself fortunate to be able to work under a dynamic leader like Ballabh, so early in my career, though only for a short period of four months.

Rampur also holds a special place in my personal life, as it was here that I found my life partner, Reeta, and the two of us got engaged soon after. Her brother Ajay, who was posted in the local branch of the Central Bank of India, played an important role in bringing us together. I had earlier been engaged to a girl in Meerut when Ajay first approached me, and he was disappointed that he would not be able to act as matchmaker. Providentially, however, my earlier engagement did not last, so I sent feelers to Ajay that I was single again. He quickly arranged a meeting between his sister and me in the presence of both our families at Paul Hotel at Meerut, which was, in those days, perceived as the most happening place in the city for a rendezvous of this kind. It was love at first sight for me and Reeta. We enjoyed a brief courtship at Rampur, thanks to Ajay, who was living there with his wife, which, given our conservative families, would otherwise have been sacrilege. My sister initially had strong reservation about my marrying a girl from a small town. The simplicity and humbleness of Reeta's parents had left a deep impression on my mind and I was convinced that some of it would have definitely been passed on to their children. It eventually proved to be a right call.

During my probation period of two years, my posting at Pratapgarh Agriculture Branch proved to be the most challenging because I failed to get a house there for my short tenure of just three months. Hence, I had to stay in a dingy and unhygienic hotel at a rent of Rs 6 per day. Pratapgarh and development seemed antithetical to each other, and here I got a glimpse of the real poverty and backwardness that was plaguing eastern Uttar Pradesh even after 35 years of Independence. Indeed, this small town seemed like a microcosm of the poor and marginalized parts of the country where people were constantly battling hardships and adversity. The only diversion from the boredom of Pratapgarh, was my fortnightly visit to Allahabad to meet my sister-in-law, Seema, who was doing her post-graduation there and had a charming personality.

Mauranipur, an Ultra Conservative Town Near the Temples of Love

The last branch where I was posted for training was Mauranipur in the Bundelkhand area, which lies on the route between Jhansi and Khajuraho in Madhya Pradesh, the latter being home to temples famous for their architectural symbolism and eroticism. Bundelkhand was quite a conservative place where the *purdah* system was still prevalent. I joined the Mauranipur branch about two months before my marriage and was thus keen to find a suitable accommodation there. Finally, I zeroed in on a two-room set with a kitchen, but faced a hurdle when the landlord refused to let it out to me as I was a bachelor. However, when I told him about my impending marriage and my intention to bring my wife to Mauranipur, he reluctantly agreed to accept me as a tenant. Later, I learnt that he had quoted a rent that was twice the market rate in the hope that I would reverse my decision, but much to his disappointment, I agreed to the higher rent. After our wedding, my wife moved in with me in Mauranipur. It was not customary in this conservative town for husband and wife to walk together or even be seen together in public places or cinema halls. We found it difficult to follow this tradition, and were conscious of all eyes on us even when we visited the market for errands. Ironically, this ultra-orthodox town was located only 60 km away from Khajuraho with its temples of love and sensuality! Barring its old-fashioned environment, Mauranipur offered us a memorable stay, as it symbolized our first home post-marriage, and also because the landlord's family took good care of us, treating me almost like a younger brother.

I received my confirmation letter after two years of probation and my only desire at the time was to be posted to a place that was connected to Meerut by train. As luck would have it, one position of Field Officer was falling vacant at Naini, the twin town of the more famous city of Prayagraj or Allahabad, as it was called, and the Regional Manager agreed to post me there after some persuasion. I was really excited at my transfer this time, landing at Naini by the Sangam Express, which would take me directly to Meerut after an overnight journey. Being the site of the confluence of three rivers, the holy Ganga, Yamuna, and the now extinct Saraswati, Prayagraj also has a huge religious significance. I decided to buy a scooter for regularly commuting from Allahabad to Naini. And that brings us to another story. It was not easy to get a scooter in those days because of the huge demand–supply gap, and consequently there was a long waiting list for the hugely popular Bajaj scooter, which was available instantly only by paying a hefty premium. Many people had, in fact, made a small fortune by booking Bajaj scooters and selling them at a premium. However, scooters made by the UP Government-owned corporation, Vijay Super Scooters, were easily available, and this scooter became my first mode of personal transport after I managed to get a vehicle loan from SBI that was offered exclusively to the bank staff. Indeed, the only experience in consumer financing for public sector banks in those days was the disbursement of loans to staff for the purchase of vehicles, consumer durables, and housing under a highly complex scheme. This scenario changed dramatically only after the advent of new generation private sector banks in the mid-1990s. Naini became a landmark posting for me in more ways than one—it was my first after completion of probation, first after marriage, and also the location where I bought my first private vehicle.

First Lessons in Credit Management

I also learnt my first lessons in handling SSI credit at Naini. The city had three large public sector undertakings, namely, Indian Telephone Industries, Bharat Pumps and Compressors Ltd, and Triveni Structurals Ltd, apart from a whole host of small-scale industries that were mainly ancillaries of these three large units. All the three units were running in losses, as a result of which most of the ancillary units were also suffering financially. The law and order situation in Naini was also grim, with many local mafias constantly meddling into the affairs of corporates and creating labour problems. One of the local mafiosi and dreaded gangsters was a man named Bhukal Maharaaj, who reportedly enjoyed a monopoly on all government and railway contracts. He had allegedly bought one of the bottling plants of Coca Cola at gunpoint for just one rupee from a Delhi-based Sikh family. To his credit, however, he was running the unit with the help of professionals. I was forced to visit his place once to get the renewal documents signed. The place was surrounded by gunmen and Bhukal had a larger-than-life aura around him. In contrast, I had a lean and thin gait. He took one look at me and disparagingly remarked that I needed to build my physique, for which he suggested that he would arrange for an accommodation for me near his place and ensure a daily supply of milk! With my heart in my mouth at the prospect of spending time near this gangster, I hurriedly obtained his signatures on the documents, and rushed out of the place, hoping never to encounter him again. When he subsequently hosted a grand reception for his son's marriage, he invited the who's who of the State government. Receiving an invite for the wedding reception of Bhukal's son was perceived as an honour for the invitees.

Bhukal, whom I had the opportunity to deal with once, was not the only desperado I came across during my banking career. There were quite a few villages around Naini, including one called Arail, which was allegedly full of people with criminal records and villainous antecedents. It was common for bankers to get some threat or the other from such people. In fact, on one occasion, a gentleman called Purwar, one of the respectable small-scale unit owners in the packaging industry, was sitting with me when a customer from Arail, who wanted a loan sanctioned, threatened me with dire consequences if I did not facilitate the sanction for his loan. Purwar advised me not to succumb to his pressure because if I did, my tenure would become miserable. Although such incidents instilled a lot of fear in me, I listened to Purwar's advice, refusing to buckle under any threats or pressure, which eventually helped me to overcome my fear of unsavoury clients and their demands.

My follow-up for recovery of loans was, however, very strong and one of the borrowers once compared me to a Pathan. Although this description did not fit my personality, it became an asset to project such a strong trait for ensuring timely recovery of many loans. It also came in handy when I decided to auction a transformer manufacturing unit that had been set up with the help of a loan from our bank but had become sick. The unit had been established by three executives who had left their cushy jobs at General Electric to set up a small-scale unit. Delayed payments and other issues with the UP government, which was one of their clients, had led to the unit becoming sick. That incident occurred many years ago but the situation has not changed over the years, and the delayed payments and disputes between suppliers and government departments continue to be the main reason for industrial sickness and the prevalence of a high level of NPLs in banks. Auctioning a unit in the mafia-infested town of Naini was not an easy task because the bidders were being threatened. Our auctioneer, an Allahabad-based firm, however, managed to get a few serious bidders. I was the only one present on behalf of the bank. The auction continued the entire day. When the auction was completed at the end of the day, another problem arose as some local mischievous elements started demanding money to enable the buyer to load the plant and machinery bought by him. It was after three hours of bargaining between the buyer and these anti-social elements that the trucks were allowed to depart from the site of the auction. I returned to the bank branch at around 10 p.m. to the relief of the branch manager, who had been waiting there for me anxiously. I learnt many useful lessons in the management of credit and non-performing loans the hard way on my very first regular posting.

First Taste of Power

After about 18 months, I was transferred to the personnel department at the local head office in Lucknow, where I handled industrial relations, dealing with staff unions and matters pertaining to service conditions. The personnel department has always been considered to be a power centre in the bank and is consequently hardly liked by anyone. At the time when I joined this department, trade unionism was at its peak in banks and the union leaders enjoyed a huge clout. The president of the All India

Staff Federation, popularly known as Panditji, belonged to the Lucknow circle. Whenever he visited Lucknow, it was quite a sight to see staff members falling over each other to touch his feet. Since he was considered to be more powerful than even the circle management, all efforts were made to generally keep him in good humour in order to ensure the smooth functioning of the branches in Lucknow circle, covering the eastern, central, and western parts of Uttar Pradesh. Very few leaders of the staff unions enjoyed a good understanding of staff matters and labour laws, which allowed them to be tough negotiators. The rest were all piggy-backing on these main leaders, benefiting from their reflected glory.

During my tenure in Lucknow, the level of computerization in banking was very low as only certain back-end activities were computerized. In retrospect, it would be fair to say that the pervasive fear among the unions that computerization would lead to their complete marginalization was not totally unfounded. The foundation of large-scale computerization in public sector banks was laid by the historic fourth bipartite settlement signed in 1984. Being in charge of industrial relations, I was quite actively involved in its implementation. The personnel department was one of the sections that led the way in computerization, and there was palpable excitement when the department got its first PC XT with DOS as the operating software. I also wrote a few small programs using dBase 3. The thrill of writing a successful software programme is difficult to describe. The programming skills I developed at that time always prove to be useful whenever the development of any new programme is discussed in the bank even today. In fact, the programming team has, at times, expressed surprise at the unique insights I am able to share with them. One of the highly successful programmes that has been developed is the end-to-end digitization of the debt waiver scheme announced in 2008, when I was Deputy General Manager of the Pune zone. And my experience in programming can also be credited for the creation of the YONO app of SBI, which is till date the bank's most ambitious and successful programme.

An area of concern at SBI over the years has been its involvement in litigation with several different levels of officers. In 1979, the bank had implemented recommendations of the Pillai Committee, which placed POs in the same starting scale as that of officers promoted from among the clerical staff. Before 1979, the POs were being appointed in a grade that was one level higher than that of officers promoted from the clerical cadre. There was another channel for fast track promotion from clerical to trainee officers, who were placed equivalent to POs. The implementation of the Pillai Committee's recommendations led to huge discontent among all the three categories of officers in the bank, particularly POs and trainee officers of the 1979 batch, and promoted officers of the 1980 batch. The dispute was centred around the fixation of seniority. All the cases were being fought in the Allahabad High Court. My immediate boss at the time was K.P. Rau. Being from a family of journalists, he had excellent writing skills and could grasp all nuances and details of the service conditions for officers and staff. He was usually a quiet person but would become more loquacious after having a drink or two in the evening. He had joined the bank in 1971 and was well versed with both the politics of the unions as well as the power politics prevalent in the bank. Almost every two months, I would travel with him to Allahabad in a taxi in connection with the court cases, where we stayed in the only three-star hotel in the city, Yatri.

The bank had started paying for the officers' lodging expenses in a hotel on outstation tours only from 1983 onwards. Prior to this, the officers travelling out of station were paid only a paltry halting allowance of Rs 50 towards lodging and boarding expenses, which was grossly inadequate, and consequently, officers on outstation duty would mostly avoid staying in hotels and try to find relatives or friends to stay with. During my tours with Rau, we could afford to stay at Yatri, but found the meals to be too costly to suit our pockets. Hence, both of us would eat at the roadside *dhaba*s near the Allahabad railway station. The food there was fantastic but the place was untidy and poorly maintained. The conversations we had during these sojourns were thoroughly enjoyable and he, in a way, became my Guru in staff matters.

Two other personalities who played a dominant role in teaching the nuances of law to me were S.N. Verma, who was a senior advocate handling bank cases, and Navin Sinha, who supported him. I knew both of them from my Naini days. Navin was very sharp and could grasp the nuances of all the cases even better than Verma despite the latter's stature and experience as a senior advocate. The bank was keen to get the cases settled as early as possible because the entire process of promotions was held up due to the pending cases. Both Rau and I were privately sympathetic to the cases filed by the POs and trainee officers as we felt that injustice was being done to them, but as representatives of the bank, we had no choice but to support the bank's point of view and ensure that it was put across effectively. In view of the slow progress of resolution of the cases, the bank decided to engage Shanti Bhushan, one of the best contemporary lawyers, who had become famous after fighting the case against erstwhile Prime Minister Indira Gandhi, which she had lost, leading to imposition of the Emergency by her. Shanti Bhushan thereafter served as Law Minister in the Janata Party Government when Congress was defeated in the 1977 elections.

I remember travelling to Delhi to brief Shanti Bhushan on the bank's cases along with Navin Sinha. During those days, the New Okhla Industrial Development Area or NOIDA, as it has come to be known, was in the early stages of development. Shanti Bhushan had an amazing grasp of issues and clarity of thought. I am convinced that it was his presence in the Allahabad High Court that ensured victory for the bank. In fact, it would not be an exaggeration to say that the bank won the case more because of Bhushan's stature rather than the merit of the issue. This perhaps also applies to many other cases, wherein the outcomes are determined more by the eminence of lawyers than the actual issue at stake. I had the opportunity to experience the aura of the court on another occasion when lawyers went on strike and the bank was seeking an urgent stay in the case. The rules allow the litigant to argue without an advocate. Verma taught me what to say in the court, and as per my brief, I had to say only two sentences. However, I became so nervous in the court that uttering even those two sentences seemed like an impossible task for me. Nevertheless, we still managed to get a stay order for the bank. All these incidents taught me invaluable lessons while also honing my ability to grasp complex issues and arrive at well-thought-out solutions for complex problems.

In 1985, the bank's Annual General Meeting was held in Lucknow. It was customary for the bank to hold an Annual General Meeting by rotation at the local head office centres. The bank requisitioned the services of many junior officers like me for managing the flagship event, which would see the presence of all the top brass of the bank in Lucknow. It was a matter of great privilege for us that the Chairman of SBI was the State Guest on the occasion, and was hosted in Raj Bhawan. All the other managing directors and deputy managing directors were accommodated at Clarks Avadh, the only five-star hotel in Lucknow. For most bank staffers, including me, this was the first experience of dining in a five-star hotel. Another 'sensational' piece of news, repeated in hushed tones, was that mineral water, considered to be a luxury at that time, was being arranged for the Chairman. The Chief General Manager of the Lucknow circle was D. Basu, who had returned from a six-year-long stay in London. Unlike many senior officials who sported a snobbish attitude, Basu was very approachable and became friends with most of us, also hosting a dinner for us at his local residence, Tara Wali Kothi, which is a heritage property. This property, which was the official residence of the Deputy General Manager of the SBI main branch in Lucknow, also became a centre of controversy when the incumbent was forced to vacate it for the Chief General Manager after the local head office of the bank was shifted from Kanpur to Lucknow, and the Deputy General Manager resigned in protest. It was around this time that many of us started nurturing aspirations about becoming a Chief General Manager at least, if not the Chairman. The aura associated with the position was a huge attraction for us and we were completely in awe of the senior officers who held that position. Today, however, I wonder whether those officers and positions still command the same reverence as they did in the early days of my career, or whether times have changed, ushering in more democracy and freedom of thought among the bank staff.

First Step of The Ladder to The Top

After our victory in the promotion case, the bank could now restart and revisit the entire process as all the cases were decided in favour of the bank. For the first time, a written examination for promotion from Scale 1 to Scale 2 was introduced, which many probationary officers failed, but I successfully cleared. Our batch got its first promotion after six years. I had prepared very hard for the exam, and one of my batch mates, Suneet Mathur, even remarked that I would rise to the position of the Chairman. I am reminded of his prophecy till today. The next hurdle for me was promotion from Grade 2 to Grade 3 of the middle management. An officer who had become a Certified Associate of the Indian Institute of Bankers (CAIIB) enjoyed an advantage of one year. I was unable to clear one paper on Rural Economics, and was getting so frustrated that I wanted to give up trying. But my wife, who has always been a strong motivator when the going gets tough, persuaded me to make one more attempt, and as luck would have it, this time I managed to scrape through by securing 50 marks, which was the minimum required to pass the examination. Thereafter, I needed two attempts to clear Part 2 of the exam and became a CAIIB just in time to become eligible for Scale 3 promotions.

The promotions in the bank are very structured and one's chances of becoming the Managing Director and Chairman depend a lot on the age of the candidates at the time of entry and the chronology of all the promotions as per schedule. It is thus not enough to be meritorious alone. Luckily for me, however, there was no looking back after I achieved success in CAIIB and all my subsequent promotions fell into place, barring that from Chief General Manager to Deputy Managing Director, which took some time, though it did not impact my eligibility for subsequent appointment as the Managing Director.

Time to Move to Field Assignments

By this time, I had completed five years in the personnel department, and it was time for me to move on for a line assignment. It was with a heavy heart that I left the personnel department, which I perceived as a golden period of my career in many ways, such as allowing me to obtain a clairvoyant perspective on the working of the bank, to learn about the idiosyncrasies and styles of functioning of many senior officials, and the impact of all these factors on the bank as a whole. I was greatly influenced by all the three personnel managers who led the department over a five-year period, with all of them being very different from each other. The first of these was very tough and powerful, and hence highly respected because of his demeanour. One of my batch mates once gathered the courage to ask him about the source of his power, and pat came the reply, 'Knowledge'. The second manager, though less knowledgeable than the first, was hugely popular among the staff because of his genial ways and understanding attitude, which made him such a successful leader. And the third one, who had just returned from New York, though a novice in handling office politics, was very affable and accessible, which made up for his inexperience and naivete. I believe that this was truly the golden period of my career not only professionally but also personally as a large number of my young colleagues were posted at the local head office, and many of us became friends for life. These relationships have persevered through the years, irrespective of the ranks and positions each of us achieved in the organization. I was the last one to retire in my batch of 400.

Leaving Lucknow, I headed for my next destination, the Ranikhet branch in the Kumaon Hills. Finding a suitable accommodation in Ranikhet was very difficult, but fortunately, the negotiating skills of another colleague of mine who was transferred to Ranikhet at the same time, helped us to get two suites at Norton Hotel. It was a very picturesque location. Ranikhet, also the headquarters of the Kumaon Regiment, was a very small but picture-perfect hill town. Despite the imposition of prohibition in the Kumaon Hills because of the prevalent problem of alcoholism, we never had any problem in sourcing alcohol from the military canteens with some member of every local family being an army man. I too made friends with many local army officers, and started enjoying a drink or two with them. However, as this started becoming a regular routine, my wife decided to take matters into her hands and stopped my daily flirtations with alcohol. But for her strong intervention, I might have soon become an alcoholic! I was in Kumaon Hills only for a short period of about 18 months before I was transferred again, this time to Pilibhit as a branch manager.

The town of Pilibhit lies about 60 km north of Bareilly in what is known as the Terai Belt. A large number of Sikh families, who were displaced from their homes at the time of the Partition in 1947, have settled in the Terai belt. Through their grit and sheer hard work, they have brought prosperity to the region. Dotted with rice fields all around, the Terai Belt has virtually become the paddy bowl of India. My posting to Pilibhit came as a bit of shock because the region was known to be an operating area for terrorists, leading to a tumultuous law and order situation, as a result of which no officer was willing to go there. Kidnapping for ransom was quite common in the city, and the local bank branch also had a history of disturbed industrial relations, with conflicts with customers being a fairly common occurrence. Fearing for my safety, many friends and colleagues advised me not to join the Pilibhit branch. However, I enjoyed good personal rapport with the Regional Manager, R.K. Thapliyal, who had earlier been my Personnel Manager, and he persuaded me to take charge at Pilibhit. He argued that I had nothing to lose, and further, that if I managed the branch well, it would be a good stepping stone in my career. So, I reluctantly departed for Pilibhit. The all-round situation in the bank was pretty grim. Not only were the bank premises shabby and uncared for, but there was also an ongoing dispute with the landlord for fixation of a revised rent. All my skills in handling industrial relations were tested to the core in Pilibhit. I found that negotiating with the top Union leadership at the local head office was an easier task than dealing with not-so-disciplined staff as well as their union leaders with inflated egos. The difference between the two was like learning to drive a car by reading the guide and learning it hands-on by actually driving the car. In the first few months after my joining the branch, a major showdown with staff unions became inevitable at the time of the annual closing of books in March 1991. But I was able to establish authority as the Branch Manager. It became clear to me that according respect to the staff helps one earn a lot of goodwill, which is of tremendous use in dealing with the union leaders. There is always a group of good people who are resentful of the union leaders and thus willing to help the management covertly. I encountered many such situations later on during my career as Deputy General Manager, Pune, Head of UK operations, the CGM, Guwahati, and eventually as the IBA Chairman in finalizing a path-breaking settlement when the concept of performance-linked pay was accepted by the unions in public sector banks for the first time. The landlord of the bank premises also became a lifelong friend as the dispute around rent fixation was resolved. The living conditions in Pilibhit, otherwise, were not conducive for a comfortable life. There were regular power cuts, and many other compromises that one had to make. For instance, the exhaust pipe of the generator of our neighbours across the narrow street almost peeped into our bedroom, causing a huge amount of noise and fumes that literally got on our nerves.

The sorry state of the local telecommunication system came home to me when my father passed away. Frantically trying to reach me through telephone, but unable to do so, my brother had to eventually convey the news to me through a family acquaintance in the railways, who sent the message to the Station Master of Pilibhit station through the railways communication system, which reached me the next day. This showed how much we still rely on the human touch despite living in a world dominated by technology. I was devastated by the death of my father, and could not believe that someone so hale and hearty and fully active even at the age of 78 could suddenly be snatched from us. These thoughts ravaged my mind as I drove non-stop for eight hours from Pilibhit to Delhi to attend my father's last rites.

Entry into Handling of Corporate Credit

My term at Pilibhit was followed by the next assignment as Chief Manager at the bank's Credit Appraisal Cell in Lucknow. In those days, working in the credit department of a bank was one of the most coveted postings unlike today when officers are unwilling to take up such assignments because of the fear of harassment and being held accountable by the investigating agencies. My stint at Lucknow coincided with the initiation of reforms in the economy and the banking sector. India had already taken baby steps towards liberalization of the banking sector, which was otherwise very tightly regulated. It was the prescriptive regime of the RBI that had a say in everything, including underwriting of loans of more than Rs 1 crore, quantitative and qualitative restrictions on lending, and fixing of interest rates on loans and deposits. The Basel norms for income recognition and asset classification had just been introduced. Further, the new generation private sector banks brought in a whiff of fresh air into the banking ecosystem and there was an exodus of many executives from all levels at SBI to join these banks. I must admit that I too was tempted to follow suit but could not summon enough courage to leave my secure job and so carried on at SBI. However, my shift from being an industrial relations expert to a credit expert signified a successful change of track within the contours of my job.

The Invaluable Experience of Working Overseas

Another big dream nurtured by those joining as POs in a bank was to be selected for an overseas assignment. The charm of moving abroad has waned considerably these days because of the narrowing gap between domestic and overseas salaries, which does not compensate much for the travails of a major dislocation. However, in the 1990s, a foreign posting was seen as something to die for. Like many of my colleagues, I would wait with mounting expectation every year to see my name in the shortlist of interviewees for a foreign posting, almost losing hope till I actually got the news of my candidature for such an assignment in 1996. I was on a vacation with my family in Puducherry when I learnt that my name figured in the list of the officers called for an interview. Having worked in the personnel department for five years, I knew that this department plays a critical role in shortlisting officers as prospects for an international assignment. I also knew that I was not a favourite for the post. Every local head office of the bank had two General Managers after the reorganization exercise at the bank. I was working under the General Manager, Commercial Banking. The other General Manager, in charge of Development Banking, was considered to be more powerful as he was responsible for all the retail branches, and most of the officers recommended for the foreign posting came from the development banking vertical. My General Manager had reportedly shown his displeasure at this favouritism, and hence my name was subsequently included in the list to placate him. I got selected as Vice President, Credit, Toronto. On my way to join the Toronto posting, after 16 years of my joining the bank, I felt the same excitement that I had experienced when I got my first appointment letter as a PO. I could hardly wait to enjoy the 'new world' that would be my home for four years. My family, especially my mother, understood and rejoiced in this opportunity but could not overcome the simultaneous trepidation at what lay ahead for the family with one of its sons travelling to such a distant land.

We had to leave India before the 30 September (end of the second quarter of the financial year) for some reason that had to do with my tax compliance. And I needed a clearance from the Income Tax Department to get a passport. I had to wait a full day outside the office of the Income Tax Officer to get a No Objection Certificate (NOC). The officer who was to issue the NOC was not only rude but also greedy. Since I refused to oblige him with any gratification in return for his clearance, he found some strange logic to levy an additional tax liability of Rs 10,000 on me, a princely sum in those days. I had no choice but to pay the amount. It is incidents like this which prove how much digitization of bank processes and faceless assessments have helped in improving the lives of honest income taxpayers in the country. Every year, getting the tax refund in the account within a few days of filing the tax return shows the tremendous improvement in functioning of the Income Tax Department.

The next hurdle I faced was to actually get the passport issued. In 1996, there was no Passport Seva Kendra anywhere in the country, unlike today when such centres have been set up in several major cities across the nation, making the process of issuance of passports so simple, transparent, and efficient. Back then, the passport office was teeming with touts and it was impossible to get a passport without their help. Albeit, I did make an effort and applied directly for the passport, but there was no sign of it even as the date of my departure was edging closer. I made several visits to the passport office, trying desperately to meet the Passport Officer. He behaved like God, seeming to suggest that having a passport is not the right of every citizen but rather a largesse to be doled out at his mercy. When I failed to meet this all-important officer, I had to resort to seek help from the officer in charge of the concerned police station, who was a relation of one of my friends, and more importantly, had jurisdiction over the passport office. Yes, getting things done in India then, always hinged on one's contacts and network. The official promised me that he would get my passport delivered the same day. I then accompanied him to the passport office. The first thing he did was to round up the touts present there, and hit one or two of them with his baton, shouting, 'What is going on here, I will put each one of you in jail.' This created a lot of commotion in the passport office and had the desired impact. The Passport Officer came running out, escorting me and the police officer to his room. Visibly shaken, he apologized and promised that he would deliver mine and my family's passports to my residence the same evening, and sure enough, he did. I felt as if I had conquered Mount Everest.

The Air India flight we were on was a direct flight between Delhi and Toronto, with a stopover of 90 minutes at London. We boarded the flight amidst a lot of anxiety and excitement. We had to de-plane and board the same plane again at London. The disembarkation at London's Heathrow Airport was my first brush with the Western world, and I was mesmerized. The dazzling shops, spotlessly clean surroundings, and indeed the entire environment at the airport was in sharp contrast to the International Terminal at Delhi Airport, where the first thing anybody would notice were its shabby carpets. It was only during the following decade when many airports were built in India under public–private partnership that airports in leading Indian cities like Hyderabad, Bengaluru, Mumbai, and New Delhi became comparable to any international airport and certainly better than Heathrow.

Toronto is one of the most beautiful cities in the world. We had landed there during the fall season when the city breaks out into a riot of colour, and driving along the Don Valley parkway was a unique experience. Everything here seemed to be new and shining. It was my first experience of seeing highways and shopping malls, and my first encounter with a vastly different culture. Initially, my daughters found it very awkward to call older people or their teachers by their first names, as is the practice in Canada. For me too, things were very different in office. While officers from India addressed the CEO as 'Sir', the local staff would call him by his first name. There were no messengers and no staff to prepare tea or carry files from one desk to another in the bank office in Toronto. The officers from India had to deal with the inflated ego of the CEO. It was the first time that I learned the concept of 'returning a call'. I imbibed this habit so deeply that I always returned each and every call even after becoming the Chairman of SBI. Many people in India are surprised to learn of this habit of mine and rarely understand that it is extremely rude to not return a call, regardless of who you are. While being posted at Toronto, I also learnt to be completely independent and became capable of managing all my affairs in office without any secretarial support. I also kept my promise to my mother, returning to India after completing four years in Toronto, despite a very strong temptation to stay back and rejecting many job offers that came my way there. In between, my 80-year-old mother once travelled alone to visit us. When I had first suggested to my brother that I wanted to call her to Toronto, he remarked with disbelief, 'Do you think this is like travelling between Meerut and Delhi?' But travel she did, which was quite remarkable for a person who had no knowledge of the English language, and who had never travelled alone in the past. But she was determined to visit us, and her grit made it possible. The direct flight between Delhi and Toronto had been discontinued by then and she also had to switch to a different flight at London.

My stay in Toronto also brought into sharp focus the extreme poverty and backwardness of my country when compared to the much more advanced nations of the world, which are almost 100 years ahead of us in terms of development and prosperity. We revel in our rich culture and heritage and rightfully so, but it is high time we realized that our national pride and patriotism need to be tempered with a realistic assessment of our position in the world and how far we still have to go to enhance the welfare and well-being of all our citizens.

I returned to India from Toronto to join my next assignment in Delhi on the last day of the year 2000, standing at the cusp of a new year and a new century, and brimming with hope for a better India in the forthcoming twenty-first century. I believed that the seeds of this transformation had already been sown over the last four years, from 1996 to 2000, as high economic growth and liberalization, and the emergence of the IT industry as a major player in the country's progress were gradually changing perceptions about India and Indians across the world.

11

The Final Lap

Perseverance and Diligence Yield Results

The red letter day had finally arrived in my professional life—28 May 2015. It was the day when I received the letter from the Department of Financial Services appointing me as Managing Director at the State Bank of India.

This momentous occasion came after 35 years of my joining the bank and 19 years after I was informed of my posting to Toronto. But my journey to the top had had its fair share of ups and downs. After returning from Toronto at the beginning of the millennium, I joined the Corporate Accounts Group as Assistant General Manager, where I was responsible for dealing with some top corporate and public sector clients like the Gas Authority of India (GAIL), Bharat Heavy Electricals Limited (BHEL), Indian Farmers' Fertiliser Cooperative Limited (IFFCO), and Krishak Bharati Cooperative Limited (KRIBHCO). The interim years between my assignment at Toronto and the offer of heading the bank were wrought with frustration, at times bordering on despair. My last promotion as Assistant General Manager had happened four years ago, and the wait for promotion to the level of Deputy General Manager had lasted eight long years.

Meanwhile, officers at the bank had constantly been demanding a reduction in the waiting time for promotions. In a reactive mode, the bank came out with a policy to fast-track promotions in 2003, introducing the concept of a written test and setting up of an assessment centre for facilitating promotions to the grade of deputy general manager. But this policy did not do much to ameliorate frayed tempers as all officers wanted the service criterion to be reduced uniformly to five years and selections for promotion to be done only through interviews. I too felt that it was not appropriate to use an assessment centre to evaluate officers who had clocked more than 20 years of service for promotion. Such a centre could, at best, be used for identifying the development needs of an executive, not for determining if an officer was worthy of being promoted or not. Although initially, the bank management rejected the officers' demand for fast-tracking promotions, it subsequently accepted their suggestion as a policy measure.

This was, however, not the end of my woes. I appeared for the fast-track examination in 2003 but could not get through. A glance at the list of officers who succeeded in becoming deputy general managers through the fast-track mode shows that only one such officer, B. Sriram, could progress to the board level, rising to the post of Managing Director in 2014. A front-runner for the chairman's position, he had appeared for the interview along with me, though, having joined the bank in 1981, he was a year junior to me. He too had already missed one promotion, reaching the position of Assistant General Manager only after completing 17 years of service in 1998. My failure to clear the examination came as a big disappointment but I did not let it affect either my diligence or my commitment to the bank. My chances of reaching the top seemed to be receding but there seemed a small ray of hope. I knew that it was a long-distance race, the outcome of which would be revealed only in the last lap.

Exploring New Pastures, New Networks, and New Attitudes at the Bank

This was also the period when implementation of core banking and Internet banking had just begun in the bank. The Corporate Accounts Group had enabled the bank to ring-fence its corporate lending business. The bank had historic relations with some of the largest corporations in the country in both the private and public sectors. While the Corporate Accounts Group in Mumbai was mostly dealing with private sector corporates, its counterpart in Delhi was largely focusing on large public sector undertakings. Although I was only a mid-level executive, the power of the name of the State Bank of India opened many doors for me even at the top-most level in most corporations. I was thus able to interact with many stalwarts and senior functionaries in the corporate world, like the MD, BHEL, K.G. Ramchandran, who had a soft corner for SBI as he had himself started his career as a SBI probationer; U.S. Awasthi, who is the current Managing Director at IFFCO; and Prashanto Banerjee, MD of GAIL. Among all of them, Banerjee was quite particular about following all protocols and hierarchy, and it was difficult to get an audience with him. Professionally, however, he was quite a dynamic officer, and was constantly pushing for the adoption of technology. In fact, it was at the behest of GAIL that the bank was forced to fast-track implementation of corporate Internet banking, as the bank faced a real threat of losing the GAIL account, if it failed to upgrade its technological systems as per the expectations of Banerjee. Contrary to general perceptions, large public sector corporations like GAIL, Indian Oil Corporation, and other oil marketing companies were front-runners as far as adoption of technology for banking was concerned, whereas many private sector corporations, on the other hand, were reluctant entrants into the world of digital banking and needed a lot of persuasion to come on board the bandwagon of Internet banking.

Here, I would like to narrate what in retrospect seems like a comedy of errors but which almost cost me my job when it occurred, and the person at the centre of the incident was none other than P. Banerjee of GAIL. I had fixed an appointment for him with Alok Batra, Managing Director, Commercial Banking, at SBI. Vijayanand, Chief General Manager, Corporate Accounts Group, also accompanied Batra to the meeting. However, when all of us reached the GAIL office, Banerjee allowed only Batra to meet him and did not let Vijayanand inside his office at all. It was a highly embarrassing situation for both of us, and I became quite nervous at this turn of events, but Vijayanand reacted like a perfect gentleman and did not create any fuss, in contrast to many other bosses, may have reacted to such a goof-up.

The meeting at GAIL was almost like a watershed in my career. That day, I decided to imbibe the same qualities of decency and magnanimity exhibited by Vijayanand on the occasion, and I tried to follow his example in dealing with my colleagues and others through the rest of my career, including the three years that I served as Chairman of the bank. Thereafter, I hardly ever lost my temper in the office or scolded anyone, particularly in the presence of their juniors. My stint at Toronto and later on at London also contributed to this style of functioning, as the liberal working environments abroad allowed juniors to often retort if senior officials did not behave properly with them. My style of functioning has been in complete contrast to that of many other chairmen and managing directors, who were prone to publicly reprimanding those reporting to them, including many senior officials even at the level of deputy managing directors and chief general managers, not to speak of lesser mortals. Many senior ministers and politicians also behave in a similar manner, little realizing that admonishing their junior staff in public is counter-productive. Such bad behaviour not only lowers the dignity of both the perpetrator and the recipient, but also creates a communication gap between the senior and his subordinates, who then become apprehensive of sharing any ideas and information with their boss lest they face his ire again. I believe that all the success I have achieved throughout my professional life stems from my ability to connect with my staff at all levels, to keep my ear to the ground, and encourage people to speak up and express their views fearlessly.

Coming back to the bank's forays into networking, SBI was always the largest bank in most of the consortiums or multiple banking arrangements. Other banks like HDFC Bank were part of such consortiums but with smaller stakes. One of the senior executives at HDFC Bank once confided to me that their bank was happy at SBI taking the leadership in such consortiums and the rest of them just getting business for which they were paid a fee. Over time, private sector and public sector banks adopted contrasting models of handling corporate business. While public sector banks started pursuing funded business at competitive rates without paying any thought to the pricing of risk and capital management, private sector banks focused on fee-based business. HDFC Bank, as a matter of strategy, never took what is called a 'duration risk' and was conspicuously absent from project funding. On the other hand, ICICI Bank, because of its origin, was seen as a major player in project funding, among private sector banks, followed by Axis Bank.

A Time for Professional Commitment and Personal Catharsis

Meanwhile, my career graph at SBI was witnessing a slow but steady ascent. Finally, after an eight-year-long wait, I was promoted to the level of Deputy General Manager in 2004, after putting in 24 years of service. This was also a time for another reorganization at SBI. In 1995, the bank had created a commercial network under a General Manager, with just a few select branches to deal with the mid-sized corporates. The other General Manager at the bank was responsible for all other banking activities, including control over a vast number of widely distributed branches and 90 per cent of the manpower resources. This also led to constant friction between the two General Managers in many geographies, and the Chief General Manager had to step in, thereby wasting a lot of his time in sorting out issues of conflict between the two General Managers. Under the new structure, the bank decided to create a MCG directly under the corporate centre. The retail business and the branches were distributed equally between the two General Managers under the Chief General Manager Circle. Many of the commercial network branches were transferred to the MCG.

I was picked to perform one of the most important roles in the MCG at Mumbai, and was given the responsibility of managing a large portfolio of 500 accounts in Mumbai. As I took over this task, I noticed, for the first time, the entrepreneurial spirit of Mumbai and why it was called the 'financial capital of the country'. There were so many corporates here that had a success story to narrate, success that could be attributed, in large measure, to just having a presence in the city of Mumbai. Many of them had started small, taking an initial loan of merely Rs 1 lakh or 2 lakhs, and then had grown big with SBI's support. The list included a who's who of India's corporate bigwigs, such as Ajanta Pharma, Alok Industries, Asian Paints, Suzlon, and Bombay Rayon Fashions, to name only a few. All kinds of businesses including pharmaceutical, secondary steel producers, textile companies, and those engaged in diamond exports, were flourishing. It was a period of high growth for both professional business and personal ambitions. Investment too was surging ahead at a rapid pace. Acquiring an overseas business was the new buzzword, giving a boost to the market capitalization of many listed companies. Following in the footsteps of the Tatas and Birlas, many mid-corporates too started acquiring companies abroad without realizing that the labour laws and practices in Europe and America were very different from those in India. Many of these companies with overarching ambitions were thus led up the garden path, believing that they were buying a business at a throwaway price.

At a personal level, my happiness and professional satisfaction derived from my assignment in MCG were rudely shattered by a monumental family tragedy just a year later in 2005, which, without doubt, proved to be the darkest year of our lives. On 22 May 2005, we lost our younger daughter, who was a student of hotel management at the Manipal Academy. Devastated by this tragic loss, my wife and I slipped into deep depression, from which we were able to emerge only with the empathy and hand-holding of our close friends and relatives, who helped us to gradually rebuild our lives. But things have never been the same again, and the initial shock and grief have been replaced by a quiet and persistent sadness at the incomprehensible ways of destiny.

After about 30 months of my tenure as Deputy General Manager, MCG, it was again time for me to move on. I had spent an almost 15-year-long unbroken stretch in corporate credit. Now keen to return to retail banking, I requested for a posting as Deputy General Manager of a module. Providentially, the Deputy General Manager, Pune, was due for a change, and the Chief General Manager of Mumbai Circle, after some hesitation, decided to give me the job. The main reason for his initial reluctance was my lack of experience in retail banking, as my work in this field was limited to my three-year terms at the Ranikhet and Pilibhit branches of the bank, way back, from 1989 to 1991. An added attraction of the posting at Pune was the bungalow allotted to the Deputy General Manager of the bank there, which was counted amongst one of the best properties in Pune. In fact, at many parties and events associated with the bank, this bungalow became a reference point for my introduction.

The western part of Maharashtra, covering Pune, Kolhapur, Satara, Solapur, Ahmedabad, and Nasik, is the hub of economic activity. The city of Pune has thrived on its excellent educational infrastructure, leading to the emergence of both the IT industry as well as an automobile hub there. This also applies to the highly developed local agriculture sector, including that of horticulture, as even farmers in Pune are very progressive. I learnt this during one of my visits to Solapur, where I had the opportunity to meet a businessman called Vishwas Rao Kachare and to have lunch at his lavish farmhouse. I doubt that many industrialists would be able to own a comparable property in terms of both size and splendour. I found out that he had been an ordinary labourer, who through the sheer dint of his hard work and business acumen, had managed to become one of the largest producers of pomegranates in the western sector.

The region has also been home to several powerful and progressive politicians, who have actively promoted economic development and established many local colleges of excellence. Sharad Pawar, popularly known as 'Sahab', is venerated like a god in the region, with his photograph adorning almost every household I visited while in Pune.

Reorganization and Restructuring at the Bank

During this period, the bank was being led by O.P. Bhatt, who was an orator par excellence and could hold the staff spellbound with his speeches. Meanwhile, the implementation of core banking was in full swing. A study by McKinsey & Co had revealed that the bank had lost market share by putting branch expansion on hold. This spurred renewed activity in this area, with expansion suddenly becoming a top priority, manifested in the unrelenting pressure to open new bank branches. In the meantime, the central government announced a debt waiver. It was a massive project. I decided to use the services of a few excellent programmers on the rolls, who would facilitate complete automation of the entire process of debt waiver, and make it an error-free exercise. The initiative for this task was taken at the module level.

The bank also created a separate rural banking vertical, wherein the Circle Chief General Manager was required to report to two Deputy Managing Directors. The bank's guidelines for allowing business facilitators and business correspondents were also issued during this period. Baramati was chosen as the pilot district for implementing SBI's Business Correspondent and Business Facilitator model.

My stay as Deputy General Manager at Pune proved to be a short one, as the bank decided to discontinue the position of DGM, Module, under a reorganization plan. The announcement of such a plan came as a shock to everyone and there was huge all-round resistance to this change at the bank. I was due for promotion as General Manager, and was hoping to complete my stay at Pune, and move out from here only after being promoted. Since the position at which I had been posted here was discontinued, I was accorded a new designation as Officer on Special Duty (OSD). However, much to my chagrin, I soon realized that there cannot be a worse position than that of an OSD. The words of Rajeshwar Rao flashed in my mind, when he had warned that at times, one would feel unimportant in the bank. I decided at the time that I would never post any officer working under me as OSD at any branch of the bank, and stuck to this decision till I stepped down from office. For me, this also proved to be an important lesson about what happens in one's life and career when one is not occupying an important position in office, and it was virtually a primer on life after retirement. Despite the upheavals I faced following restructuring in the bank, however, my positions as DGM, Module and OSD offered me invaluable experience and the gumption to take many initiatives when I subsequently became Chairman.

Luckily, the travails of being an OSD were over soon, as I was promoted as General Manager, and was briefly given charge of the same network, which included the Pune and Nagpur areas. But it was just a stop-gap arrangement, as I was soon posted again, this time as Regional Head and CEO of bank's UK operations at London. It was a period of turmoil for economies all over the world. The global financial crisis of 2008 was almost at its zenith, when I landed in London on 28 February 2009. This overseas assignment, after my previous one at Toronto, was one of the few instances when the bank had posted an officer abroad a second time. A section of people in the bank were of the opinion that CEOs of the bank must have experience of working at international locations. This led to the decision, under the Chairmanship of Bhatt, to preferably post officers with previous work experience at overseas locations and to subsequently make them CEOs. I found it easy to transition into the role of the Regional Head and CEO of UK Operations, riding on my experience at the Toronto SBI branch nine years ago.

Revelling in Life and Work at London

I soon discovered that London, one of the world's topmost financial centres, thrives on networking. The Imperial Bank of India, predecessor to the SBI, had opened a branch in London City in 1921. I, along with my family, had last visited London in 1998 for a few days, and the city looked as charming now as it had in 1998. In contrast to the modern, well-planned structure of Toronto, London has an old-world charm. Further, the cities in Europe are very different from those in North America in design, architecture, and history.

My posting in London gave me an opportunity to travel across many cities of Europe. It is very difficult to say which city of Europe is more beautiful than others—London, Paris, Berlin, Vienna, Rome, Florence, Prague, Budapest—as each of them has its individual charm and tourist attractions. However, for me what made London score over the others is its language—like many fellow Indians, I found my ability to converse in English a boon when in London. Besides, the Indian businesses and diaspora were well entrenched in the UK. Reportedly, Tatas were the largest employer in the UK employing more than

50,000 employees. The city is also a favourite haunt for many film stars and industrial magnates. Among the leading Indian corporates, the Hinduja brothers, Laxmi Mittal, Anil Agarwal, and the Ruias all live in London in exorbitantly priced homes. At any given time, one can see many Indian film personalities roaming around in Washington Mayfair Hotel and at the Taj Hotels, with the former being a particular favourite for Indians visiting London because of its proximity to world famous Oxford Street. It was a matter of great pride and excitement for me to be able to live in St Johnswood, next door to the Lord's Cricket Ground. I could hear the noise emanating from most matches at the ground in my apartment. And to top it all, I had the opportunity to have lunch with none other than Sachin Tendulkar, during the Indian cricket team's trip to England while I was there. He was the brand ambassador of Lloyds Bank and I was seated at the same table as him. Sachin too gave me a lesson in humility, in diametrical contrast to the godly status he enjoys throughout India.

As I got to know the city more intimately after spending some time there, I learnt that there is a city of London within London, known popularly as the Square Mile, that houses the headquarters of many banks, law firms, and chartered accountant firms, apart from the historic London Wall, Guildhall, Bank of England, the grand St Paul's Church, Tower Bridge, and the Tower of London, among others. It also has its own mayor, known as the Lord Mayor, who is elected for a one-year term and assumes office in a grand ceremony. The Lord Mayor enjoys special status, and it is customary for him to host a banquet for the visiting heads of state. The CEO of SBI's UK operations is invariably an invitee to these banquets, which are eagerly looked forward to by one and all. Like all white-tie events, the banquets hosted by the Lord Mayor indicate the social standing of the guests, that is, whether they are titled, or members of the royal family, or enjoy some other high social status. As regards the CEO of the State Bank of India, this status was probably conferred upon this position because of the bank's presence in and around Guildhall for decades, which had made it an integral part of the city's social life. The British have kept all their traditions intact, and the infrastructure in the city too is supportive of all these traditions.

The first time I was invited to a major white-tie event in London was when the Lord Mayor hosted a banquet for the then President of India, Pratibha Patil on her visit to the UK. The invitation threw me into a dilemma, as I could not envisage missing the high-profile event but I was in no mood to spend 500 pounds to buy the requisite white tie suit for attending it. Much to my relief, I found a solution as I came to know that many shops in the city offer these suits on hire for 85 pounds, which too is not a small amount but preferable any day to the small fortune that a new suit costs. Many invitees prefer to hire the suits which come into use only on a few select occasions. Besides, the tail coat looks a bit awkward, particularly on a short person. It's also a tricky business to dress up in a white tie. In comparison, a tuxedo (black tie) is a much simpler affair!

President Patil's visit became memorable for me for another reason, offering me, as it did, an opportunity to attend a high tea hosted by the Queen at Buckingham Palace for select Indians in honour of the visiting Indian President. It goes without saying how excited I was to visit Buckingham Palace and be introduced to the Queen. All the guests first assembled in a big hall and the highlight of the evening was a performance of dances from Hindi films by a local Indian troupe. Later on, all the guests were received one by one at another entrance inside the main room by the Queen and Prince Philip. As part of the protocol, the names of all the guests are announced by an usher, and the Queen has a brief word or two with each one of them. Subsequently, during the course of the event, she makes it a point to meet all invitees individually and have a brief conversation with them. I was really impressed by the professional manner in which the entire event was conducted and the courtesies extended to the guests. We, in India, may have learnt many other things from the British but I wish we had also learnt from them how to preserve our traditions and culture with such dignity and decorum.

The social revelry in the city, however, failed to mask how drastically the financial crisis of 2008 had shaken the foundation of the City of London as a financial centre. London had earned its status as the number one financial centre in Europe due to many of its qualities and practices, including its practical and progressive legal framework; its feather-touch approach to banking regulation; the availability of top-class talent in the fields of law, accounting, banking and finance; access to a highly developed infrastructure, which in turn, attracted global talent; and above all, the dominance of English as a global language. But, during the global financial crisis, the Financial Services Authority (FSA), responsible for regulating the financial system, had to face huge criticism over bank failures. Bankers were subjected to derision and ridicule, and the high compensation structure of the top executives of the bank came under severe public criticism. It also became quite evident that the Basel framework had several inadequacies, particularly the absence of norms relating to liquidity management, and needed to be revamped.

There has always been a history of tension between the City of London (the Square Mile) and the lawmakers. The two have some sort of a love-hate relationship. This could be because the City of London was a major contributor to the prosperity of London but its influence and affluence probably fomented jealousies outside. The 2008 financial crisis provided an opportunity for people harbouring 'anti-City' feelings to strike back, and the outcome was the enactment of several laws, which led to the curtailment of bonuses paid to staff of financial institutions, and abolition of the Financial Services Authority. It also resulted in the creation of a Prudential Regulation Authority (PRA) and making the Financial Conduct Authority (FCA) responsible for the conduct of financial entities. Another far-reaching change brought about by the crisis was ring-fencing of the retail banking business in the UK, as recommended by the Independent Commission on Banking under the chairmanship of John Vickers.

A Wave of Innovation and Expansion at the Bank

Events at SBI were, however, taking a somewhat different turn. While the world was grappling with the financial crisis, the bank's CEO, Bhatt was keen on expanding SBI's international footprint. Hence, McKinsey & Co was hired again to prepare a strategy for international expansion. It was decided that retail banking in some of the geographies would be synchronized with the marketing of localized products. The bank had not been able to establish any significant presence in any country outside India. It was thus a giant in India but a pygmy in many of the overseas locations where it was operating. This could be attributed to several limitations faced by the bank, including a weak currency, relatively small size of the Indian economy and international trade, inadequacy of scale, lack of access to the latest technology, and inability to create a niche market for itself. As part of the strategy recommended by McKinsey & Co, many new offices of the bank were established keeping in view the importance of bilateral relations between India and other countries, rather than based purely on commercial considerations or business opportunities. Ironically, opening a foreign office was easier than closing one, which the bank realized some years later when it decided to rationalize its international operations!

From London to Guwahati—Office Politics at Play

I returned to India in April 2012 after three years of stay in London where I had laid the foundation of a relatively successful expansion of the retail banking business. The first call I received after landing in Delhi was from the Chief General Manager, HR, of the bank. He told me to report immediately at Guwahati Local Head Office (LHO) as Chief General Manager. Guwahati LHO covers branches in the seven states of the North-east. Although I was initially taken aback by this development, I was happy that I would at least have the opportunity to lead a circle, which is, in many ways, better than being posted at the corporate centre. But for my peers, it was a sign that I had fallen out of favour, and one of the Chief General Managers who was heading another local head office was candid enough to mention it directly to my face. His observation was not completely untrue. At least two Chairmen of the bank, A.K. Purwar and Bhatt had served in the North-east in different capacities, and both were out of favour of their superiors when they were posted to the North-east. At junior levels too, officers posted to the North-east would try hard to get their postings cancelled. Some of the issues that put people off from serving in the region were its lack of development, poor telecommunication and geographical connectivity, and law and order issues. However, these stereotyped images of the North-east were contrary to the reality. They did not take into account certain subsequent developments that had actually taken place in the states. For instance, air and road connectivity had improved tremendously, with Guwahati becoming one of the busiest airports in the country. Although extremist activities were still rife in certain pockets of the region like East Garo Hills, Bodoland, and parts of Manipur and Nagaland, most of the North-east was now, by and large, peaceful.

Within a few days of reporting at Guwahati, I realized, much to my relief, that the situation on the ground was much better than what it was perceived to be outside of the region. The state of Assam had become relatively peaceful under the septuagenarian Chief Minister, Tarun Gogoi, who was immensely popular at the time. The Guwahati–Shillong Road (popularly known as GS Road) had such a shopping hub that it could be compared to the South Extension market in New Delhi. Nature had also showered its bounties on the state in abundance. The picturesque drives from Guwahati to Tawang, Aizawl to Silchar, Dimapur to Kohima, and Guwahati to Kaziranga were mesmerizing enough to take one's breath away. Local politicians and bureaucrats, including chief ministers and chief secretaries of all the states were all very accessible to the common people and could be approached informally. Even the local people are generally of a docile nature, making me wonder how they could ever take up arms and resort to militancy. I also quickly realized that the staff in the bank at Guwahati were sincere but could not be pushed beyond a point. They work at their own pace (called '*lahe lahe*' in local parlance) but are very simple and committed. All these unique characteristics of the region allowed me to forge a strong bond with the North-east during the 18 months I spent there. Later, when I was promoted to the top post at the bank, the highest number of congratulatory messages I received were from the people I had befriended and interacted with during my posting at Guwahati, all of whom treated me as one of them. Deeply committed to this bond, I always remained accessible to the people of the North-east even after becoming the Chairman of the bank.

As a city, Guwahati has the dual attraction of a unique culture and a diverse geography. The mighty Brahmaputra, the only river considered to be a male river, popularly believed to be the son of Brahma, the creator, flows through Guwahati. The city's Kamakhya Temple, dedicated to mother goddess Kamakhya, is one of the oldest of the 51 *Shakti Peeth*s in the country. According to the *Kalika Purana*, Kamakhya Temple was built at the place where the genitals of Sati fell after Lord Shiva danced with her corpse. Apart from being replete with tourist spots, the North-east is also known to be culturally very advanced. Thus, I consider myself really fortunate to have been posted in the region, and irrespective of the negative perceptions of my colleagues, I will always carry fond memories of my 18-month-long stay in Guwahati.

Rise of Women Power in Indian Banking

For me, it was a welcome change that Arundhati Bhattacharya took over as Chairperson of SBI in October 2013. In the over 200-year-long history of the bank, Bhattacharya was the first woman to become its chairman—she preferred to be addressed as such, not as the 'chairperson'. Within a few days of her taking over, I was transferred as the Chief General Manager, Project Finance, because the new chairperson felt that my skills would be best utilized in a credit-related role. I performed this role during a brief tenure of just 10 months from October 2013 to August 2014. Thereafter, on my promotion as the Deputy Managing Director, I was appointed as the Managing Director, SBI Capital Markets, where I remained till 26 May 2015, the date when I was appointed as Managing Director in the bank.

With the appointment of Bhattacharya, it became a triumvirate with Chanda Kochhar and Shikha Sharma who dominated the banking in India for several years till 2018. All were charismatic leaders in their own way and it is rather sad that currently none of the banks in the public or private sector is headed by a woman leader.

Trajectory of My Career Back on Track

As with my past promotions, my appointment as Managing Director too began with a hitch. My first round of interview was with the then Secretary, DFS who was chairing the interview board. Before my appointment could be finalized, there was a change at the helm of affairs, with Adhia taking over as the Secretary, DFS, and it was decided to hold my interview again. The position of the Managing Director had fallen vacant in October 2014, but my appointment was finalized only after a gap of nine months. It was an extended period of anxiety for me, with my emotions and expectations alternating between hope and despair during those nine long months. One positive action by the government after the constitution of the banking board has been the declaration of the results on the same day of holding of the interviews. I earnestly wish that this process could also be streamlined for appointments to ensure their timely implementation. Unfortunately, till date, there is no concept of succession planning in public sector banks, and positions at the level of the ED/CMD often remain vacant for months together.

As regards the appointment of the Chairman of SBI, however, the effort has always been to declare the appointment closer to the date when the term of the outgoing Chairman is scheduled to end. The Banking Board Bureau has adopted a commendable practice of declaring the name of the successful candidate on the date of the interview itself. At the time of selection of Arundhati Bhattacharya's successor, the interviews were held well in advance in July 2017. But the Banking Board Bureau decided to keep the name of the successful candidate a secret and announced it only after a four-month-long wait on 3 October 2017. The probable reason for this delay could be that declaring the name of the appointee so much in advance could dilute the authority of the existing incumbent. This policy is in contrast to the succession planning executed in private sector organizations, where the process of identifying the top official's successor starts at least a year in advance. All this highlights the urgent need to re-look at the entire process of selection of full-time directors, chairmen, and government nominees as well as the compensation structure of key management personnel in public sector banks, failing which it would be difficult for these banks to become competitive and survive in a tough environment.

Before taking over as the Chairman of SBI, I had already spent about two-and-a-half years as Managing Director. Initially, for six months, I had been overseeing compliance and was scheduled to take over as the Managing Director, Commercial Banking on the retirement of the incumbent, Pradeep Kumar in October 2015, as had been promised to me by the then Chairman. However, there was a last moment change in this decision, and I was asked to take charge of the National Banking Group, which handles the retail banking business of the bank, covering 22,500 branches, 95 per cent of the liabilities and around 45 per cent of the loan book, and all the alternate channels including Internet and mobile banking. I later came to know that B. Sriram, who was Managing Director, National Banking, at the time, had been quite keen to handle commercial banking in order to improve his profile, which led to this last-minute change in allocation of duties.

Since I had spent a large part of my career in corporate banking, this change at the eleventh hour did not affect me unduly and I readily accepted the new responsibility assigned to me. In retrospect, I can say that working in that position proved to be of immense benefit for me, as during my tenure, many far-reaching policy changes were initiated. These included the approach to lending to SMEs, which had earlier come to a halt because of perpetration of frauds and a high incidence of NPLs, as well as other matters concerning customer service and digitization, all of which I was able to take further when I became the Chairman of the bank.

Retirement

The day finally dawned—6 October 2020, the day when I completed my three-year term at SBI. After being at the helm of the bank for three years and a devoted employee for more than three decades, it was finally time for me to say goodbye to my beloved organization. However, my satisfaction at rendering long years of service to the bank was tempered by the sadness I felt at the pain and suffering that our workforce faced at the hands of the raging pandemic. However, as one team, we had been able to wade and navigate through the worst phase. Although the restoration of normalcy was still a distant hope, I could take some solace from the fact that we had managed to strike a fine balance between employee well-being, operational priorities, and discharging our duty towards the nation and communities at large. And I was leaving with a sense of fulfilment as I had been able to not only bring many of my hopes and aspirations for the bank to their logical culmination but also to offer to my colleagues a human touch and a caring environment that would sustain even when I was no longer there at the bank. This was the best retirement gift that I could have hoped for.

Appendix I

The Enron Dabhol Power Project[1]

The Supreme Court closes cases of alleged corruption involving politicians, bureaucrats, and corporates in the Enron-Dabhol power project, noting the inordinate delay in the case which was filed in 1997. The apex court had, in 1997, admitted the petition of the Centre for Indian Trade Union (CITU) challenging a Bombay High Court order upholding the Power Purchase Agreement (PPA).[2]

The Dabhol mega power project, worth US$3 billion, was set up in Maharashtra by the Dabhol Power Company (DPC), a subsidiary of Enron, incorporated in India with ownership of 80 per cent by Enron and 10 per cent each by GE and Bechtel. The DPC was intended to build a naphtha- and LNG-based thermal power plant in Maharashtra on a Build, Own, and Operate Basis. GE provided the generating turbines to DPC, Bechtel constructed the physical plant, and Enron was assigned the task of managing the project through Enron International.

In December 1993, DPC and Enron Group entered into a PPA with the Maharashtra State Electricity Board (MSEB) for the generation of 2015 MW of power. As per the agreement, MSEB was to pay both the capacity charges (based on availability) and the energy charges. The cost of fuel was also passed on to MSEB. Enron Fuels International was appointed as the fuel manager and was responsible for identifying the least cost fuel supplier. While MSEB exercised control on this process, DPC needed the MSEB's approval for these fuel purchase contracts. The project also had an integrated Liquefied Natural Gas (LNG) terminal with a regasification facility.

Enron's pre-contract estimate of the 'all in' tariff (the cost per unit taking into account both the capacity and energy charges, assuming a power dispatch at 90 per cent of the plant capacity) had been 6.91 US cents/kWh (equivalent to Rs 2.07/kWh at that time). By April 1993, this was adjusted to make the estimate Rs 2.45/kWh. However, the tariff was subject to a number of variables, including the price of fuel, the rupee–US$ exchange rate, and the level of dispatch required by the MSEB. The payment obligations of MSEB were guaranteed by both the Government of Maharashtra and, subject to a cap of roughly US$300 million, by the Central Government.

In February 1996, Maharashtra and Enron announced a new agreement, with the following contours and terms of reference:

- Enron was to cut the price of the power by over 20 per cent and the total capital costs from US$2.8 billion to US$2.5 billion,
- DPC's output would increase from 2015 MW to 2184 MW.
- There would be a sale of 30 per cent equity interest in the project by Enron to an MSEB affiliate for US$137 million, reducing Enron's interest in DPC to 50 per cent. MSEB's 30 per cent interest was subsequently diluted to roughly 15 per cent upon its failure to contribute to further equity investments.
- Both parties committed formally to develop the second phase of the project. The first phase achieved the Commercial

Operation Date in May 1999, almost two years behind schedule, and construction was started on Phase II of the project. All these delays led to an increase in the cost of the project to US$3 billion.

By July 2000, MSEB was being charged a tariff of about Rs 7.80/kWh due to the high prices of naphtha and the non-availability of LNG, signifying a more than three-fold increase in the pre-contract projections. Meanwhile, in view of the skyrocketing costs, MSEB stopped making payments to DPC, whereafter DPC sent MSEB a notice of arbitration in May 2001. By late 2001, DPC and Enron Group had run into financial and other difficulties, and they could not continue operation of the plant.

The various roadblocks in its implementation indicate that the project has faced issues like poor financial health of the promoter, increase in project costs, delays in organizing the LNG facility, non-availability of fuel, and a PPA counter-party dishonouring its commitment to the project, all of which led to the closure of DPC, and it was placed under the control of a Receiver appointed by the High Court of Bombay.[3]

The Government of India and the Government of Maharashtra considered various alternatives to revive DPC in view of the huge investments that had already been made in the project. Ultimately, in July 2005, Ratnagiri Gas and Power Pvt. Ltd (RGPPL), an SPV, took over the project. RGPPL had shareholdings from several leading public sector organizations, including the National Thermal Power Corporation (NTPC), Gas Authority of India Limited (GAIL), various financial institutions, and the State Electricity Utility of Maharashtra. On 6 October 2005, the assets of the 1967.08 MW project, along with the LNG terminal of 5 MMTPA and the associated infrastructure facilities, were taken over by the RGPPL. While NTPC was entrusted with the responsibility of running the power plants, GAIL was made in charge of managing the gas-related infrastructure and supply of gas.

During the period October 2006 to July 2007, the Central Commission approved[4] tariff for sale of infirm power from the generating station utilizing liquid fuel from time to time. In 2007, the distribution licensee executed a PPA including the terms for determining the tariff consistent and the scheme for revival of the project was finalized.

The project had a PPA of 95 per cent of its capacity with the Maharashtra State Electricity Distribution Company Limited (MSEDCL), and 2 per cent each with the Union Territories of Dadra & Nagar Haveli and Daman & Diu, and of 1 per cent with the Electricity Department of Goa. RGPPL was allocated gas from the KG D6 block of Reliance Industries Limited (RIL) and the marginal gas fields of the Oil and Natural Gas Corporation Limited (ONGC).

In the meantime, MSEDCL had wriggled out of the 'Take or Pay' agreement and refused to buy power from Reliance Gas Pipelines Limited (RGPL) on technical grounds. The fact was that because of the increase in the price of gas, the tariff was working out to be much higher than that of coal-based thermal power plants and there was no way that MSEDCL could pass on such a high tariff to its end-consumers.

Hectic efforts were thus made to resolve the issue in the year 2014. The main proposal was to demerge the company into two, with plans for the power company to be owned and managed by NTPC, and the port and the LNG infrastructure to be managed by GAIL. However, NTPC was strictly opposed to this and a meeting between the then chairman of SBI, Arundhati Bhattacharya, and Chairman, NTPC, Arup Roy Choudhary, had ended in a deadlock. NTPC always felt that they would not be able to run the power plant and would be saddled with a huge liability if they agreed to manage the plant. In an attempt to break the deadlock, I requested for a meeting with the NTPC Chairman as a last-ditch effort to save the deal. SBI Capital Markets prepared a demerger scheme, according to which the shareholding pattern in the demerged entities was kept identical to the shareholding pattern in the existing company. I met I.J. Kapur, Director, Technical, at NTPC, and was able to convince him that the proposed demerger scheme was not detrimental to the interests of NTPC, because no change was proposed in the shareholding pattern. It was a forward movement but the road ahead was not an easy one, mainly because of the involvement of so many players, including NTPC, GAIL, MSEDCL, the Government of Maharashtra, the Indian Railways, lenders, and various regulatory commissions. But for an effective intervention by the Prime Minister's Office (PMO), there was little chance of the mess around RGPPL being resolved. Following are details of the proposed demerger scheme of Dabhol power plant.

Demerger of the Power and R-LNG Blocks (2016–18)[5]

- The demerger of the power plant and the R-LNG terminal was envisaged for resolution of funding constraints for carving out a sustainable debt, in order to achieve value creation and a dedicated focus.
- The key aspects of the demerger scheme were

    a) hiving off of the R-LNG terminal assets into separate SPVs, that is, Konkan LNG Private Limited or KLPL, with mirror shareholding as RGPPL;
    b) transfer of the debt of Rs 3310 crore out of a total debt of Rs 8907 crore to R-LNG SPV, with the balance remaining in RGPPL;
    c) retaining a debt of Rs 5597 crore in RGPPL, comprising an unsustainable debt of Rs 3697 crore, which was to be converted into 0.01 per cent Cumulative Redeemable Preference Shares (CRPSs);
    d) refinancing of the sustainable debt in KLPL and RGPPL, based on the 5/25 scheme of the RBI; and

e) proposal of an investment plan of Rs 2519 crore in KLPL, to be funded through a mix of debt and equity in the ratio 1:1, under the 5/25 scheme.

The sequence of events post the proposal for the demerger scheme and its implementation was as follows:

- KLPL was incorporated in December 2015 as a wholly owned subsidiary of RGPPL.
- The demerger scheme of RGPPL was approved by the National Company Law Appellate Tribunal (NCLAT) vide an order dated 28 February 2018, with the appointed date being 1 January 2016, thereby transferring the LNG undertaking from RGPPL to KLPL.
- The demerger scheme came into being with effect from 26 March 2018. Accordingly, the LNG business and all its associated assets and liabilities have been transferred to KLPL by RGPPL, with a mirror shareholding as of RGPPL.

Post Demerger (2018–21)

- As per the Demerger Business Plan of RGPPL, the CRPS against the unsustainable portion of loan of Rs 3696.68 crore was offered to lenders in August 2018.
- However, Canara Bank withdrew from the 5/25 scheme (including the conversion of debt into CRPS), and sought a fresh resolution plan under the revised framework of the RBI for resolution of the stressed assets.
- Canara Bank did not agree to the lenders' views and filed a petition in September 2018 before the NCLT for initiating the corporate insolvency resolution process under IBC.
- NCLT was not inclined to entertain Canara Bank's petition at this stage as per the interim order of the Supreme Court to maintain status quo in the case of the RBI circular dated 12

February 2018, and dismissed Canara Bank's petition as non-maintainable at this stage.

- The Supreme Court pronounced its order on 2 April 2019 wherein it declared the RBI circular dated 12 February 2018 as *ultra vires* as a whole, having no effect in law.
- Subsequently, in August 2019, RGPPL issued CRPSs of Rs 3695.12 crore to lenders, including Canara Bank, for the portion of unsustainable debt.

Resolution—Consensus Building

- Post the demerger due to cross-holding and promoter issues, the Power and R-LNG blocks were not operating at optimal levels, and a long-term solution to the power block was not forthcoming.
- It was thus decided to adopt a focused approach on KLPL (the R-LNG block) by mandating 100 per cent control by GAIL and on RGPPL's power block by NTPC.
- It was decided to swap the cross-holdings of GAIL in the RGPPL power block and NTPC in KLPL's R-LNG block. However, this could not be achieved due to valuation issues.
- Various meetings were held between the promoters, including GAIL and NTPC, representatives of the Government of India and lenders to resolve the issues.

    - *One-time Settlement of KLPL*: In March 2020, KLPL completed a one-time settlement of debt with the lenders by paying a consideration of Rs 2700 crore to settle the outstanding dues, including debt and outstanding interest, of Rs 3813.07 crore. The lenders also transferred their entire existing equity shares of KLPL, amounting to Rs 1194.41 crore, in favour of GAIL on 27 March 2020.

- *One-time Settlement of RGPPL*: In December 2020, RGPPL completed a one-time settlement of debt with the lenders by paying a consideration of Rs 890 crore to settle the outstanding dues. The lenders also transferred their entire equity stake of 35.47 per cent in RGPPL in favour of NTPC on 31 December 2020. All the tranches of CRPS were redeemed as on 31 December 2020.
- *Share-Purchase Agreement*: On 24 February 2021, GAIL and NTPC executed the share-purchase agreement through which GAIL acquired the entire shareholding of NTPC in KLPL and NTPC acquired the entire shareholding of GAIL in RGPPL.

These proposals and demergers brought an end to the saga of the ill-fated Dabhol power plant. An assessment of the entire course of events in this episode indicates that the only fault which could be attributed to lenders is that they supported an important project at a time when the Indian economy was just opening up and the country, suffering huge power shortages as it was, was not ready for such an ambitious project that could derail the entire reform process.

The Fate of Ultra Mega Power Projects in Gujarat: Another Misadventure

Background—Plant Set-up and PPA History

(i) *Tata Power Mundra Plant (4150 MW)*: Pursuant to the Government of India's policy on Ultra Mega Power Projects (UMPP) formulated in 2005–2006, bids were invited for the development of two UMPPs—one based on imported coal and another based on captive coal. These UMPPs were to be awarded to the developers as part of the tariff-based competitive bidding route, under Section 63 of the

Electricity Act, 2003. As part of this initiative, the Mundra UMPP, based on imported coal, was awarded to the Tata Group, which acquired the shareholding of Coastal Gujarat Power Limited (CGPL). Thereafter, CGPL executed the PPA with the states of Gujarat (1805 MW), Maharashtra (760 MW), Haryana (380 MW), Punjab (475 MW), and Rajasthan (380 MW) in April 2007.

(ii) *Adani Power Mundra plant (4620 MW)*: In the year 2006–2007, Gujarat Urja Vikas Nigam Limited (GUVNL) invited bids for the supply of power under the long-term PPAs. Following the tenders floated by GUVNL, Adani Power Limited (APL) was selected for supplying 2000 MW, that is, 1000 MW each under Bid 01 and Bid 02. The PPA under Bid 01 was based on imported coal. The 1000 MW PPA under Bid 02, on the other hand, was based on a commitment from Gujarat Mineral Development Corporation (GMDC) for the supply of coal from the Morga-II coal block. However, in view of the non-execution of the Fuel Supply Agreements (FSAs) by GMDC, APL had to resort to an alternate arrangement, depending upon imported coal from Indonesia. It was envisaged that APL would set up its 4620 MW Mundra plant in four phases, including 4x330 MW in Phases I and II, 2x660 MW in Phase III, and 3x660 MW in Phase IV, in the Kutch district of Gujarat. The 1980 MW Phase IV project has a tie-up with Mahanadi Coalfields Limited (MCL) for the provision of 6.4 MTPA, or 70 per cent of the total capacity of the Phase IV project.

In 2006, Haryana Power Generation Corporation Limited (HPGCL) invited bids for the procurement of 2000 MW of power under the long term PPA in terms of the Case 1 model of the then existing Competitive Bidding Guidelines. Following the tenders floated by HPGCL, APL was selected to supply 1424 MW for this plant from its Phase IV project.

APL entered into two PPAs of 1000 MW each with GUVNL in February 2007, and two other PPAs of 712 MW each with Uttar Haryana Bijli Vitran Nigam (UHBVN) and Dakshin Haryana Bijli Vitran Nigam (DHBVN) in August 2008.

(iii) *Essar Power Salaya Plant (1200 MW)*: Essar Power Gujarat Limited (EPGL) was selected to supply 1000 MW of power, under Bid 03, from its 1200 MW (2x600 MW) thermal power plant located in the Salaya district of Jamnagar, Gujarat. Consequently, EPGL executed a PPA with GUVNL in February 2007 for the provision of 1000 MW of electricity.

PPA Tariff Premise and Dependence on Indonesian Coal

The tariffs quoted by CGPL, APL, and EPGL in their respective bids, were predominantly based on the usage of imported coal from Indonesia. Coal supply from Indonesia was available in a certain price range, keeping in view the past as well as the then prevailing market trends pertaining to imported coal pricing in Indonesia over the past 40 years. Further, the coal supplies from Indonesia were found to be competitive as compared to the other sources due to comparatively lower ocean transportation costs. Therefore, these companies tied up for the receipt of their coal supplies from Indonesia. APL also acquired a small mine (Bunyu) in Indonesia whereas Tata Power acquired a 30 per cent stake in large Indonesian coal mines.

Change in Indonesian Regulations

In 2010, the Indonesian government effected significant regulatory changes in coal pricing for the calculation of export and royalty/tax. As per the new regulations, Indonesian coal was to be exported only at global benchmark prices. This policy change by the Indonesian government had a direct impact on the financial viability and sustainability of the projects in India that were based on the use of Indonesian coal as fuel. Further, coal prices also increased in the other countries exporting it, notably Australia and South Africa, thereby making it financially unviable to import coal from such alternate sources too.

These changes in the pricing methodology came into effect in September 2011. The Indonesian government further directed that all the existing supply agreements with Indonesian mining firms would also be brought in line with this new benchmark by September 2011. The prices that had initially been agreed upon for these projects in the FSAs thus had to be revised and aligned with the new benchmark prices linked to the coal price indices, as per the directions of the Government of Indonesia.

In view of these radical changes in Indonesia, several planned thermal projects in India, such as the Krishnapatnam UMPP and the Salaya Phase II project, which were intended to be based on the use of Indonesian coal as fuel, had to be abandoned. Consequently, the project generators started incurring huge losses in the process of supplying power under their PPAs.

Regulatory Process Post-2011 till the Energy Watchdog Judgment of April 2017

In 2011, APL and CGPL approached the Central Electricity Regulatory Commission (CERC), seeking relief for these unforeseen events, under the terms of the PPA. Since EPGL was supplying only to GUVNL under a long-term PPA, it approached the Gujarat Electricity Regulatory Commission (GERC) in 2012. The claims before the CERC were primarily based on assertions of 'Change in the Law' and/or Force Majeure, as per the provisions of the PPA. Following is a brief overview of the regulatory process and the sequence of events under it:

- *The CERC Order of April 2013*: Through its orders dated 2 April 2013 and 15 April 2013, the CERC refused to grant relief based on the PPA provisions on Force Majeure or

'Change in Law', to APL and CGPL, respectively. However, it directed that a committee should be formed to recommend compensatory tariff for APL and CGPL through a consultative process.[6]

- *Constitution of the Deepak Parekh Committee*: This committee was formed by the Government of Gujarat following the above-mentioned directions of CERC. The committee was formed with the distribution companies, APL and CGPL, and the respective State governments, along with an independent financial analyst of repute, for which SBI CAPS and Devi Singh, Director, Indian Institute of Management, Lucknow, were appointed. The committee was headed by eminent banker, Deepak Parekh. In its report of August 2013,[7] the committee also recommended the application of an appropriate methodology for computing the compensatory tariff package.
- *The CERC Order of February 2014:* In consideration of the recommendations made by the Deepak Parekh Committee, CERC passed an order on 21 February 2014, delineating the formula as per which compensatory tariff was to be granted as a relief to counter the hardships caused by the increase in coal prices due to the change in the Indonesian legal regime. CERC passed this order under its special regulatory powers, as defined in Section 79 of the Electricity Act.[8]
- *Appeal before the Appellate Tribunal for Electricity (APTEL)*: Aggrieved by the order passed by the CERC, GUVNL, the Haryana distribution companies, and the consumer representative groups appealed before APTEL.
- *APTEL Order of April 2016*: Following the above appeal, APTEL passed a final order on 7 April 2016 setting aside the orders passed by CERC under Section 79. It also postulated that no relief could be offered under the 'Change in Law' provision of the PPAs. However, APTEL held that the promulgation of the Indonesian law resulting in an

unprecedented enhancement in the cost of imported coal, constitutes a Force Majeure event. Accordingly, APTEL directed CERC to compute compensation payable to the generating companies concerned with the affected projects under the Force Majeure provision of PPAs.[9]

- *The CERC Order of December 2016*: CERC passed an order on 6 December 2016 granting relief to the concerned parties under the Force Majeure provisions of the PPA, as directed by APTEL.[10]
- *Appeal in the Supreme Court*: Aggrieved by the directions issued by APTEL, the consumer representative groups, that is, Energy Watchdog and the energy group Prayas, along with the distribution companies, amongst others, filed appeals before the Supreme Court.
- *Supreme Court Order of April 2017 (Energy Watchdog Judgment)*: The Supreme Court passed the Energy Watchdog Judgment on 11 April 2017, findings of which are given in subsequent paragraphs.

Formation of a Working Group

Subsequently, the Government of Gujarat referred the matter to the Government of India, seeking timely resolution of the problems being faced by the generating companies, as well as the procurer states and the lenders. Thereafter, the Ministry of Power convened a meeting of the lenders, developers, and officials of the procurer states on 20 June 2017 to discuss options for resolving the financial distress being faced by the generating companies.

It was decided at this meeting that a Working Group would be constituted to evaluate and recommend options for ensuring the sustained operation of the projects. The Working Group consisted of all members of the procurer states and lenders represented by Punjab National Bank and Canara Bank, with SBI acting as a convener of the Group.

The final report prepared[11] by the Working Group, after carrying out discussions and deliberations over a course of meetings, was circulated by SBI on 10 January 2018. SBI also submitted a request for the constitution of a High Power Committee (HPC) to review the report and make recommendations for resolving these issues.

Formation of a High Power Committee

The Government of Gujarat approached the Government of India, seeking coordination of the process of resolution of issues related to power projects based on the use of imported coal. Responding to this, the Government of India issued a letter dated 13 April 2018, wherein it granted the Government of Gujarat in its capacity as the lead procurer in the three imported coal projects based in Gujarat, liberty to examine the issues in detail and take further action for their resolution.[12]

The Government of Gujarat then constituted the HPC through its Energy and Petrochemicals Department. R.K. Agrawal, a retired judge of the Supreme Court of India was appointed as the Chairman of the Committee, while S.S. Mundra, former Deputy Governor, RBI, and Pramod Deo, former Chairman, CERC, were the other two members of the HPC. Post its constitution, the HPC held meetings on the issue at stake with lenders, procurers, State government officials, and consumer representative groups. The Committee submitted its report to GUVNL on 3 October 2018.[13]

All the stakeholders, particularly the procurers and consumer representative groups, were of the view that any resolution process should be finalized only after considering the interests of all the stakeholders. Thus, after carefully examining and analysing the views and suggestions of all the stakeholders, the HPC arrived at a solution aiming to ensure a balance of equities for all the stakeholders. The contours of the resolution package suggested by the HPC are discussed in detail below.

Contours of the HPC's Resolution Package

- *Fuel Cost*: The fuel cost was to be made fully pass-through on a landed cost basis. It was proposed that there should be a ceiling on the coal price, with a stipulation to cap the Free on Board (FOB) coal cost at an HBA[14] of US$110/tonne of coal. This cap was to be reviewed after every five years.
- *Lenders' Sacrifice*: It was recommended to reduce the capacity charge by 20 paise per unit in all three projects. This was done to bring overall tariff down after permitting fuel cost as pass-through. Lenders were expected to reduce the debt to accommodate a discount of 20 paise/unit discount in the capacity charge. The following was an estimation of the debt reduction for the various stakeholders:

  - CGPL—Rs 4,240 crore;
  - APL—Rs 3,821 crore; and
  - EPGL—Rs 1,154 crore.

However, it was estimated that the lenders' sacrifice could be higher for EPGL as they might have had to reduce the outstanding debt, as on 31 March 2018, by around Rs 2,324 crore, excluding the undisbursed loan of Rs 250 crore, in order to make the debt sustainable after implementation of this scheme. Over and above this, there was an invoked Bank Guarantee (BG) of Rs 250 crore and devolved Letters of Credit (LCs) of Rs 481 crore.

- Further, the lenders would also need to reduce the interest rate in the projects.

- *Developers' Offerings*: The promoters were expected to sacrifice their past losses up to the cut-off date of 15 October 2018. In addition, the developers were urged to share the profits accruing to them from the mines owned by them in Indonesia. The developers were also asked to increase the plant availability threshold to 90 per cent and offer an extension of the PPA tenor by ten years.

Developments Post-HPC Report Submission

GUVNL filed a petition in the Supreme Court seeking clarity on the amendment of the PPA as per the HPC's recommendations while keeping in view the earlier Energy Watchdog judgment dated 11 April 2017. The Supreme Court, vide its order dated 29 October 2018, permitted the procurers to approach CERC for adoption of the HPC recommendations and also noted that such a proposed amendment shall not be in contravention of its previous judgment.[15]

After the Supreme Court judgment, GUVNL executed Supplemental PPA (SPPA) with Adani Power Mundra Limited for both the PPAs (Phase I/II and Phase III). Then, GUVNL filed a petition with CERC for approval of these SPPAs. CERC in its order[16] dated 12 April 2019 approved the changes suggested in SPPA to be effective from 15 October 2018.

Adani Power had filed a petition in the Supreme Court for termination of the PPA for Phase III of the project (1000 MW) with GUVNL, citing the absence of a FSA with GMDC. Thereafter, the Supreme Court passed an order on 2 July 2019, stating that the validity of the PPA stood terminated with effect from 4 January 2010, thereby allowing the company to approach CERC for determination of a compensatory tariff (including interest on delays in making the payment), payable to it from the date of supply of electricity by it to GUVNL.[17]

In response to this order, GUVNL discontinued scheduling or power offtake during Phase III of the project with effect from 10 July 2019, and filed a review petition with the Supreme Court on 29 July 2019, requesting the latter to review its earlier decision on cancellation of both the PPA and the SPPA. This review petition of GUVNL was, however, dismissed by the Supreme Court for Bid II PPA cancellation vide its order dated 3 September 2019.[18]

Apart from its review petition before the Supreme Court, GUVNL also filed a petition with CERC on 1 August 2019, for recalling its order dated 12 April 2019, which allowed approval of the SPPA for Phases I, II, and III of the project.[19] Meanwhile, GUVNL issued an appeal that the SPPAs signed as per the HPC recommendations should be declared as void and not enforceable. Further, GUVNL made the plea that APL had breached the SPPA terms when it proceeded to claim relief for the past period up to 14 October 2018 as per the Supreme Court Order dated 2 July 2019. Accordingly, GUVNL has sought refund of the principal amount it had paid as per the SPPA, with interest.

In response, the company wrote a letter to GUVNL to offer power at the applicable tariff under the SPPA dated 5 December 2018. The company also filed a petition with CERC for compensation under Section 62 for Bid II PPA on 2 September 2019. Presently, the company is selling power on a merchant/bilateral basis for Phase III of the project.

- *Essar Power Salaya Plant (1200 MW)*: As per the recommendations of the HPC, EPGL signed an SPPA with GUVNL on 1 March 2019, and subsequently GUVNL approached GERC for approval of the SPPA on 27 March 2019.
- GERC issued a final order in the matter on 27 April 2020. In this order, GERC made various deviations from the HPC's

recommendations and terms of the SPPA.[20] Aggrieved by this order, EPGL filed a petition in APTEL against this order.

- However, the Government of Gujarat, vide its resolution[21] dated 12 June 2020, revoked the earlier resolution dated 1 December 2018. As per this new resolution, the Government of Gujarat was directed to devise separate strategies for these three projects. As regards APL, on the other hand, it was advised to pursue revocation of the amended PPA. And in the case of EPGL, it was asked to follow the terms as per the GERC order. On the basis of the GERC order, EPGL has agreed to the execution of a revised SPPA. It has also filed an application for withdrawing its petition from APTEL challenging the GERC order. However, the revised SPPA is yet to be signed, at the time of going to the press.

Major Findings by Regulatory Orders/Committees

Findings as per the CERC Order of April 2013:[22]

a. No case was made out in favour of the generator under the Force Majeure clause or the 'Change in Law' clause of the PPAs. However, CERC observed that ways and means need to be found to compensate the petitioner for any loss or additional expenditure incurred by it.
b. Sharing of coal mine profits—It is well known that the company earned a profit from the coal mines in Indonesia on account of the benchmark price resulting from the Indonesian Regulation corresponding to the quantity of the coal being supplied for the project. The net profit less Government taxes and cess should thus be factored and passed on in full to the beneficiaries of the compensatory tariff.
c. Sale beyond target availability—The possibility of sharing the revenue accruing from the sale of power beyond the target availability to third parties may be explored.

d. Use of low-Gross Calorific Value (GCV) coal—There is a need to examine the possibility of using coal with a low GCV for the generation of electricity without having an impact on the operational efficiency of the generating stations.

Findings of the Deepak Parekh Committee:[23]

a. The generators, APL and CGPL must be compensated for historical losses on account of under-recoveries of energy cost, effective from the Scheduled Commercial Operation Date (SCOD).
b. The Deepak Parekh Committee proposed a formula for the computation of prospective compensatory tariff. This compensatory tariff was to be recovered in the following three steps: (i) Provisional Compensatory Tariff to be charged vide a monthly bill; (ii) Actual Compensatory Tariff to be calculated at the end of the particular year; and (iii) Truing up/reconciliation of Provisional Compensatory Tariff at the end of each financial year based on the audited financial statements, with adjustment for actual/normative fuel energy expenses and sharing of profits from the Indonesian mining companies pertaining to coal supplied under the respective Coal Supply Agreements (CSAs).
c. It was also recommended that third-party sale of power beyond the target availability of 80 per cent may be permitted (after making requisite modifications in the PPA), and the profits from such a sale may be shared equally between the generator and the procurers.
d. It was further recommended that the usage of low-GCV coal may not be commercially beneficial at the then prevailing prices and in any event, it is expected to adversely affect the performance of the plants in the long run, thereby leading to extra costs.
e. The procurers and generators were urged to jointly pursue options for reduction in duties and taxes with the concerned authorities.

f. The lenders were advised to explore options of a reduction in interest rates, extending the moratorium on principal payment for a period of two to three years, and elongation of loan repayment tenor to reduce the hardship of capacity charges on the generator.

Findings as per the CERC Order of February 2014:[24]

a. Recovery of past losses—It was held that the generators would be entitled to a provisional lump sum compensation for the period from SCOD till 31 March 2013.
b. Compensatory tariff formula—The formula for calculating the compensatory tariff from April 2013 onwards, which was to be provided on a monthly basis, was also specified in the said order. It was also directed that the excess realization towards third-party sale above the availability of 80 per cent (after adjusting energy charges including compensatory tariff and incentive) shall be shared in the ratio 60:40 between the procurers and generators.
c. It was directed that the actual profit from the coal mining operations in Indonesia be calculated on the basis of the total incremental revenue after payment of taxes and royalty as per the Indonesian Regulations 2010 and the incremental mining cost in proportion to the coal used for the generation of contracted power under the respective PPAs.
d. CERC also advised for the usage of low-GCV imported coal blended with high-GCV imported coal. It was further directed that the generators and procurers would jointly continue to pursue all possible options with the concerned authorities for reduction in duties and taxes on fuel. Gains made by the generator on account of any possible reductions shall be passed on to the consumers in reducing the tariff through 'Change in Law' provision in PPA.

e. It was also held that the procurers and the generators shall jointly continue to pursue all the possible options in terms of approaching lenders to achieve a reduction in interest rates, extending the moratorium on repayment of the principal amount for a period of two to three years, and possible extension of the loan repayment tenor to reduce hardship on capacity charges.
f. CERC was of the view that the generators should also share the burden of the hardship caused due to the escalation of coal prices in the Indonesian market, and in this context, directed for an adjustment in the tariff towards sacrifice of the Return on Equity (ROE) based on the equity investment of the respective contracted capacity, as on the SCOD.
g. It was stipulated that CERC would review the compensatory tariff after a period of three years unless the same had been withdrawn earlier.

Findings as per the APTEL Order of April 2016:[25]

a. CERC had no power to vary/modify the tariff or otherwise grant compensatory tariff to the generating companies dehors the provisions of the PPAs.
b. Change in the term 'law' event—APTEL held that the term 'law' referred only to Indian laws and there was no scope whatsoever to insert foreign law in the said definition.
c. Force Majeure event—The increase in the price of coal on account of the intervention by the Indonesian Regulations 2010 as also the non-availability or short supply of domestic coal in the case of APL constitute a Force Majeure event in terms of the PPA.
d. The petitions were remanded back to CERC with instructions for it to assess the extent of the impact of the Force Majeure event on the TPPs of APL and CGPL, and to provide them such relief as may be available to them under their respective PPAs.

Supreme Court order of April 2017 (Energy Watchdog Judgment):[26] The Supreme Court passed the Energy Watchdog Judgment on 11 April 2017 with the following major observations:

a. The change in the Indonesian legal regime dealing with the price of coal cannot be construed either as a Force Majeure event or as a 'Change in Law' event under the relevant PPAs.
b. CERC had general regulatory powers under Section 79 of the Electricity Act. However, these regulatory powers could be exercised only in a situation wherein no guidelines had been framed under Section 63 of the Electricity Act, or wherein the guidelines do not deal with a given situation.
c. Accordingly, the Supreme Court concluded that the financial distress being faced by the promoters of the two projects could not be addressed or resolved within the framework of the terms of the PPAs as they stood, nor was there a possibility of a recourse to the general regulatory powers of CERC under Section 79 of the Electricity Act.
d. The Supreme Court thus set aside APTEL's judgment dated 7 April 2016 as well as the CERC orders following the said judgment and thereafter directed CERC to examine the matter afresh and determine what relief should be granted to those power generators that fall within the ambit of the change in Indian law provision of the relevant PPA, as per the findings mentioned in this judgment.

Findings of the Working Group:[27]

a. The five states procuring power from these projects, that is, Gujarat, Maharashtra, Rajasthan, Haryana, and Punjab, are critical states with regard to power generation in the country, as due to their high demands for electricity, they are placed in the top bracket of the spectrum of the electricity consumer states in India.

b. The capital cost of these projects (in Rs crore/MW) was significantly lower than the costs of other comparable coal-based power projects that had either been completed recently or were presently in the implementation/planning phase.
c. It was stated that the average rates in the exchange market had been in the range of Rs 2.5/unit to Rs 4.25/unit during the period November 2016 to October 2017, and that they were moving towards the average tariff discovered in Case 1 bidding in the recent past. Further, an analysis was carried out on volume data for electricity trading on the Indian Energy Exchange (IEX) from 1 April 2017 till 18 December 2017, which showed that the clearing price went above Rs 4/unit whenever the purchase quantity was higher than quantity available for sale. In view of this analysis, it was stated that in a scenario wherein these projects are not operational [which are capable of generating approximately 61.2 BUs at a Plant Load Factor (PLF) of 85 per cent], the exchange prices would significantly increase as the quantum of power being supplied presently, that is, approximately 44.6 BUs, in the system was not sufficient to meet the existing demand.
d. Competitive Analysis—Projects are placed very high in the merit order of their respective procurer states at the prevailing tariff, and even with a pass-through of the variable tariff at the enhanced Indonesian coal prices, the projects would continue to be competitively placed in their respective Merit Order Dispatch (MOD).
e. The Working Group recommended a full pass-through of the coal cost to the procurers. In order to mitigate the additional costs accruing to the procurers, it was suggested that the procurers may ask the generators for certain benefits like enhanced plant availability, availability of untied capacity, and power availability beyond the tenor of the PPA.
f. Conclusion—It was suggested that the contentious issues may be addressed via: (1) Change in ownership with effect from

31 March 2017, or (2) Revision in the PPA without a change in ownership. The 'way forward' was thus for the concerned states to take the requisite approval from the competent authorities, after which the lenders could be apprised of the same, if required. A tripartite agreement could thus be executed between the procurers, lenders, and developers, covering the roles and responsibilities of each of the parties involved.

Findings of the High Power Committee (HPC):[28]

a. Shutting down these projects would have severe ramifications for all the stakeholders, including the consumers. Further, there was a consensus, including among most of the consumer representative groups, that these projects need to be salvaged, and with reasonable efforts, be allowed to be rehabilitated and continue operations. This is because the consequences of the alternative option of allowing these projects to shut down and be scrapped has very significant adverse financial and economic consequences.
b. It is also widely recognized, including by the procurers and consumer representatives, that these projects are highly efficient, as most of the units are state-of-the-art and entail the use of advanced technology in their functioning, which makes them both cost-effective and environmentally beneficial. Further, an analysis of the operational parameters affirms that these projects offer a saving of at least 18.5 per cent in coal utilization, as compared to the other existing generating plants of older vintage in the state.
c. The HPC laid down the broad contours of the revision in the PPA based on an equal contribution from all the stakeholders, including a pass-through in the coal cost, reduction in the capacity charge to be facilitated by the lenders, and sharing of the mining profit by the developers. The HPC

also recommended the implementation of other beneficial measures like the extension of tenor, tie-up of free capacity, and ensuring higher availability of power.

The entire case history shows divergent views taken by different authorities and an inordinate delay in finding a satisfactory solution, jeopardizing huge investments made in setting up the power generation capacity in a power-starved country. Lenders can't foresee such a situation while appraising the projects. Based on their not-so-happy experience, the natural tendency is to go into shell and keep away from financing any new project. The need for infrastructure financing in India is huge and some of these issues, need to be ironed out to attract fresh investment.

Appendix II[1]

Resolution of Essar Steel: A Trailblazer

The resolution of the Essar Steel case through the IBC process has been one of the most high-profile cases in the country, wherein the lenders not only achieved a full recovery of their outstanding amounts but managed to recover Rs 12,000 crores over and above the principal from Laxmi Mittal with regard to connected accounts like Uttam Galva Steels Limited (henceforth Uttam Galva) and KSS Petron Limited (henceforth KSS Petron). Albeit, it must be pointed out that the lenders had to face legal challenges and many other obstacles in the recovery process that were related to IBC.

Legal Issues around IBC

First Round of Litigation Regarding Admission

- Essar Steel (India) Limited (ESIL) was one of the top 12 stressed assets referred to by the RBI for initiation of the Corporate Insolvency Resolution (CIR) process under the provisions of the Insolvency and Bankruptcy Code, 2016, in June 2017.

- The above referral by the RBI was challenged by ESIL before the High Court of Gujarat on the grounds that the referral by the RBI was arbitrary, unreasonable, and manifestly unjust for having singled out ESIL, especially when a debt structuring plan for ESIL was under discussion with the Joint Lenders' Forum.
- The writ petition was dismissed by the High Court vide its order dated 17 July 2017 inter alia citing the following facts:

    - The RBI did not discriminate against ESIL and the basis for the referral was based on cogent reasons (that is, the amount of debt exposure being more than Rs 5,000 crores and at least 60 per cent of the same being classified as a non-performing asset).
    - There is no embargo on the initiation of the CIR process even when a debt restructuring plan is at an advanced stage.

- Thereafter, the application under Section 7 of the Code was admitted by the Hon'ble NCLT, Ahmedabad Bench on 2 August 2017.

Second Round of Litigation Regarding Ineligibility under Section 29A

Under IBC, a Resolution Applicant was originally defined as any person who submits a resolution plan. Intriguingly, the Resolution Applicant could also be the existing promoter. Hence, this became both a sensitive and politically controversial issue. It could theoretically lead to a situation, wherein many defaulting promoters would have been able to keep or gain control of their units at deep discounts. This necessitated the insertion of

Section 29A on eligibility criteria, which successfully prevented such situations but which, in turn, led to a lot of disputes and delay in the resolution of stressed assets.

As regards the Essar Steel case, the first round of the resolution plans submitted by Arcelor Mittal India Private Limited (henceforth Arcelor) and Numetal Limited (henceforth Numetal) were found to be ineligible by the Resolution Professional (RP) overseeing the resolution of the case.

Arcelor was held to be ineligible under Section 29A(c) of the Code, as Arcelor Mittal Netherlands (henceforth AM Netherlands) was found to have been the promoter or one that exercised control over two other companies, namely, Uttam Galva and KSS Petron, whose accounts were classified as NPLs for more than one year prior to the commencement of the CIR process.

Numetal was held to be ineligible under Section 29A(c) of the Code, as Rewant Ruia was the ultimate shareholder of Aurora Enterprises Limited (AEL), a shareholder of Numetal. Further, Ravi Ruia, the father of Rewant Ruia, was a promoter of ESIL, which was classified as an NPL for a period of more than one year prior to the commencement of the CIR process.

The decision of the RP was challenged but upheld by NCLT, NCLAT, and eventually even the Supreme Court of India. Mercifully, however, at the request of the CoC, and in order to ensure complete justice under Article 142 of the Constitution as also because the law on Section 29A was being laid down for the first time, both Arcelor and Numetal were given one more opportunity to '*pay off the NPAs of their related corporate debtors*' within two weeks of the judgment. Thereafter, the CoC was allowed to consider the plan of Vedanta along with the plans of Arcelor and Numetal, subject to the clearance of their overdue amounts. The Supreme Court, however, made it clear that if eventually none of the resolution plans was approved, ESIL would go into liquidation.

Key Legal Principles Settled by the Supreme Court

Lifting of the Corporate Veil: The Supreme Court invoked the principle of 'lifting the corporate veil' to determine the ineligibility of the applicant submitting a resolution plan. After analysing the jurisprudence on the principle of the corporate veil, the Supreme Court held that, '*where a statute itself lifts the corporate veil, or where protection of public interest is of paramount importance, or where a company has been formed to evade obligations imposed by the law, the court will disregard the corporate veil. Further, this principle is applied even to group companies, so that one is able to look at the economic entity of the group as a whole.*'

Hence, the Supreme Court held that the Code itself contained language of wider import intending to implicate all the persons who may act arm-in-arm with the person submitting the resolution plan. Accordingly, it was imperative to lift the corporate veil to unravel the actual persons behind Numetal, that is, the looming presence of Rewant Ruia as well as the fact that AM Netherlands had a presence in both Arcelor as well as Uttam Galva and KSS Petron.

Management and Control: In view of the disqualification contained in Section 29A(c) inter alia, as regards any entity that an RA is in management and control of, the Supreme Court stated that control in terms of Section 29A(c) is to be interpreted to mean positive control, that is, controlling the management or policy decisions of a company or appointing a majority of the directors, and not negative control, that is, having the power to block actions.

Ultimate Decision on Eligibility of RAs under Section 29A Rests with the CoC: The Supreme Court held that the role of the RP was only to place before the CoC his *prima facie* opinion on whether an RA was rendered ineligible under Section 29A. The RP is, therefore, not empowered to decide on the eligibility of an RA.

The ultimate decision on the disqualification of an RA for reasons of ineligibility under Section 29A rests with the CoC.

Compliance with Timelines: The Supreme Court held that the consequence of not adhering to strict timelines as prescribed under the Code, was the liquidation of the corporate debtor. However, the Supreme Court laid down the principle of exclusion of time to state that the time spent in litigation be excluded from calculating the timelines under the Code.

Third Round of Litigation Regarding Plan Approval

The final negotiated resolution plan of Arcelor was approved by the CoC on 25 October 2018 by a majority of 92.24 per cent after clearance of dues by Arcelor in relation to the NPL accounts of Uttam Galva and KSS Petron.

The application for approval of the plan was filed before NCLT on 26 October 2018. Objections to the plan inter alia were filed by the operational creditors and Standard Chartered Bank (which was a member of the CoC), alleging discrimination and differential treatment by the CoC.

Separately, an application was also filed by Essar Steel Asia Holdings Limited (ESAHL) and certain other shareholders of ESIL before NCLT, requesting for issuance of directions to the CoC to consider a settlement plan that was submitted after the approval of the Approved Resolution Plan. The said application was, however, dismissed by NCLT vide its order dated 29 January 2019 by holding it to be 'not maintainable' as inter alia the Hon'ble Supreme Court allowed only a limited window of consideration.

NCLT passed an order dated 8 March 2019 approving the resolution plan. However, while approving the resolution plan, it made some suggestions, and observations, and decided to render advice that encroached upon the commercial wisdom of the CoC.

Following were the major findings under the NCLT Order:

- *Suggestion for modification of the resolution plan to re-allocate certain amounts from the allocations made to the secured financial creditors under the Approved Resolution Plan:* In the applications filed by the operational creditors raising objections against alleged discrimination, NCLT suggested that 15 per cent of the amount being proposed under the Approved Resolution Plan towards payments to the secured financial creditors be distributed among other operational creditors and other stakeholders who are going to receive *nil* amount.

  Accordingly out of the total amount of Rs 42,000 crores being proposed by AM, it was suggested that an amount of Rs 6,300 crores be apportioned towards payment to operational creditors with claims of more than Rs one crore.
- *Registration of claims of operational creditors:* In the applications filed by operational creditors whose claims had been admitted by the Resolution Professional at a notional amount of Re 1, for being contingent in nature (*in accordance with Regulation 14 of the CIR Regulations*), the NCLT held that the Resolution Professional does not have the power to adjudicate the claims submitted before it.

  Accordingly, the NCLT directed the Resolution Professional to 'register' the claims of certain operational creditors amounting to approximately Rs 14,000 crores, whose claims had been admitted at a notional value of Re 1. However, this order created uncertainty as the Code only envisages 'admission' or 'rejection' of a claim and the concept of 'registration' is outside the purview of the Code.
- *Treatment of Standard Chartered Bank to be at par with the other secured financial creditors:* In the application filed, Standard Chartered Bank claimed inter alia discrimination in the amounts allocated to it by the CoC, as it was ostensibly paid only 1.7 per cent of its total admitted

claim in comparison to about 90 per cent recovery for the remaining secured creditors. NCLT thus directed that Standard Chartered Bank should be treated at par with the other secured creditors.

The above direction was passed without taking into account the intelligible criteria applied by the CoC to determine distribution based on the nature, quality, and value of the security interest available to Standard Chartered Bank and the other secured creditors.

- Accordingly, NCLT suggested and advised the CoC to relook into its decisions and consider distribution of the amount on a pro rata basis on all the admitted claims of the financial creditors, including Standard Chartered Bank. Thereafter, post the deduction of the 15 per cent amount (suggested for payments to operational creditors), it proposed the distribution of the remaining 85 per cent amount on a pro rata basis amongst all the secured financial creditors.

Proceedings before NCLAT

The NCLT order of 8 March 2019 was challenged before NCLAT by Standard Chartered Bank, the CoC, as well as various operational creditors.

NCLAT, vide its order dated 4 July 2019, disposed of the appeals with the following findings:

- *Belated Admission of Claims of the Operational Creditors:*

In the appeals filed by the operational creditors whose claims had been admitted by the resolution professional at a notional amount of Re 1, for being contingent in nature (in accordance with Regulation 14 of the CIR Regulations), and thereafter directed to be registered by the Adjudicating Authority, NCLAT admitted these additional claims of operational creditors.

The above claims were admitted at a highly belated stage and without any sound reasoning, and in a majority of the instances, without consideration of the reason for the rejection of the same by the Resolution Professional. Consequently, the admitted operational debt of approximately Rs 5,074 crores swelled up to approximately Rs 19,719.20 crores.

Allowing Disputed Claims to Be Agitated Even Subsequent to the Approval of the Resolution Plan

- NCLAT also dealt with the objections regarding a stipulation in a resolution plan extinguishing all future, contingent, and unknown claims, and thereafter making it binding upon the corporate debtor and its employees, members, creditors, guarantors, and other stakeholders involved in the resolution plan.
- NCLAT held that in the cases in which NCLT or NCLAT could not decide the claim on merit, the appellants are allowed to raise the issue before an appropriate forum in terms of Section 60(6) of the Code against a corporate debtor under the management of the RA.

The Code Does Not Envisage the Formulation of a Subcommittee and Delegation of the Powers of the CoC to Such Subcommittee Is Bad in Law

As regards the objection of Standard Chartered Bank that the subcommittee formed by the CoC for negotiations with Arcelor was *ultra vires* the Code, NCLAT held that a subcommittee is unknown and against the provisions of the Code, and no provision under the Code or the regulations permit constitution of a subcommittee.

Distribution of the Resolution Proceeds Does Not Fall Within the Commercial Domain of the CoC

- NCLAT held that the CoC is required to look only into the viability and feasibility of the resolution plan, and the CoC has not been empowered under the Code to decide the manner in which the distribution is to be made between one or more creditors.
- NCLAT also held that a resolution plan, which delegates the powers related to distribution of amounts to the CoC, would be contrary to Section 30(2) of the Code read with the regulations thereunder.

There Can Be No Classification amongst Financial Creditors on the Basis of Security

- On the basis of a reading of Sections 5(7) and 5(8) of the Code (*definition of financial creditor and financial debt respectively*), NCLAT held that no distinction is made between one or other 'Financial Creditor', and they cannot be sub-classified as 'Secured' or 'Unsecured Financial Creditor' for the purpose of preparation of the resolution plan by the RA.
- Accordingly, NCLAT held that the distribution under the Approved Resolution Plan providing different percentages of payment to and amongst the secured creditors, the unsecured creditors, and the operational creditors, was discriminatory in nature.
- Therefore, NCLAT proceeded to modify the terms of the Approved Resolution Plan and re-distributed the resolution proceeds equally amongst all the financial creditors and operational creditors.

Proceedings before the Supreme Court

- The NCLAT order of 4 July 2019 was challenged by the CoC and other members of the CoC before the Supreme Court of India.
- Thereafter, the Supreme Court, vide its judgment dated 15 November 2019, held the as follows here.

Limited Jurisdiction of the NCLT/NCLAT

- The Supreme Court held that NCLT and NCLAT have been vested with the limited powers of judicial review under the Code, which can, in no circumstances, trespass upon a business decision of the majority of the CoC.
- The limited judicial review during approval of a resolution plan is to ensure both compliance with the mandatory provisions of Section 30(2), and also that the CoC has taken into account the balancing of interests of all the stakeholders, including operational creditors.
- If, on facts, the CoC has not considered these interests, NCLT/ NCLAT can advise the CoC to re-examine the provisions, but cannot substitute an Approved Resolution Plan. Accordingly, NCLAT's modifications to the distribution of proceeds were set aside.

The CoC Has the Power to Decide Distribution—Commercial Wisdom Upheld

The insolvency resolution is ultimately in the hands of the majority vote of the CoC, and the CoC, while deciding on the 'feasibility and viability' of a resolution plan, can obviously decide on all aspects of the plan, including the manner of distribution of funds among the various classes of creditors.

Full freedom and discretion has been given to the CoC to classify creditors and to pay secured creditors based upon the value and nature of their security. However, the commercial wisdom of the CoC should be exercised in a manner so as to balance the interests of all stakeholders and to ensure fair and equitable treatment of all classes of creditors. Accordingly, the distribution of funds inter-se creditors as approved by the CoC was upheld (wherein Standard Chartered Bank was treated differently from the other secured creditors on account of it holding a grossly undervalued security).

Separately, on account of the NCLAT judgment of 4 July 2019, which completely disregarded the security interest and essentially brought to naught the entire basis of financial lending in India, SBI made necessary representations to the Government. This ultimately resulted in the promulgation of the Insolvency and Bankruptcy Code (Amendment) Act, 2019, which inter alia clarified that the value and nature of security interest and the priorities prescribed under Section 53 of the Code would be relevant factors even during the CIR process.

Primacy of Secured Creditors Upheld

- The Supreme Court held that equal treatment cannot be stretched to treat unequals equally.
- The law is not such that financial creditors and OCs, or secured and unsecured creditors, must be paid the same amounts, percentage-wise, under the resolution plan before it can pass muster.
- The CoC, in its commercial wisdom, can approve differential payments to different classes of creditors, while also negotiating with a prospective RA for better or different terms, which may also involve differences in the distribution of amounts between different classes of creditors.

- Equitable treatment has to be accorded to each creditor, depending upon the class to which it belongs: secured or unsecured, financial or operational.

Accordingly, the Approved Resolution Plan was upheld and the allegation of the OCs (that they should be paid the same percentage as FCs in the plan) was rejected.

Undecided/Disputed and Future Claims

- The Supreme Court held that a successful RA cannot suddenly be faced with 'undecided' claims after the resolution plan submitted by him has been accepted, as this would amount to the popping up of a hydra head, which would throw into uncertainty the amounts payable by the successful RA.
- All claims must be submitted to and decided by the RP so that a prospective RA knows exactly what has to be paid to be able to then take over and run the business of the corporate debtor.
- A successful RA ought to be provided with a clean slate after taking over the corporate debtor and cannot be burdened with undecided/disputed claims after resolution as the same is contrary to the objective of predictability.
- On the basis of the above, the Supreme Court overturned the order of NCLAT wherein the latter, post the conditional approval of Arcelor's resolution plan by the NCLT, had admitted additional operational claims of approximately Rs 14,000 crore, which were contingent or disputed in nature. A resolution plan can extinguish the right of subrogation of the guarantors as in the following points.
- As per the Code, once a resolution plan is approved by the CoC, it shall be binding on all the stakeholders, including the guarantors. This provision ensures that the successful RA starts running the business of the corporate debtor on a fresh slate, as it were.

- Therefore, if the resolution plan provides that the claims of the guarantor on account of subrogation shall be extinguished (including the promoter guarantees), then the same would be binding on the guarantor. Accordingly, the resolution plan of Arcelor, which extinguished the right of subrogation available to the Ruias (as guarantors), was upheld.

The CoC May Constitute a Subcommittee for Performing Administrative Functions

- The CoC may constitute a smaller subcommittee or core committee of select lenders to negotiate with the RA and perform other ministerial and administrative actions, as long as such actions are ultimately approved and ratified by the CoC.
- However, the subcommittee cannot exercise the powers of the CoC with regard to actions under Section 28(1) that have a vital bearing on the business of the corporate debtor or for the approval of a resolution plan under Section 30(4). Such powers cannot be delegated by the CoC.
- Accordingly, the objections raised about the role performed by the subcommittee of the CoC of ESIL in negotiating the resolution plan with Arcelor were dismissed.
- Additionally, keeping in view the concerns raised by the RAs across various CIR processes, including the RA in the CIR process of ESIL, the firm assisted SBI in making representations to the government. This culminated in the introduction of Section 32A within the framework of the Code, thereby ensuring that the RAs take over the company without any past criminal liabilities.

Other Challenges Faced and Decisive Action Taken by the Lenders to Overcome Them

Keep the Company as a Going Concern

Resolution of the Essar case took more than two years. During this period, it was important to keep the company as a going concern to preserve its value.

SBI, the lead bank, requested all the major working capital lenders to implement a Holding on Operation. A system was thus introduced whereby a report on LCs established by all the banks, under a Holding on Operation, against the credit received by them, would be circulated every Monday to ensure that all the key lenders were participating in the process. However, many lenders, particularly ICICI Bank and IDBI Bank, were not keen to participate in the process.

The matter was discussed a number of times in a consortium and in the CoC. In the end, SBI, Canara Bank, and Union Bank did most of the heavy lifting of opening of the LCs/Bank Guarantees as part of the Holding on Operations.

It was decided and documented that such requests for opening LCs would be countersigned by the RP and the CoC would be periodically apprised of these developments.

Implementation of the TRA Mechanism

The company was sceptical that a Trust and Retention Account (TRA)/escrow mechanism would work smoothly in such a large company. They, in fact, believed that it would hamper the smooth functioning of the company. The SBI mapped the cash flows of the company, and details of the collection and pooling accounts and the entire cash flows were collected at the end of the day at SBI's Hazira branch. The company used to give debit requests in the TRA account one day in advance, which was approved by the lenders' agent, Ernst & Young, who had been appointed by the consortium. For other critical payments, the company would submit requests to the TRA auditor, giving a window of three to four hours to approve the transactions. Ernst & Young submitted a monitoring report to the lenders.

After admission into the NCLT, the RP adopted the same TRA mechanism with his agent, Alvarez & Marsal, replacing Ernst & Young as the TRA monitoring agency.

Intervention with the Group Companies for Keeping the Company as a Going Concern

Essar Steel was dependent on other group companies, viz., Essar Steel and Essar Power, for continuing as a going concern, as post its admission into the Corporate Insolvency Resolution Procedure (CIRP), many group companies would often stop support, at the behest of their promoters. The top management of SBI thus intervened with the promoters of these companies a number of times to keep Essar Steel as a going concern.

Decision to Form the Core Committee

ESIL had 29 lenders, and it was difficult to bring all of them on a common platform for taking multiple decisions. The RP also had to individually contact all the lenders for any decision. At this time, in a CoC meeting, SBI suggested the formation of a core committee consisting of two public sector banks (SBI and IDBI) and two private sector lenders (ICICI and Edelweiss). The inclusion of Edelweiss in the proposed core committee would ensure representation of the interests of debt buyers like Asset Reconstruction Companies (ARCs) and Stressed Asset Funds, who had purchased Essar debts. The core committee could have multiple telecalls during the day (Microsoft Teams and Webex were not in vogue those days), enabling the RP and his team to decide on various operational and resolution-related issues. It was mandated by the CoC to take decisions on their behalf. The decisions of the core committee were to be ratified by the CoC. Even the Supreme Court upheld the decision to have a core committee.

The core committee also played a critical role in explaining the RfP terms to the RAs and in negotiating the key terms with them.

Mechanism for the Payment of Legal Fees

ESIL was a highly litigated matter. The Insolvency and Bankruptcy Board of India (IBBI) has prohibited lenders from recovering their legal costs from the cash flows of the company. This meant that the legal cost had to be shared among the lenders on a pro rata basis. However, it was often difficult to collect funds from all the lenders in time. This prompted the senior counsel to issue a threat that it would stop representing the CoC if they were not paid in time.

It was then agreed that the legal cost would be paid by the four core committee lenders, and the core committee would be reimbursed on a pro rata basis from the first dip in the resolution proceeds. A CoC resolution was approved to this effect. The mechanism helped the lenders pool in the requisite resources for fighting the legal battle. The lenders also agreed to pool funds from the resolution proceeds towards payment of future legal dues.

Permission to the Company to Discount Bills outside the Consortium/CoC

All sale bills, under LCs were discounted by the consortium lenders. However, no lender was agreeable to discount the non-LC bills. The company was able to bring a proposal from Axis Bank and Deutsche Bank for discounting these bills. The CoC laid down two conditions before these banks, viz., firstly, that the bills have to be discounted on a non-recourse basis, and secondly, that the discounted proceeds have to be transferred to an escrow account. Both Axis Bank and Deutsche Bank agreed to these conditions, thus helping ESIL to ramp up its sale during the CIRP period.

Acknowledgements

The idea of writing my memoirs was planted in my mind by Suhel Seth at a social event in 2019. I was petrified at the idea; I am well able to write or dictate office notes, but could I write a book?

After completing my term as Chairman of SBI, I had ample time at my disposal and was wondering what to do. COVID-19 ensured that I had to abandon all my plans and settle for a long vacation. I thus ended up spending time with my grandchildren and socializing with some members of my extended family. Being confined to the home for a long period instilled courage in me to try and fructify the idea planted in my mind by Suhel Seth.

There are many people who supported me in writing this book. My first thanks, of course, go to Suhel for his encouragement.

I am particularly grateful to Anupma Mehta for developing this book right from its inception through her editorial interventions, keen insight, and comprehensive research-based inputs. She worked tirelessly, producing drafts of the various chapters while adhering to the challenging timelines for the project. Indeed, her collaboration was instrumental in bringing to life my story, which I have great pleasure in sharing with my readers.

My thanks also go out to Premanka Goswami, Executive Editor at Penguin Random House India, who reviewed the draft of the book and suggested many structural changes transforming the quality of the manuscript.

Supratim Sircar, Executive Vice President, SBI Capital Markets Ltd; Akash Lal, Senior Partner at McKinsey & Co.; and Atul Kumar, Chief Ethics Officer at SBI, have made valuable contributions in putting together the chapters on Non-Performing Loans, YONO, and Human Resources.

I would like to thank veteran journalist Tamal Bandyopadhyay, who read the manuscript and provided detailed comments, which resulted in many improvements in the final output. Others who offered many helpful suggestions and honest feedback on reading the book include Anil Khandelwal, Former Chairman of the Bank of Baroda; Rajat Gupta and Puneet Goel, IAS; Gopal Jain, Senior Advocate; and Nishant Parikh, Joint Managing Partner, Trilegal. My sincere thanks go out to all of them.

I also benefited from the support of several of my outstanding colleagues while I was at the helm of affairs at SBI.

I was also fortunate that the second line of command at the level of Deputy Managing Directors at the bank was equally strong. It was for the first time in the history of public sector banking in India that SBI provided as many as six Managing Directors to other public sector banks.

Very strong succession planning at SBI ensured that I never felt the void created by the exit of so many senior officials of the team.

The bank also has a very strong Board of Directors, comprising such eminent personalities as Pushpendra Rai, Purnima Gupta, Basant Seth, Sanjeev Malhotra, Bhaskar Pramanik, Girish Ahuja, and Chandan Sinha. All of them were members of the Board for most of my tenure, and offered their guidance and support in improving risk management, corporate governance, technology architecture, and overall cleaning up of the balance sheet. My special thanks to all of them. Among these, apart from Pushpendra Rai, the other directors have since retired on completion of their respective terms.

I would be remiss if I do not offer my gratitude to Rajiv Kumar, ex-Secretary, and Debashish Panda, the current Secretary, Department of Financial Services, who were consecutive Government nominees on the Bank's Board of Directors. They guided me and stood solidly with me in difficult times such as during the handling of the issues relating to Jet Airways and Yes Bank. Many initiatives relating to financial inclusion and outreach programs were successfully implemented at the bank under their guidance. I also worked very closely with Pankaj Jain, Additional Secretary, Department of Financial Services, for preparing a relief package for the industry when it was reeling under the impacts of the COVID-19 attack.

I was also very ably supported by my Executive Secretary, D. Munshi, and two Personal Assistants, Pradeep Rao and Melisa, who were working in the Chairman's Secretariat.

Last but not the least, I am grateful to Reeta Agarwal, my wife; Pratiksha Agarwal, my daughter; and Sameer, my son-in-law, for their constant support and succour during the challenging period of conceptualization and creation of this book. And finally, I am eternally thankful to my two young grandsons, Rihansh and Sarang, whose childhood joie de vivre always kept me relaxed and motivated during this period.

Notes

Chapter 3: Non-Performing Loans: Are the Bankers Villains?

1. Report in *Mint* dated 14 November 2018.
2. Mercom India report on the Power Minister's statement in the Lok Sabha, matter batch WP 9844/2019.
3. Unstarred Question No. 931, answered on 25 November 2019 in the Rajya Sabha.

Chapter 5: Baptism by Fire

1. Please refer to https://www.ndtv.com/business/kerala-opposes-state-bank-of-travancore-merger-with-sbi-1417368 (accessed on 18 June 2021).
2. Save SBT Forum vs Union of India on 14 March 2017.
3. Save SBT Forum vs Union of India on 14 March 2017.

Chapter 6: Challenges of Captaining a Large Ship

1. Later on, after extensive consultation with staff across the bank, the acronym STEPS was redefined to mean:

S Service
T Transparency
E Ethics
P Politeness
S Sustainability

2. SBI annual report, 2018.
3. The term 'Dirty Dozen' was originally coined to allude to 12 leading adult entertainment stars in the US film industry. The term was controversially adopted by the news channel CNBC to refer to 12 un-named companies, most likely in the steel and power sectors, which represent a quarter of India's US$120 billion bad loan problem, as estimated by the RBI. The Central Bank also ordered lenders, including SBI, to tip these dozen companies into bankruptcy proceedings following the advent of the insolvency regime in May 2017. This move was seen as an attempt by the RBI to clean up the system and defend its credibility in the face of rising NPLs.
4. On 2 April 2019, the Supreme Court of India delivered a judgment in the case of Dharani Sugars and Chemicals Ltd and held that the revised framework is ultra vires of the constitution.
5. As per the financial results of the bank as on 31 March 2021.

Chapter 7: From a Legacy Bank to a Tech-Savvy Bank—The YONO Vision

1. https://www.business-standard.com/article/markets/yono-earnings-recovery-key-triggers-for-sbi-goldman-sachs-macquarie-121011300403_1.html (accessed on 18 June 2021).

Appendix I

1. For full access to the figures cited here, please refer to CERC Petition No. 155/MP/2012; dates of hearing: 8 November 2013 and 13 November 2013; date of order: 21 February 2014.

2. *Economic Times*, 11 April 2019.
3. CERC Petition No. 155/MP/2012.
4. Ibid.
5. From the scheme of arrangement filed in the High Court of Delhi, company application number 142 of 2016.
6. Central Electricity Regulatory Commission (CERC), New Delhi, Petition No. 155/MP/2012; date of hearing: 08 November 2013; date of order: 21 February 2014.
7. Committee Report for CERC (August 2013), shared by CERC for public consultation. Available in archive of CERC website.
8. Central Electricity Regulatory Commission (CERC), New Delhi, Petition No. 159/MP/2012, member date of hearing: 13 November 2013; date of order: 21 February 2014.
9. Full bench judgment in the Appellate Tribunal for Electricity (APTEL) dated 7 April 2016 in case of Adani Group (Appeal No. 100 of 2013 and Appeal No. 98 of 2014 and others) and CGPL Group (Appeal No. 151 of 2013 and Appeal No. 97 of 2014 and others). Available on APTEL website.
10. CERC order for Petition No. 155/MP/2012 (dated 7 December 2016) in case of Adani Power Limited (APL) and CERC order for Petition No. 159/MP/2012 (dated 7 December 2016) in case of Coastal Gujarat Power Limited (CGPL). Available on CERC website.
11. Refer clause 4 of CERC order in Petition No. 374/MP/2018 (dated 12 April 2019) in case of Gujarat Urja Vikas Nigam Limited (GUVNL). Available on CERC website.
12. Refer to Clause 3.6 of CERC order in Petition No. 1807 of 2019 (Gujarat Urja Vikas Nigam Ltd vs Essar Power Gujarat Ltd and others) dated 27 April 2020. Available on CERC website.
13. Refer to Clause 127(c) of CERC order in Petition No. 374/MP/2018 (dated 12 April 2019) in case of Gujarat Urja Vikas Nigam Limited (GUVNL). Available on CERC website.
14. Harga Batubara Acuan; reference price of coal published by Indonesian government.

15. Supreme Court Judgment in M.A. Nos 2705–2706 of 2018 in Civil Appeal Nos 5399–5400 of 2016 (Energy Watchdog vs CERC and others) dated 29 October 2018
16. CERC order for Petition No. 374/MP/2018 (dated 12 April 2019) in case of GUVNL. Available on CERC website.
17. Supreme Court Judgment in Civil Appeal No. 11133 of 2011 (Adani Power Mundra Limited vs GERC and others) dated 2 July 2019.
18. Supreme Court Judgment in Review Petition (C) No. 2012 of 2019 in Civil Appeal No. 11133 of 2011 (GUVNL vs Adani Power Mundra Limited and others) dated 3 September 2019.
19. Record of Proceeding in CERC with respect to Petition No. 250/MP/2019 (GUVNL vs Adani Power Mundra Ltd. and others), dated 15 October 2019. Available on CERC website.
20. CERC order in Petition No. 1807 of 2019 (Gujarat Urja Vikas Nigam Ltd vs Essar Power Gujarat Ltd and others) dated 27 April 2020. Available on CERC website.
21. Government of Gujarat Resolution No.: CGP-12-2018-166-K, Energy and Petrochemicals Department, dated 12 June 2020.
22. CERC order for Petition No. 155/MP/2012 (dated 2 April 2013) in case of Adani Power Limited (APL) and CERC order for Petition No. 159/MP/2012 (dated 15 April 2013) in case of Coastal Gujarat Power Limited (CGPL). Available on CERC website.
23. Committee Report for CERC (August 2013), shared by CERC for public consultation. Available in archive of CERC website.
24. CERC order for Petition No. 155/MP/2012 (dated 21 February 2014) in case of Adani Power Limited (APL) and CERC order for Petition No. 159/MP/2012 (dated 21 February 2014) in case of Coastal Gujarat Power Limited (CGPL).
25. Full bench judgment in the Appellate Tribunal for Electricity (APTEL) dated 7 April 2016 in case of Adani Group (Appeal No. 100 of 2013 and Appeal No. 98 of 2014 and others) and CGPL Group (Appeal No. 151 of 2013 and Appeal No. 97 of 2014 and others).

26. Supreme Court Judgment in Civil Appeal Nos 5399–5400 of 2016 (Energy Watchdog vs CERC and others) dated 11 April 2017.
27. Refer to Clause 4 of CERC order for Petition No. 374/MP/2018 (dated 12 April 2019) in case of GUVNL. Working Group was constituted of members of all procurer states, banks represented by Canara Bank, Punjab National Bank with State Bank of India acting as convener to find a solution through consultative process.
28. Refer to Clause 6 of CERC order for Petition No. 374/MP/2018 (dated 12 April 2019) in case of GUVNL. The Government of Gujarat constituted a High Power Committee for reviewing the report of Working Group and obtaining its recommendations, with regard to resolution of the issues of the imported coal-based power projects located in the State of Gujarat. The HPC comprised of (i) Hon'ble Justice R.K. Agrawal, former Justice of Hon'ble Supreme Court; (ii) Sh. S.S. Mundra, former Deputy Governor, RBI and; (iii) Pramod Deo, Former Chairman, CERC.

Appendix II

1. Disclaimer: These case studies are only examples and the problem is not specific to the states mentioned. This is the situation that seems to be prevailing everywhere.